STILL COLD WAR?

STILL COLD WAR?
PERSPECTIVES ON INTER-KOREAN PEACE AND RECONCILIATION

Published in 2021 by Seoul Selection, Inc.
B1, 6 Samcheong-ro, Jongno-gu, Seoul 03062, Korea

ISBN: 979-11-89809-49-2 93340

Phone: 82-2-734-9567
Fax: 82-2-734-9562

E-mail: hankinseoul@gmail.com
Website: www.seoulselection.com

STILL COLD WAR?

PERSPECTIVES ON INTER-KOREAN
PEACE AND RECONCILIATION

Edited by Woo-Young Lee and Sunghee Kim

Seoul Selection

CONTENTS

This book is an anthology of articles on national reconciliation on the Korean Peninsula, where military tensions following the Korean War (1950–1953) have yet to be resolved. To be specific, this collection of studies explores the psychological and emotional aspects of inter-Korean relations.

Although the world is entering a new age of conflict called the New Cold War or Second Cold War, Korea is still stuck in the first one. In other words, the Cold War on the Korean Peninsula—specifically, the geopolitical tension between the US-led liberal democratic world and socialist North Korea—continues despite the fall of the Eastern bloc in the late 20th century. However, this is not to say that the New Cold War—the conflict between China and the United States—does not affect the Korean Peninsula; if anything, this new rivalry, with China's support of North Korea, overlaps the old ideological strife in the region. Thus, the lingering geopolitical tension in Korea is not merely a national problem but an international one that extends both Cold Wars.

The two Koreas—North and South—have lost their way to national reunification in a labyrinth of global conflict. International communities led by the US, China, and Russia (formerly the Union of

Socialist Soviet Republics or USSR) have tackled "Korean problems"—notably, North Korea's nuclear program. However, their efforts have proved fruitless. Neither the six-party talks on North Korea's nuclear program nor the US's strategies for North Korea (e.g., information operations and strategic patience) have worked. Moreover, the South Korean public has been losing interest in national unification over the last decade as the gap in the economy between North and South widens. As a result, the peace talks in Korea have reached a stalemate.

However, the present work examines the possibilities of peace and reconciliation on the Korean Peninsula, focusing on subjective elements such as emotion and psyche—not objective factors such as the international environment—in inter-Korean relations. *Maŭm*, a Korean word meaning mind and heart, is the key concept upon which all the studies in this book draw. Understanding each other's *maŭm* could be a vital prerequisite for peace and reconciliation between the two Koreas.

In 2012, the Simyeon Institute for North Korean Studies (SINKS) at the University of North Korean Studies launched a 10-year project on North and South Koreans' *maŭm* in relation to each other: in other words, their emotional attitudes toward each other. The National Research Foundation of Korea (NRF) funded this project, selecting SINKS as a participant in the Social Sciences Korea (SSK) program through which the NRF promotes research in the field of social sciences. Thus, scholars affiliated with SINKS have produced hundreds of academic articles and dozens of books about emotion and *maŭm* in inter-Korean relations. The articles in the present work are a small portion of this research project, spanning from 2012 to 2021.

This book represents neither a particular approach nor methodology. Instead, it seeks to foster diverse perspectives, embracing various conceptual, normative, and empirical research on inter-Korean relations. Thus, this work aims to promote the global discussion on Korea, a region suffering from the two Cold Wars.

Editors
Woo-Young Lee (University of North Korean Studies)
Sunghee Kim (Soongsil University)

Previous Versions

The articles in this book were originally published in various journals. They have been revised and reprinted with permission.

Chapter 1

Lee, Woo-Young, and Hayeon Lee. Previously published as "The Perception of the Integration of North and South Korea." *Historical Social Research* 44, no. 4 (2019): 293–307.

Chapter 2

Park, Ju Hwa, and Kap-sik Kim. Previously published as "Ethnic Identification Matters." *Asian Perspective* 43, no. 4 (2019): 673–697.

Chapter 3

Kwon, Young-Mi, and Ju Hwa Park. Previously published as "Peace through Cooperation or Peace through Strength? How to Achieve Peace in the Very Intractable Conflict Society." *Historical Social Research* 44, no. 4 (2019): 269–292.

Chapter 4

Jung, Jin-heon, and Eun-jeung Lee. Previously published as "Division and Unification: Seen through the Eyes of Korean Migrants in Berlin." *Historical Social Research* 44, no. 4 (2019): 308–324.

Chapter 5

Lee, Bongki, and Hannes B. Mosler. Previously published as "The Elephant in the Room: Problems and Potentials of the Workers' Party of Korea in a Korean Unification Scenario." *Historical Social Research* 44, no. 4 (2019): 325–246.

Chapter 6

Kim, Tae-Kyung. Previously published as "The Making of the "Reader-People" in the 1950–1960s North Korean Socialist Literature." *Asian Perspective* 44, no. 4 (2019): 699–719.

Chapter 7

Koo, Kab Woo. Previously published as "The Discursive Origins of Anti-Americanism in the Two Koreas." *Asian Perspective* 41, no. 2: 291–308.

Chapter 8

Lee, Woo-Young, and Kim Myoung-Shin. Previously published as "Inter-Korean Integration Mirrored in Division Films: Changing Collective Emotion in South Korea Toward Inter-Korean Integration." *North Korean Review* 13, no. 2: 24–47.

Chapter 9

Choi, Sunkyung. Previously published as "Remaking a Transborder Nation in North Korea: Media Representation in the Korean Peace Process." *International Journal of Communication* 14 (2020): 1376–1397

1. The Perception of the Integration of North and South Korea

Woo-Young Lee and Hayeon Lee

(University of North Korean Studies)

Abstract

This study describes South Koreans' general perceptions of the integration of North and South Korea through a survey of 500 adults living in South Korea. Multiple-choice questions were asked on the participants' general ideas about the reunification of North and South Korea, the type of Korean reunification they support or are opposed to, the type of Korean reunification they see as most probable, the pros and cons of reunification, and necessary factors for reunification. Additionally, we examined the differences in the perception of Korean reunification among subgroups based on participants' demographic information (i.e., gender, age, political orientation). The main results are as follows. First, the predominant understanding of reunification was "geographical integration of the Korean Peninsula," followed by "establishment of economic partnerships or communities" and "restoration of common identity." Meanwhile, there were differences among participants with regard to the details of Korean reunification. This suggests that when we discuss the attitudes toward integration of North and South Korea, differences in people's perceptions should be considered.

Keywords

social integration, Korean reunification, integration of Korean mindsets

There is a growing interest in the integration of North and South Korea as the relations between the two countries have been growing positive after the 2018 PyeongChang Winter Olympics. How could Korean reunification be possible at the sociocultural level? Further, how could *an integration of Korean mindsets* be possible among those who make up an integrated Korean society? To answer these questions, it is necessary to consider the general perception of the integration of North and South Korea among their peoples. How do people perceive the integration of the two Korean societies? Do various subgroups and demographics in each society hold similar or different attitudes on Korean reunification? If members of subgroups have different attitudes toward Korean reunification, how can we resolve these differences of opinion and construct an integrative society? The answers to these questions will be stepping-stones toward the understanding of the perceptions of Korean reunification and will point the direction towards the integration of Korean mindsets. In this research, our major purpose is to describe the perceptions of Korean reunification among South Koreans.

The perceptions of Korean reunification can be understood at various dimensions: North and South Koreans' beliefs about each other (stereotypes about North and South Koreans), attitudes toward the social systems (political or economic systems) of North and South Korea, perceptions about inter-Korean relations, or attitudes and expectations toward Korean reunification. Most previous research (e.g.,

Chun and Jo 2000, H. S. Kim 2002, Yoon and Chae 2010) focused on the stereotypes and prejudices North and South Koreans held about each other. In addition, major surveys conducted annually ask people about their perceptions and attitudes toward Korean reunification.

A survey about Korean reunification conducted by the Korea Institute for National Unification (KINU; J. H. Park, M. K. Lee, and Cho 2017) asked participants questions on their general attitude toward Korean reunification ("How necessary do you think Korean reunification is?"), their specific attitudes and emotional responses toward reunification ("Although North and South Koreans share a common ethnic identity, it is not necessary to construct one country"; "I am comfortable thinking about reunification"), and their behavioral intentions in relation to reunification ("I am in favor of raising taxes for reunification"). Participants answered these questions on a scale from 1 to 5 (1 = not at all; 5 = very much). Participants also selected statements that best corresponded with their opinions on the processes of Korean reunification. These included statements on the timeframe for reunification ("need not be unified" vs. "pursue at a flexible pace" vs. "as soon as possible"), preferred method for reunification ("gradual unification through negotiation" vs. "radical unification through direct action" vs. "other"), reason for reunification ("because North and South Korean share a common ethnic identity"), and necessary conditions for reunification ("improvement of North Korea's economic status").

A second survey on the perception of Korean reunification was conducted by the Institute for Peace and Unification Studies (IPUS; Jeong et al. 2018). This survey also asked participants about their general attitudes towards Korean reunification through questions such as "How necessary do you think reunification between North and South Korea is?" (1 = not at all; 5 = very much), with follow-up questions on specific perceptions of reunification, similar to KINU's survey. In addition, they asked participants about their preferred political system for an integrated society of North and South Korea (response options included "based on the system of North Korea vs. South Korea," "a compromise between systems of North and South Korea," and others).

The two surveys have attempted to quantify the range of attitudes towards Korean reunification, in addition to gauging the general population's thoughts on specific aspects and methods of integration. Based on these surveys, researchers can describe and summarize the numeric data from participants and examine statistical hypotheses about the differences between participants based on their characteristics (gender, age, educational background) and the relations among variables.

However, there are limitations for understanding people's perceptions about various forms of Korean reunification and their attitudes toward it, because it cannot be verified which type of reunification is represented in each person's mind. For example, it is not possible to identify through the survey questions above what South Koreans generally consider "the reunification of North and South Korea" to be—whether they consider it a geographical integration on the Korean Peninsula, or the construction of one unified political and economic system, or a social and cultural integration of North and South Koreans. Those aspects of Korean reunification could occur independently rather than simultaneously (Cha 2000). In addition, specifically regarding the integration of the political and social systems of the two Koreas, it is possible that respondents have different attitudes (e.g., preference, perceived feasibility, and behavioral attention) toward each process and the outcome of Korean reunification. Therefore, in the interpretation of previous research, it is necessary to give concern to the possibility that each participant responded to attitudes on Korea reunification based on their own individual perceptions. In fact, there are in-depth analyses based on the above surveys which compared the attitudes towards Korean reunification (B. R. Kim and Choi 2012) between North and South Koreans, and other research examined the effect of demographic factors on the perception of legitimacy and feasibility of Korean reunification among South Koreans (N. Y. Lee 2014). Both pieces of research were limited in that they sought answers to questions about general attitudes toward Korean reunification without specifying the type and manner of reunification. In other words, it is possible to interpret these findings from various angles, such as whether differences in region, age, or political orientation predict attitudes toward reunification, or whether variations in attitudes are the result of differences in the perception of reunification in accordance with individual demographic factors.

Furthermore, the various and often conflicting opinions on Korean reunification among South Koreans pose another limitation in establishing common goals about how Korean society would be integrated at the community level. Perceptions of reunification can be different depending on people's ideology and political/economic status, as well as their perception of situational factors such as changes in inter-Korean relations. Hence, in order to discuss the perceptions of reunification, it is necessary to analyze various perceptions and attitudes towards those aspects first (H. O. Kim 2001, 79–104). Additionally, if there are different perceptions of Korean reunification between members of society, there is the possibility that conflict will arise between subgroups, resulting from a lack of understanding of the differences in perception (Kang 2004, 55–100). Therefore, to construct social agreement on Korean reunification, it is necessary to verify concrete perceptions of inter-Korean integration by members of society and identify commonalities and differences between the perceptions that exist within each subcommunity.

However, to the best of our knowledge, there has been no empirical study about the various perceptions and attitudes regarding Korean reunification attempting to verify the differences among people in Korean society. Through this research, we tried to understand the perceptions of Korean reunification and to verify whether South Koreans' ideas and attitudes on reunification differ depending on demographic variables such as age, gender, and political orientation. Specifically, we obtained a more detailed understanding of their perception of Korean reunification by asking what they think reunification between North and South Korea means, what their attitudes toward each type of reunification (i.e., constructing one country, a federation, or a national union) are, why they support or oppose reunification, and what would be required for reunification. Each question had various response options to facilitate an accurate expression of participants' thoughts. Participants were then categorized according to their age, gender, and political orientation, and we analyzed whether there were statistical differences in responses between subgroups. The following section details the methods and results of this study.

Participants

Five hundred people (250 female, mean age = 39.75, SD = 11.03) who are living in South Korea were recruited via an online survey with monetary rewards. The survey was conducted in March 2018, after the PyeongChang Winter Olympics.

Measures

– The perception of Korean reunification

To understand the perceptions of Korean reunification, the question "What do you think reunification of North and South Korea means?" was asked with nine response choices. Participants selected three responses which corresponded with their opinions. The nine response options were as follows: (1) geographical integration on the Korean Peninsula, (2) establishment of a single political system, (3) establishment of economic communities, (4) expansion of social and cultural exchanges, (5) restoration of common ethnic identity, (6) psychological harmony between North and South Koreans, (7) South Korea's absorption of North Korea, (8) North Korea's absorption of South Korea, and (9) other (open-ended).

– Most preferred or opposed type of reunification

To identify the most preferred or opposed type of reunification, we asked two questions: "What type of reunification do you prefer?" and "What type of reunification do you oppose?" We presented five choices for each question, from which participants selected the one that most closely matched their opinion. The choices presented were as follows: (1) establishment of a single political system based on South Korea, (2) establishment of a single political system based on North Korea, (3) establishment of a single state through a federation between North and South Korean governments, (4) a union of the nation between North and South Korea, and (5) other (open-ended).

– Most feasible type of reunification

To determine perceptions of the type of reunification that is most likely to occur, we asked: "What kind of reunification do you think is most likely to happen in the current situation?" We presented five choices, the same as presented in the previous question (*the most preferred or opposed type of reunification*) to the participants, from which they selected the one that most closely corresponded with their opinion.

– Reasons for supporting reunification

To determine why participants support Korean reunification, we asked: "Why do you think North and South Korea need to be unified?" We presented nine choices, from which respondents selected the three that were closest to their opinions. The views presented were as follows: (1) because we are one group as the Han ethnicity, (2) to eliminate the threat of war, (3) to make Korea a stronger country, (4) to resolve the problems of separated families, (5) to improve the life of North Koreans, (6) to contribute to world peace, (7) because the majority of Koreans want reunification, (8) for no particular reason, and (9) other (open-ended).

– Reasons for opposing reunification

To determine why participants oppose Korean reunification, we asked: "Why do you think the two Koreas should not be unified?" We presented nine choices, from which respondents selected the three that were closest to their opinions. The views presented were as follows: (1) North and South Korea have had different histories for too long, (2) there is no possibility of war between North and South Korea, (3) reunification interferes with South Korea becoming a stronger country, (4) aversion to the North Korean regime, (5) the financial burden on South Korean in reunification, (6) the state of division is favorable to maintaining the power order of the world, (7) many people do not want reunification, (8) no particular reason, and (9) other (open-ended).

– Necessary factors for reunification

To determine the factors necessary for reunification, we asked: "What do you think is necessary for reunification?" We presented nine choices, from which respondents selected the three that were closest to their opinions. The views presented were as follows: (1) improvement in North Korea's political/economic situation, (2) improvement in South Korea's political/economic situation, (3) improvement in South Koreans' perceptions of reunification, (4) improvement in North Koreans' perceptions of reunification, (5) establishment of peaceful relations between North and South Korea, (6) international agreement by China, the United States, and so on, (7) expansion of political and economic exchanges between North and South Korea, (8) expansion of inter-Korean social/cultural/interpersonal exchanges, and (9) other (open-ended).

Once the responses to the main questions were completed, participants responded to a question on their political orientation (1 = liberal; 7 = conservative). The survey ended with questions about their place of birth, age, occupation, and academic background.

Results
– Demographic information of participants

Of the participants, 38.8% were from Seoul and 16.4% from the capital area (Gyeonggi-do). Other major cities (Busan, Daegu, and Incheon) followed with 6–7% each. There were no statistically significant differences in cross-analysis in place of birth based on gender and age group, $ps > .282$.

The mean (M) of the political orientation of participants was 3.63 and the standard deviation (SD) was 1.40. There was no statistically significant difference in the level of political orientation by age group, $p = .095$. Male responses ($M = 3.87$, $SD = 1.45$), however, indicated more conservative as compared to females ($M = 3.40$, $SD = 1.31$), $F(1,498) = 14.31$, $p < .001$. Meanwhile, we checked the score distribution to form a subcategory of respondents' overall political orientation. The percentages for liberal (one to three-point response), moderate (four-point response), and conservative (five to seven-point response) were 43.5%, 33.8%, and 22.7%, respectively. There was no statistically significant difference in the response rates for liberal, moderate, and conservative orientations by age group, $p = .481$, but there was a statistically significant difference in the response rates for liberal, moderate, and conservative orientations by gender, $\chi2(2) = 19.63$, $p < .001$. Specifically, the response rates for liberal, moderate, and conservative political orientations among males were 43.9%, 45.2%, and 67.8%, respectively. Among females, the response rates for liberal, moderate, and conservative political orientations were 56.1%, 54.8%, and 32.2%, respectively. There was a gap between males and females in the response rate for conservative orientation.

In the analysis of the main questions, we described the results of the participants' overall responses, as well as whether the response rates and details varied according to age group (20s, 30s, 40s, 50s), gender (male, female), and political orientation (liberal, moderate, conservative). (See Appendix for the full results of this question and the results for age group, gender, and political orientation.)[1] To compare the response rates according to age group, gender, and political orientation, a chi-square test (and a chi-square test for multiple responses) was performed based on the question.

– The perception of Korean reunification

The most common idea associated with Korean reunification was the "end of geographical division on the Korean Peninsula" (average 57.5%), followed by "establishment of an economic partnership or community" (average 47.1%) and "restoring the common ethnic identity of the two Koreas" (average 48.4%). The differences in

---

1   In the cross-analysis to determine the difference in response rates according to age group, gender, and political orientation, responses of "other" and "60s" age group were excluded because of their small number. A small number of each cell in the chi-square analysis leads to low validity of results when 20% or more of the total number of possible frequencies is less than five. The "other" response rate in this survey was 1.1% on average and 0.2–3.0% in each question.

response rates by age, gender, and political orientation were statistically significant, age group $\chi^2(24) = 36.40$, $p = .050$, gender $\chi^2(8) = 17.76$, $p = .023$, political orientation $\chi^2(16) = 34.79$, $p = .004$. Descriptions of each analysis areas follows.

First, by age group, those in their 20s thought of reunification as the "end of geographical division on the Korean Peninsula" (average 56.0%); "establishment of a single political community" (average 46.0%); and "expansion and integration of social and cultural exchanges" (average 46.0%). The response rates were low for "restoration of common ethnic identity" (average 39.0%) and "establishment of economic communities " (40.0%). Meanwhile, for those in their 30s–50s, the second and third most common responses were "restoration of common ethnic identity" (average 51.5%) and "establishment of economic communities" (average 49.5%). This can be interpreted as a reduced awareness in people in their 20s of "restoration of common ethnic identity" or "establishment of economic communities " as compared to those in their 30s–50s.

Next, by gender, the most frequent response for both males and females was "end of geographical division on the Korean Peninsula" (average 58.0%). There were differences in their second and third most frequent responses. Males responded in the order of "establishment of economic communities" (average 49.6%) and "restoration of common ethnic identity" (average 46.8%) while females responded in the order of "restoration of an ethnic identity" (average 50.8%) and "expansion of social and cultural exchanges" (average 49.6%).

Next, by political orientation, the response rates for liberal, moderate, and conservative groups were all in the order of "end of geographical division" (average 58.9%), "restoration of common ethnic identity" (average 49.2%), and "expansion of social and cultural exchanges"(average 47.7%). However, for "psychological harmony between North and South Koreans" the response rate was lower in conservatives (20.3%) than in liberals and moderates (average 36.5%). For "South Korea's absorption of North Korea" (35.6%) and "North Korea's absorption of South Korea" (9.3%), the response rate was higher in conservatives than in liberals and moderates (24.6% and 2.6%, respectively). Thus, conservatives are less likely to recognize reunification as serving the purpose of "psychological harmony between North and South Koreans" than liberals or moderates, whereas they are more likely to perceive reunification as the absorption of one country by another.

– Most preferred type of reunification

The most preferred type of reunification was "establishment of a single political system based on South Korea" (average 56.9%). The second highest was "establishment of a single state through a federation between North and South Korean governments " (average 25.6%). In this analysis, the difference in response rates by age group was statistically significant, $\chi2(9)= 17.26$ and $p = .045$. Specifically, for those in their 20s, the response rate for "establishment of a single political system based on South Korea" (average 71.7%) was more than three times that of the second highest, "establishment of a single state through a federation between North and South Korean governments " (average 18.2%). However, for those in their 30s–50s, the response rate for "establishment of a single political system based on South Korea" (average 52.0%) was about half that of the total responses. The response rate for "establishment of a single state through a federation between

North and South Korean governments" (average 28.1%), which was half that of the most frequent response, ranked second. This means that the most preferred type of reunification was almost the same among those in their 20s (South Korean system-based unification). However, people in their 30s–50s can be interpreted as having relatively diverse opinions (federal system, national union, etc.) on Korean reunification.

– Most opposed type of reunification

The most opposed type of unification was "establishment of a single political system based on North Korea" (average 76.4%). In this analysis, the difference in response rates by gender and political orientation was significant, gender $\chi2(3)= 8.01$, $p = .046$, political orientation$\chi2(6) = 12.58$, $p = .050$. By gender, for males and females alike, the primary response was "establishment of a single political system based on North Korea." However, females opposed this type of reunification more vociferously (average 81.9%) than males (average 71.6%). The analysis based on political orientation showed that the primary response for liberals, moderates, and conservatives was "establishment of a single political system based on North Korea." However, liberals (81.8%) had a higher response rate for "establishment of a single political system based on North Korea" than conservatives (average 71.8%). In other words, female and liberal South Koreans are most likely to be opposed to reunification based on the North Korean regime.

– Most feasible type of reunification

The type of reunification respondents considered most likely was "establishment of a single state through a federation between North and South Korean governments " (average 33.7%). This was followed by "a union of the nation between North and South Korea " (average 30.9%), and "establishment of a single political system based on South Korea" (average 30.7%). For this question, there was no statistically significant difference in response rates by age, gender, or political orientation, *ps* > .118. Thus, South Koreans see these ways of reunification as equally feasible regardless of their age, gender, or political orientation.

– Reasons for supporting reunification

The highest response rate among the reasons why the two Koreas should achieve reunification was for "to eliminate the threat of war" (average 78.6%). This was followed by "because we are one group as the Han ethnicity" (average 53.1%), and "to make Korea a stronger country" (average 52.6%). Analysis of the difference in response rates by age group showed that the overall difference was not significant, p = .200. However, for "because we are one group as the Han ethnicity," those in their 20s (average 40.0%) showed a lower response rate than those in their 30s–50s (average 57.4%). This is a result consistent with the response rate for "restoration of common ethnic identity," which was lower for those in their 20s than in their 30s–50s.

Differences in response rates by gender and political orientation were statistically significant, gender $\chi 2(8) = 18.41$, $p = .018$, political orientation $\chi 2(16) = 32.34$ and $p = .009$. A summary of each analysis is as follows. First, by gender, for males and females, the same responses ranked first to third: "to eliminate the threat of war," "because we are one group as the Han ethnicity," and "to make Korea a stronger country." Meanwhile, for "to resolve the problems of separated families," the response rate of females (average 44.8%) was higher than that of males (average 36.0%). For those who selected "for no particular reason," males (average 6.4%) had a higher response rate than females (average 2.0%). Second, the analysis based on political orientation also showed that liberals, conservatives, and moderates had the same order of responses from first to third. However, for "to eliminate the threat of war," moderates (average 86.3%) had a higher response rate than conservatives (average 68.6%). On the contrary, for "to improve the life of North Koreans," conservatives (average 37.3%) had a higher response rate than moderates (average 23.8%).

– Reasons for opposing reunification

The highest response rate among the reasons why the two Koreas should not achieve reunification was for "aversion to the North Korean regime" (average 85.4%). This was followed by "the financial burden of the South Koreans for reunification " (average 81.1%) and "North and South Korea have had different histories for too long" (average 66.7%). In this question, the difference in response rates by political orientation was statistically significant, $\chi 2(16)= 34.84$, $p = .004$. Specifically, for "aversion to the North Korean regime," liberals (average 90.2%) had a higher response rate than conservatives (average 77.1%). As for "there is no possibility of war between North and South Korea" (average 14.9%), moderates (average 14.9%) had a higher response rate than liberals (average 6.1%). Most liberal South Koreans oppose reunification because of an "aversion to the North Korean regime," and the percentage of people who think "there is no possibility of war" is relatively low.

Based on the fact that the response rate for the top three answers was approximately 78%, we could infer that reasons for why the two Koreas should not achieve reunification were relatively converged. Also, the third most common answer, "North and South Korea have had different histories for too long," can be seen as contradicting the second most common answer, "because we are one group as the Han ethnicity," among pro-reunification reasons. Although South Koreans believe they share a common identity with North Koreans, they simultaneously feel an aversion to North Korea because of the fact that they have experienced different historical events over the past 70 years.

– Necessary factors for reunification

The highest response rate for factors required for unification was for "improvement in North Korea's political/economic situation" (average 67.3%). This was followed by "establishment of peaceful relations between North and South Korea" (average 47.4%) and "expansion of political and economic exchanges between North and South Korea" (average37.8%). In this question also, the differences in response rates by age group, gender, and political orientation were all statistically significant: age group $\chi2(24) = 47.28, p =.003$, gender$\chi2(8) = 37.04, p < .001$, political orientation $\chi2(16) = 28.61, p = .027$. Descriptions of each analysis are as follows.

First, by age group, those in their 20s responded in this order: "improvement in North Korea's political/economic situation " (average 78.0%), "improvement in North Koreans' perceptions of reunification" (average 48.0%), and "international agreement by China, the United

States, and so on" (average 45.0%). Response rates for "establishment of peaceful relations between North and South Korea " (average 41.0%) and "expansion of political and economic exchanges" (average 28.0%) were relatively low. Among those in their 30s–50s, the following were the second and third highest responses: "establishment of peaceful relations"(average 49.5%) and "expansion of political and economic exchanges" (average 41.1%). In sum, there was a difference between those in their 20s and those in their 30s–50s with regard to what was considered a requirement for reunification. Those in their 20s were relatively more concerned about changes in North Korea (political/ economic situation and improved perceptions) than people in their 30s–50s, who were concerned with inter-Korean exchanges and improved relations between the two nations.

Next, by gender, males and females both ranked "improvement in North Korea's political/economic situation" (average 66.8%) first, and the second highest response was "establishment of peaceful state relations" (average 49.0%). However, there were differences in the third highest response: while for males it was "international agreement by China, the United States, and so on" (39.6%), for females it was "expansion of political and economic exchanges" (40.8%). In addition, females (36.0%) had a higher response rate than males (22.4%) for "expansion of inter-Korean social/cultural/interpersonal exchanges." In other words, females consider direct exchanges between the two Koreas a requirement for reunification.

Next, by political orientation, liberals, moderates, and conservatives all ranked the following first and second: "improvement in North Korea's political/economic situation" (average 66.9%) and "establishment of peaceful relations" (average 48.7%). However, there was a difference in the third highest response: "expansion of political and economic exchanges" (average 43.5%) for liberals, "improvement in North Koreans' perceptions of reunification" (average 38.1%) for moderates, and "international agreement by China, the United States, and so on" (average 42.4%) for conservatives. In addition, for "expansion of inter-Korean social/cultural/interpersonal exchanges," liberals (average 35.0%) showed a higher response rate than moderates and conservatives (average 23.9%). In sum, liberals consider direct inter-Korean exchanges (political/economic, social/cultureal/interpersonal) the main requirement for reunification when compared to other political orientations.

Discussion

In this study, we sought to understand the general perceptions of Korean reunification and verify whether these perceptions varied according to demographic variables such as age, gender, and political orientation. We surveyed 500 adults living in South Korea, questioning them about their ideas of Korea reunification, their attitudes toward each type of reunification, and reasons for favoring/opposing reunification and the requirements for it. We provided multiple choices for each question, allowing them to choose more than one. By doing so, we examined South Koreans' perceptions of integration between North and South Korea in more specific terms.

The main results of this study are summarized as follows. First, with regard to the general idea of reunification, "end of geographical division on the Korean Peninsula" was the dominant answer regardless of age, gender, or political orientation. However, people in their 30s–50s mostly chose "restoration of common ethnic identity" and "establishment of economic partnerships or communities" as a meaning of Korean reunification, but those in their 20s showed relatively low levels for this perception. This result was similar to the result of reasons for favoring reunification. For one of the reasons for favoring reunification, "because we are one group as the Han ethnicity," the response rate by those in their 20s was lower than those in their 30s–50s. This suggests that South Koreans in their 20s are actually less aware of the common ethnic identity of the North and South Koreas than those in their 30s–50s.

Meanwhile, the most preferred type of reunification was that based on the South Korean system. Those in their 20s showed a response rate of over 70%, while those in their 30s–50s showed a rate of around 50%. The rest of those in their 30s–50s preferred other types of reunification, such as the federal system (around 28%) or a national union (around 14%). It is suggested that different age groups have different preferences for reunification models. Meanwhile, the type of reunification South Koreans most strongly oppose is that based on the North Korean regime. While females and liberals tended to show the highest response rates in this regard, more than 70% of all respondents were against unification based on the North Korean system. Noteworthy is that unlike the type of reunification participants most preferred or opposed, the most feasible type of reunification showed an even response rate of 30% for federation, national union, and South Korean system-based reunification. There were also no differences in response rates based on age, gender, or political orientation for the most feasible type of reunification. Various interpretations are possible with regard to this. The assessment of the feasibility of a particular event may depend on the circumstances or social context in which the actual event is occurring rather than on the demographic factors of an individual. Or, it may depend on how members access relevant information about the event. Therefore, future research examines the factors that affect the perceived feasibility of Korean reunification and suggest an agreement between various perceptions of Korean reunification among society members could be made.

Finally, on why people supported or opposed Korea reunification, the most popular reason for the support of reunification was "to eliminate the threat of war," and for the opposition, it was "aversion to the North Korean regime." Noteworthy is that the second reason for supporting Korean reunification was "because we are one group as the Han ethnicity," and the third reason for opposing Korean reunification was "North and South Korea have had different histories for too long." This suggests that South Koreans simultaneously experience alienation and familiarity with regard to North Korea; they are conscious of the different historical experiences since the division even though they recognize that they shared common in-group identity. Expanding on this, when emphasizing the reason for reunification, it is necessary to stress the common ethnic identity between North and South Koreans as well as accurately identify the differences in historical and cultural experiences for reducing their aversion to each other. In other words, for an integrated society and culture, it is necessary for people from two countries to understand and respect differences among each other.

In sum, regarding South Koreans' general perceptions of integration of North and South Korea, it was confirmed that there were differences in how people think of reunification and their beliefs towards specific aspects of reunification depending on age, gender, and political orientation. Future research is necessary to expand the results of this study to include teenagers and senior citizens in South Korea, as well as people from North Korea. Also, it is possible to analyze longitudinal data to verify whether perceptions of integration of North and South Korea are maintained or changed at various timepoints depending on the rapidly changing situation between the two Koreas. In addition, while this study focused on the perceptions of Korean reunification, future studies could further focus on the interpretation of inter-Korean relations (hostile rivalry and antagonism vs. friendly partner for cooperation, governance, support, or assistance vs. partner with equal status and common identity) as well as examine the details of mutual recognition and attitudes toward each other. Given the fact that perceptions of integration of North and South Korea may vary depending on the interpretation of inter-Korean relations or the influence of mutual recognition and attitudes between the South and North, identifying the makeup of perceptions and verifying the correlations among various factors could be the focus of future research.

Furthermore, in addition to demographic factors and political orientation, it is necessary to seek the psychological variables affecting the perception of integration of North and South Korea and other related attitudes. By exploring individual characteristics that consist of political attitudes (e.g., universal values; H. J. Kim, Y. Park, and S. H. Park 2015; Schwartz, Caprara, and Vecchione 2010) or levels of common in-group identity between two countries (e.g., the Han ethnicity identification; Yang 2009), it is possible to suggest a direction that allows members of society to form a shared belief about Korean reunification. Universal values (Schwartz 1992, 1994) which represent, for example, beliefs regarding the individual behaviors that are considered desirable (e.g., benevolence, universalism, power, achievement), can be seen to have an effect on perceptions of integration of North and South Korea. It can also be inferred that one's general ideas about and preference for or against a certain type of reunification will change depending on the level of common in-group identity between North and South Korea. We can predict that with high levels of identification on the common in-group identity (Han ethnicity) of North and South Koreans, people will more strongly prefer the form of reunification based on a single country or political and social system. Future studies need to verify the effectiveness of these psychological variables in the recognition of the integration of North and South Korea based on more specific research.

References

Kang, Won-taek. 2004. "An empirical analysis of the ideological nature of the South-South conflict." In *South-South Conflict Diagnosis and Resolution.* Edited by Kyungnam University Institute for Far Eastern Studies. Changwon: Kyungnam University Press.

Kim, Byung-ro, and Kyung-hui Choi. 2012. "Comparative Analysis of Attitudes toward the Unification of North and South Korea." *Journal of Peace and Unification Studies* 4: 101–139.

Kim, Hyun-ok. 2001. *South Korea's reunification consciousness and conflict structure.* The Korean Sociological Association Symposium.

Lee, Nae-young. 2014. "What Determines Korean Perception and Attitude on National Unification? Searching for the new analytical model." *Peace Studies* 22: 167–206.

Kim, Hyeon-jeong, Yeongock Park, and Sang-hee Park. 2015. "Basic psychological characteristics, political attitudes, and candidate choice: A path model analysis." *The Korean Journal of Social and Personality Psychology* 29: 103–132.

Kim, Hai-sook. 2002. "A Survey on the Relationship Between Values and the Attitudes Toward North Koreans." *The Korean Journal of Social and Personality Psychology* 16: 35–50.

Park, Joo-hwa, Min-kyu Lee, and Won-bin Cho. 2017. *National survey of people's consciousness toward inter-Korean integration.* Korea Institute for National Unification.

Yang, Kye-min. 2009. "The Factors Influencing the Korean Adolescents' Attitude to Minority Groups." *The Korean Journal of Social and Personality Psychology* 23: 59–79.

Yoon, In-jin, and Jung-min Chae. 2010. *Mutual recognition of North Korean defectors and South Koreans: Focusing on identity and social and cultural adaptation.* North Korean Refugees Support Foundation.

Chun, Woo-young, and Eun-kyung Jo. 2000. "Stereotypes of North Korea and Psychological Distance Toward Unification." *The Korean Journal of Social and Personality Psychology* 14: 167–184.

Jeong, Keun-sik, Sun Kim, In-cheol Moon, Young-hoon Song, Dong-jun Jeong, Dong-jun Cho, Ja-hyun Chun, Jung-mi Hwang, Hee-jung Kim, Jung-ok Lee, and Soo-jin Lim. 2018. *Unification Perception Survey, 2017.* Institute for Peace and Unification Studies.

Schwartz, Shalom H. 1992. "Universals in the Content and Structure of Values: Theoretical Advances and Empirical Tests in 20 Countries." *Advances in Experimental Social Psychology* 25: 1–65.

Schwartz, Shalom H. 1994. "Are There Universal Aspects in the Structure and Contents of Human Values?" *Journal of Social Issues* 50: 19–45.

Schwartz, Shalom H., Gian Vittorio Caprara, and Michele Vecchione. 2010. "Basic Personal Values, Core Political Values, and Voting: A Longitudinal Analysis." *Political Psychology* 31: 421–452.

2. Ethnic Identification Matters

Ju Hwa Park, Kap-sik Kim

Abstract

We aim to verify how identification (South Korean identification and ethnic identification) directly and indirectly influences attitudes toward unification through the perception of North Korea (hostile vs. cooperative). Based on nationwide survey data (N = 1,000), we investigated the structural relationships among the variables using a structural equation model. The research results revealed (1) that ethnic identification and South Korean identification, and cooperative perception and confrontational perception toward North Korea, were found to be distinguishable concepts; (2) that ethnic identification has a direct effect on positive attitudes toward unification and also has an indirect effect on the attitude through a cooperative perception toward North Korea; and (3) that South Korean identification has a direct but negative influence on positive attitudes toward unification but does not have significant influence on perception toward North Korea. The implications of the research were discussed.

Keywords

identity, identification, attitude toward unification, perception toward North Korea

Introduction

Since the division of the two Koreas, two different state systems have existed on the Korean Peninsula. However, both South Korea and North Korea have denied the legitimacy of the other Korea seeking unification in the cause of a modern nation-state (C. S. Chun 2009). Such discrepancy between the cause and the reality is also found in the inconsistency between South Korea's constitution and its unification plan. While the constitution presumes that the two Koreas form a homogeneous nation-state, the National Community Unification Formula (NCUF), the South Korean government's official unification plan, recognizes that there are two state systems on the Korean Peninsula (Jeong 2017).

To achieve a unified nation-state, South Korea and North Korea have pursued their respective system's superiority. Based on such superiority, the two Koreas have both tried to establish one modern nation-state by bringing down and absorbing the other. This has inevitably led the two Koreas to emphasize ethnic identification and state identification at the same time: the former for the cause and the latter to justify the means of building a modern nation-state.[1] The contradiction of seeking a homogeneous nation under heterogeneous systems has strengthened ethnic identification and state identification.

Until recently, the inconsistency between ethnic identification and South Korean identification gained little attention. The first possibility

---

1 In this research, identity refers to an individual's or a group's fundamental and defining features found only in the individual and his/her in-group but not in others and out-groups, while identification indicates the degree of the individual identifying with the group he/she belongs to (A. Reber and E. Reber 2001).

could be that ethnic identification, a normative value, had been much stronger than South Korean identification, an instrumental value. That is, people often believed that South Korea was a nation-state and thus there was no difference between ethnic identification (or identity) and South Korean identification (or identity). Empirical studies have raised the question as to whether South Koreans distinguish between national identification and South Korean identification (Chung and S. M. Lee 2011; J. M. Hwang 2010; K. I. Yoon 2017). In the same vein, N. Y. Lee (2011) argued that national identification is a part of South Korean identification.

The second possibility has to do with limitation of empirical research. Attitudes toward unification or the tendency to support unification are highly normative. In other words, people find it difficult to give answers opposing the need for building a homogeneous nation-state or implying their South Korean identification rather than ethnic identification. However, recent studies suggest South Korean identification, or an awareness of heterogeneity, is increasingly growing, as opposed to the normative value (I. J. Yoon and Song 2011; Jeong 2017).

The fundamental cause of the divide between ethnic identification and South Korean identification lies in the separation of the two Koreas. Nevertheless, little research has been done on how ethnic identification and South Korean identification influence attitudes toward the separation. This research explores how ethnic identification and South Korean identification impact attitudes toward unification through structural equation modeling (SEM).

Identity

A national identity defines the category of the state or group to which an individual belongs. To put it another way, it distinguishes between "our people" and "others" outside of the group (Kang 2011). It is about people's conviction and sentiment toward the criteria which determine their nationhood and is thus considered the most important cultural factor behind people's civil rights (Brubaker 2009; Jones and Smith 2001). Therefore, it has great significance in providing criteria necessary to distinguish between the in-group and out-groups and it also determines the strength of one's nationhood within the in-group.

Most studies on national identity have focused on the two qualities of nationhood, the civic-territorial quality and the ethnic-genealogical quality (Kunovich 2009; Jones and Smith 2001; Smith 1991). While the civic-territorial quality is centered on statutory and institutional rights and obligations as well as whether the person resides in territory, the ethnic-genealogical quality is more about blood ties and linguistic and cultural elements. With the assumption that the ethnic-genealogical quality refers to national identity and the civic-territorial quality is South Korean identity, previous studies examined the influence of the two identities on ordinary Korean citizens' sense of distance, openness, and citizenship of diverse minority groups, such as North Korean defectors, compatriots in other countries, people with dual citizenship, migrant workers, marriage immigrants, and Korean Chinese (S. D. Baek and An 2013; Chang 2010; Y. E. Choi and Nam 2014; Chung and S. M. Lee 2011; K. Kim and N. Yoon 2012; K. I. Yoon 2017; I. J. Yoon and Song 2011).

Then, what effects do people's national identity and South Korean identity have on their attitudes toward unification? It appears reasonable to say that one's state identity, or the criteria for one's nationhood, is not enough to predict one's attitudes toward unification or policy preference regarding North Korea. First of all, an intuitive contradiction found in the previous studies on the two identities and openness to diversity makes it difficult to make a generalization. Prior studies on national identity and openness to diversity found that a stronger ethnic-genealogical quality made openness toward diversity weaker, while a stronger civic-territorial quality made it stronger (S. D. Baek and An 2013; S. H. Shin, Hur, and Kashima 2012). Furthermore, I. J. Yoon and Song (2011) reported that people with strong civic-territorial as well as ethnic-genealogical qualities demand both qualities for others to have citizenship, which means they are the least open to diversity. In this context, it can be assumed that people with strong national identity and strong South Korean identity at the same time, who account for the vast majority of the total South Korean population, are among the least open to diversity and thus negative about unification.

Second, empirical research does not support the general idea that ethnic identity has a positive correlation with attitudes towards unification but South Korean identity has a negative correlation. K. Kim and N. Yoon (2012) found that ethnic identity had nothing to do with the tendency to support unification but that South Korean identity had a positive correlation with the tendency to support unification. S. D. Baek and An (2016) showed that people with a stronger ethnic identity were more negative about paying a unification tax, which also runs counter to the intuitive idea.

Why is it difficult to predict people's tendency to support unification based on their civic-territorial quality and ethnic-genealogical quality?

Among others, it is because the two qualities' theoretical validity has yet to be proven empirically. Research has found mixed results on whether there is a clear boundary between the two qualities. While S. D. Baek and An (2013) and I. J. Yoon and Song (2011) found that the two qualities could be distinguished from each other, K. I. Yoon (2017) found the two qualities to be unitary. Meanwhile, the question remains as to whether the results of Western studies are applicable to Asian countries other than Korea (Choe 2016; Chung and S. M. Lee 2011; H. S. Kim, S. S. Choi, and H. J. Kim 2011; S. H. Shin, Hur, and Kashima 2012).

Rather than a national identity, one of the strongest indicators that helps predict people's attitudes toward unification is their emotional solidarity with North Korea, or ethnic identification (N. Y. Lee 2014). The next section takes a look at ethnic identification and state identification, two examples of emotional identification and solidarity with the nation and the state, and their relationship with attitudes toward unification.

Identification

While identity is individuals' subjective perceptions toward their groups' prototypes, identification is their subjective perceptions toward the distance between them and their groups' prototypes. Social identity is defined as the social category one perceives to belong to or the aspects of the person's self-image derived from the social group (Tajifel and Turner 1979). In short, one's identification with one's group can be defined as the degree of attachment the person has with the group and the extent to which the person identifies with the group and perceives similarities with the group. In this context, people's ethnic (South Korean) identification can be interpreted as the degree of their attachment to the ethnicity (South Korea), perceived similarities with members of the ethnic group (South Korea), and identification with the ethnicity (South Korea).

Building upon the social identity theory, the self-categorization theory highlights the cognitive process of developing social identification (Turner et al. 1987). More specifically, the theory assumes that just like individuals develop their identification based on commonalities and differences with others, they develop social identification after perceiving overall similarities with other members of their group and overall differences from members of other groups. This means that the prototype of the group becomes part of the concept of oneself.

The social identity theory is based on the assumption that individuals are motivated to raise their self-esteem. Raising one's respect for the group that represents the person's self-image is an important strategy to enhance one's self-esteem, and this explains why people tend to favor their in-group and discriminate against out-groups (Brewer 1979; McGarty and Penny 1988). The existence of a group's prototype as a part of one's self-image means that norms of the group are likely to influence one's world view and information processing. Using the group's norms instead of personal norms makes information-processing easier, but this can lead to de-individualization, stereotypes, blind sympathies, group-centrism, and group thinking (Turner et al. 1987).

In their research on the effects of ethnic identification and South

Korean identification on the tendency to support unification, J. Jung, Hogg, and H. S. Choi (2015) predicted a positive correlation between ethnic identification and attitudes toward and the tendency to support unification and a negative correlation between South Korean identification and attitudes toward and the tendency to support unification. However, only the effects of ethnic identification are found significant according to a survey of university students in Korea. The survey shows that people with stronger ethnic identification have more positive attitudes toward unification, while people's South Korean identification does not have any effect on their attitudes toward unification. N. Y. Lee's study (2014) found that people with greater ethnic identification were more optimistic about the need for unification and its feasibility. S. D. Baek and An (2016) and S. K. Lee and C. W. Lim (2016) also reported that people's ethnic identification and perceptions toward unification were in a positive relationship. Based on conjecture above, a positive correlation between ethnic identification and attitudes toward unification can be predicted with the following hypothesis:

Hypothesis 1a. Ethnic identification will show a positive relationship with attitudes toward unification.

While the relationship between ethnic identification and attitudes toward unification is relatively clearly predictable, the relationship between South Korean identification and attitudes toward unification is ambiguous according to previous studies. As mentioned above in Jung et al. (2015), the only research that examines the effects of South Korean identification on attitudes toward unification failed to prove their prediction on the effects of the former on the latter. However, the study has limitations in that it focuses only on university students and that the authors simply use support for engagement policy as a measure of attitudes toward unification. Consequently, the prediction that South Korean identification would be in a negative relationship with attitudes toward unification is still valid.

Studies on the effects of South Korean identity, not South Korean identification, on attitudes toward unification have also shown mixed results. Some studies found that people who put more emphasis on the citizen's identity—complying with South Korean laws and institutions, speaking Korean language, and maintaining South Korean nationality—as requirements to become a South Korean citizen had more positive attitudes about unification (S. D. Baek and An 2016). By contrast, S. K. Lee and C. W. Lim (2016) reported greater citizen's identity meant less support for unification.

Then what relationship can be presupposed between South Korean identification and perceptions toward unification? Jung et al. (2015) did not provide theoretical grounds for their prediction on a negative relationship between South Korean identification and attitudes toward unification. The social identity theory suggests that people with strong South Korean identification would be more South Korean-centric and have more negative stereotypes about the out-group, North Korea. Such prediction in the social identity theory has been proven in Korean society according to Jeong (2017). Jeong reported that superiority over North Korea and the isolationist idea had been growing in South Korean society. Based on the discussions above, the following prediction is possible:

Hypothesis 1b. South Korean identification will show a negative relationship with attitudes toward unification.

Perceptions Toward North Korea

Previous studies appear to agree that people's perceptions toward North Korea are the most important variable in predicting their attitudes toward unification. G. Kim (2007) argued that perceptions toward North Korea were the number one factor dividing people over issues related to unification with North Korea and North Korean policies. In other words, whether people see North Korea as a target of cooperation and aid or a target of vigilance and hostility determines their preference for unification and particular policies toward the North. In Korean society, ideological belief is mostly explained by the attitudes toward North Korea (Han 2016). In the same vein, H. J. Kim, Y. Park, and S. H. Park (2015) found that people's perceptions toward North Korea were the strongest predictor of voting behavior. S. Y. Jung and Y. H. Kim (2014) argued that perceptions toward North Korea were the most fundamental prerequisite for discussions on attitudes toward unification and policies toward North Korea. Given the results of prior studies on perceptions toward North Korea (see J. Park, M. Lee, and Cho 2017 for the overview of the prior studies), it can be predicted that people with positive attitudes toward North Korea are positive about unification, while those with negative attitudes toward North Korea are negative about unification.

However, recent research on perceptions toward North Korea has shown that the perceptions are not as simple as a binary question of being positive or negative. Rather, they can be two-dimensional with the positive axis and the negative axis crossing one another (H. J. Kim, Y. Park, and S. H. Park 2015; T. Kim, Namkung, and Y. Yang 2003; J. Park and M. Lee 2011; Y. Shin 2010; B. S. Lee 2015; W. Y. Chun and Jo 2000; S. Y. Jung and Y. H. Kim 2014; Jang and J. S. Kim 2015; J. H. Hwang 2011). That is, people can have both positive and negative perceptions toward North Korea at the same time. For example, Y. Shin (2010) argued that South Koreans have an ambivalent attitude toward North Korea. On the one hand, it threatens the citizens' survival and safety, and on the other hand, the North Korean people can also be brothers and compatriots. Such ambivalence has been reflected in South Koreans' support for policies toward the North. J. Park , M. Lee, and Cho (2017) found that South Koreans' preferences for unification and North Korea policies were better explained by the ambivalent perceptions toward the North than the simplistic perceptions toward the North.

Then, it can be presupposed that people's perceptions toward North Korea are not simplistic but ambivalent, which can be cooperative and hostile at the same time, and that the two perceptions can influence attitudes toward unification in a relatively independent manner. More specifically, the following hypotheses can be made:

> Hypothesis 2a. Cooperative perceptions toward North Korea will show a positive relationship with attitudes toward unification.
> Hypothesis 2b. Hostile perceptions toward North Korea will show a negative relationship with attitudes toward unification.

Identification, Perceptions Toward North Korea, and Attitudes Toward Unification

There has been no empirical research on the effects of people's identification on their attitudes toward North Korea. N. Y. Lee (2014) included perceptions toward North Korea as a subdimension of ethnic identification, assuming that people who perceived North Korea as a target of cooperation and aid were more likely to have stronger ethnic identification. This assumption is clearly plausible as a hypothesis, but it has never been verified empirically. According to the social identity theory, people with strong ethnic identification are more likely to see North Korea as an in-group. In other words, ethnic identification and homogeneous ethnic identification in that the two Koreas are the same ethnicity are likely to have a positive correlation although there is a debate whether the two identifications are different concepts (K. M. Yang 2009).

By contrast, people with strong South Korean identification are more likely to regard North Korea as an out-group. State identification is expressed as the subdimension of both patriotism and blind patriotism, as proven empirically. (See Y. Shin, Hur, and Kashima 2012 for more detailed discussions on state identification.) In general, people's patriotism means their emotional attachment to or constructive support for their country's citizens, while blind patriotism is about people's belief that their country's citizens are more superior than other countries' citizens (Roccas, Klar, and Liviatan 2006). No previous studies have examined whether Koreans' patriotism and blind patriotism can be distinguished from one another and how strong they are. However, in the context of empirically proven ideas on state identification, people with strong South Korean identification are more likely to see North Korea as an out-group and thus a target of vigilance and hostility.

Considering all of the discussions above, the following hypotheses can be made on the effects of ethnic identification and South Korean identification on perceptions toward North Korea:

> Hypothesis 3a. Ethnic identification will show a positive relationship with cooperative perceptions toward North Korea.
> Hypothesis 3b. Ethnic identification will show a negative relationship with hostile perceptions toward North Korea.
> Hypothesis 4a. South Korean identification will show a negative relationship with cooperative perceptions toward North Korea.
> Hypothesis 4b. South Korean identification will show a positive relationship with hostile perceptions toward North Korea.

All of the hypotheses made in this study can be presented as the research model in figure 2.1. As shown in figure 2.1, the goal of this research is to test the hypothesis that ethnic identification and South Korean identification have direct effects and at the same time indirect

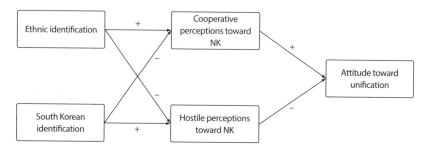

Figure 2.1. Research Model

effects, by means of perceptions toward North Korea, on attitudes toward unification.

Method

To test the hypothesis, this research utilized data from "Korean Peninsula Peace Research (2): Psychology of Peace," conducted in 2018 by the Korea Institute for National Unification (KINU).

– Participants

The research was conducted using the method of one-on-one interviews with 1,000 male and female adults aged 19 and older across the country. The sample was extracted through proportionate quota sampling by gender, age, and region.

– Measures

Identification. To measure ethnic identification and South Korean identification, four questions selected from those used by Jung et al. (2015) were used: "Do you feel similar to members of the Korean people (South Korean citizens) overall?"; "Do you identify with the Korean nation (South Korea)?"; "Do you feel happy about the fact that you are a member of the Korean nation (a South Korean citizen)?"; "Do you feel attached to the Korean nation (South Korea)?" The answers were measured on a scale of 1 point to 9 points (1 = "Not at all"; 9 = "Definitely").

To find out if ethnic identification and South Korean identification were two independent concepts, a factor analysis (a principal factor analysis and the oblique rotation method) was conducted, and the analysis found that the two identifications were two separate factors. South Korean identification's internal consistency (Cronbach's α) was .88 and that of ethnic identification was .93.

Perceptions toward North Korea. Perceptions toward North Korea were measured to find out if people considered it a target of support, cooperation, vigilance, or hostility on a scale of 0 points to 11 points (0 = "Not at all"; 10 = "Very much"). According to a factor analysis, people's perceptions could be divided into two factors: a target of support and cooperation, and a target of vigilance and hostility. The former was named cooperative perceptions, and the latter hostile perceptions. The internal consistency of the two factors were .49 and .86, respectively.

Attitudes toward unification. To measure attitudes toward unification, four statements were used: "The unification of the two Koreas is necessary"; "There is no need to bother to unify the two Koreas if there is no risk of war"; "It is not necessary to achieve one state because the two Koreas are homogeneous"; and "If I have to choose between unification and the economy, I would choose the economy." The Cronbach's α was .69.

Results

– Descriptive statistics and correlation

Pearson's correlation analysis was applied to figure out the relationships among ethnic identification, South Korean identification, cooperative perceptions toward North Korea, hostile perceptions toward North Korea, and attitudes toward unification. According to the analysis, all variables but the correlation between South Korean identification and attitudes toward unification were significantly correlated at the level of .01. The correlation coefficient, significance probability, average, and standard deviation for each set of variables are presented in table 2.1.

Table 2.1. The correlation Coefficient, Average, and Standard Deviation For Each Set of Variables

	1	2	3	4	5	M(SD)
1	—					6.41 (1.40)
2	.46**	—				7.04 (1.15)
3	.11**	.15**	—			6.94 (1.95)
4	−.22**	−.11**	−.24**	—		6.38 (2.18)
5	.16**	.00	.27**	−.13**	—	2.91 (0.70)

Note. 1. Ethnic identification   2. South Korean identification   3. Cooperative perception
4. Hostile perception   5. Attitudes toward unification ** $p < .01$

– Model-based test

The hypothesis of this study is that ethnic identification and South Korean identification will have direct effects on attitudes toward unification and that perceptions toward North Korea will serve as a mediator variable. The causal structural relations among the variables were tested after the conversion of a conceptual research model into a measurement model. After achieving the test results showing that the fit of the measurement model was acceptable, the structural model was tested, followed by the assessment of the mediator effects.

− Measurement model test

The measurement model test is designed to assess the quality of measurement by checking if latent variables are properly measured with measurement variables. In this research, the method of maximum likelihood (ML) estimation was used to assess the model fit. Among various measurement indices to assess the model fit, $\chi2$ is the only indicator that offers statistical significance, but it is not recommended because it is greatly influenced by the number of subjects. Absolute fit indices are used to examine how well measurement variables fit to the data, and the most representative of them include goodness of fit index (GFI), adjusted goodness of fit index (AGFI), root mean square error of approximation (RMSEA), and standardized root mean square residual (SRMR). Recently, the argument that GFI and AGFI are not appropriate as model fit indices is gaining ground, but they are still widely used (Kenny 2015). The recommended acceptance criteria for both GFI and AGFI is at least .90. For RMSEA, .05 and lower means good model fit, .08 and lower is fine model fit, .10 and lower is average model fit and .10 and higher is bad model fit. For SRMR, the recommended acceptance criterion is .08 and lower. The comparative fit index (CFI), normed fit index (NFI), and Tucker-Lewis index (TLI) are among the most frequently used relative indices to show how well the suggested model explains the data compared with the worst model. All of the three indices' recommended acceptance criteria are at least .90 (Hong 2000).

According to the measurement model test, the measurement model fit of this study is statistically acceptable. Moreover, all of the parameter estimates between latent variables and measurement variables ranged between .46 and .98 and were statistically significant at the .001

significance level. This means that all of the measurement variables are acceptable to measure the latent variables, which leads to a conclusion that there is no problem with testing the structural equation model with the measurement variables (Bae 2011).

– Structural model test

The structural model is presented in figure 2.2 and path coefficients are presented in table 2.2. The fit of the structural model is χ2 (93, N=1,000)= 470.89, $p<.001$, with NFI= .94, GFI= .95, AGFI= .92, TLI= .94, CFI= .95, SRMR= 0.062 and RMSEA= .064, showing that the fit is overall acceptable.

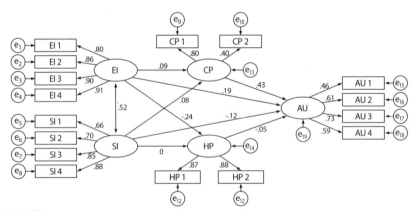

Figure 2.2. Structural Model

EI: Ethnic identification

SI: South Korean identification

CP: Cooperative perception

HP: Hostile perceptions toward North Korea

AU: Attitudes toward unification

Both paths, the one from ethnic identification to cooperative perceptions toward North Korea (β=.09, p<.10) and the one from ethnic identification to hostile perceptions toward North Korea (β=-.24, p<.001) were found to be significant. By contrast, all of the paths from South Korean identification to any perceptions toward North Korea were found to be insignificant. For the paths from cooperative perceptions to attitudes toward unification (β=.43, p<.001), from hostile perceptions toward attitudes toward unification (β=-.05, p<.05), from ethnic identification to attitudes toward unification (β=.19, p<.001), and from South Korean identification to attitudes toward unification (β=-.12, p<.05), they all were found to be significant.

Table 2.2. Path Coefficients of the Structural Model

			B	β	SE	CR	p
Ethnic identification	→	Cooperative perceptions	.05	.09	.03	1.68	†
Ethnic identification	→	Hostile perceptions	−.34	−.24	.06	−5.75	***
South Korean identification	→	Cooperative perceptions	.06	.08	.04	1.58	—
South Korean identification	→	Hostile perceptions	−.01	.00	.07	−0.10	—
Cooperative perceptions	→	Attitudes of unification	.21	.43	.03	6.63	***
Hostile perceptions	→	Attitudes of unification	−.01	−.05	.01	−1.33	*
Ethnic identification	→	Attitudes of unification	.06	.19	.02	3.86	***
South Korean identification	→	Attitudes of unification	−.04	−.12	.02	−2.51	*

†p < .10. *p < .05. ***p < .001.

This study proposes a single research model by assuming only a suggested model without competitive models. In conformity with the initial hypothesis, the direct and indirect paths from ethnic identification to attitudes toward unification and the direct path from South Korean identification to attitudes toward unification were all found to be statistically significant. However, all of the paths from South Korean identification to any perceptions toward North Korea were found to be statistically insignificant, going against the hypothesis. Based on the results, the method of post-hoc model modification was adopted to remove paths found insignificant and redesign the model, according to which Modification Model 1 was designed.

Model comparison was implemented as a process of examining the difference in model fit indices including χ^2 ($\Delta\chi^2$) between the research model and Modification Model 1. The results of model comparison are presented in figure 2.3. As Correction Model 1 is nested in the research model, a difference test was conducted to compare the two models. The difference between the research model and Correction Model 1 was $\Delta\chi^2=1.97$ ($\Delta df=2$), smaller than the critical point of 3.84, implying that the difference in the two models' values was not significant. When the difference between two models is significant, the model with a smaller degree of freedom is selected. When the difference is insignificant, suggesting that there is no difference in two models' internal inconsistency, the simpler model with a larger degree of freedom is preferred according to the principle of simplicity. Following the principle of simplicity, the correction model is found to be more appropriate. However, as the path coefficient from hostile perceptions toward North Korea to attitudes toward unification was found to be insignificant in Correction Model 1, it was removed and Modification Model 2 was designed. According to the results of comparison between

Modification Model 1 and Modification Model 2, Modification Model 2 was found to be more appropriate as in figure 2.3.

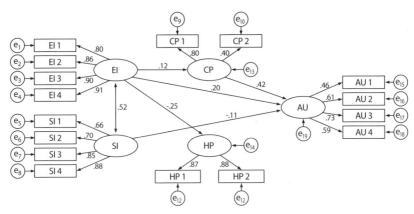

Figure 2.3. Final Model

Table 2.3. Model Fit indices for the Measurement Model, Research Model, and Correction Models

	χ^2	df	NFI	GFI	AGFI	TLI	CFI	SRMR	RMSEA	$\Delta\chi^2$
Measurement model	654.29***	94	.92	.92	.88	.91	.93	.054	.077	—
Research model	470.89***	93	.94	.95	.92	.94	.95	.062	.064	—
Modification Model 1	472.86***	95	.94	.94	.92	.94	.95	.063	.063	1.97
Modification Model 2	475.05***	96	.94	.94	.92	.94	.95	.063	.063	2.20

***p < .001.

Indirect Effect Test

A bootstrap hypothesis test was used to see if the indirect effects among latent variables in the structural model were statistically significant. This method is a way to obtain an accurate estimate of the standard error of mediator effects. To implement the testing, 2,000 pieces of data generated through random sampling from raw data (N=1,000) were used in parameter estimation with the 95% confidence interval. The results are displayed in table 2.4. The results show that both the direct effects of ethnic identification on attitudes toward unification (β=.197, p<.05) and the indirect effects through cooperative perceptions toward North Korea (β=.05, p<.05) are all significant.

Table 2.4. Direct and Indirect Effects Of Each Variable on Attitudes Toward Unification (N=1,000)

	Direct effects	Indirect effects	Total effects
Ethnic identification → Cooperative perceptions	−.245**		−.245**
Ethnic identification → Hostile perceptions	.122**		.122**
Ethnic identification → Attitudes toward unification	.197*	.051*	.248*
South Korean identification → Attitudes toward unification	−.107		−.107*
Cooperative perceptions → Attitudes toward unification	.416**		.416

***p < .05. **p < .01.

Discussion

This research aims to find psychological variables that are at play between people's identification and attitude toward unification, and to understand if the variables show a structural relationship among one another. To elaborate, this study sets a hypothetical structural relationship and verifies it to show how ethnic identification and South Korean identification influence attitudes toward unification when perceptions toward North Korea come into play as a mediator.

The first hypothesis about the relationship between the two identifications and the attitude toward unification is supported, as the direct paths from the identifications to attitude toward unification are statistically significant, respectively. It is consistent with existing research that show the higher one's ethnic identification is, the more positive one's attitude toward unification is. (Jung et al. 2015; N. Y. Lee 2014; S. K. Lee and C. W. Lim 2016). Current research shows that the higher South Korean identification is, the more negatively people react to unification, which is in line with Jeong (2017) but not with Jung et al. (2015). As we mentioned above, our study used more relevant questions and representative samples than Jung et al. (2015), so we cautiously argue that our results are more valid and reliable.

The second hypothesis is regarding the perception toward North Korea and the attitude toward unification. It is subdivided into two sub-hypotheses: (1) cooperative perception toward North Korea has a positive relationship with the attitude toward unification, and (2) confrontational perception against North Korea has a negative relationship to the attitude toward unification. The results reveal that there is a direct relationship between cooperative perception toward North Korea and attitude toward unification. However, it is not supported that a confrontational perception against North Korea leads to a negative perception of unification.

Hence, our research found that perceptions of North Korea have a discriminatory influence on attitudes toward unification, which is not inconsistent with existing research that has presumed a linear relationship between perception toward North Korea and attitude toward unification. Rather, the research is consistent with other recent research showing that the two perceptional dimensions on North Korea play independently (J. Park, M. Lee, and Cho 2017). The final hypothesis that ethnic identification has a positive influence on cooperative perception toward North Korea but has a negative influence on hostile perception was supported. On the other hand, neither paths from South Korean identification to cooperative perception nor to hostile perception toward North Korea were found statistically significant.

One possible explanation about the non-effect of South Korean identification on perception of North Korea is that what evokes South Korean identification may not be social comparison with North Korea but with other nations such as the US, Japan, or China. South Korean identification would have been formed by the pride coming from the global reputation South Korea holds. Again, further studies are necessary to investigate various aspects of South Korean identification. Taken together, ethnic identification influences attitude toward unification directly and also indirectly through cooperative perception. South Korean identification directly influences attitude toward unification.

The implications of the current study are as follows. First, our study verified how identification influences attitude toward unification. Compared to much research that has been conducted on identity to see how important "nation" is as a qualification for being Korean, little has been conducted on identification.

Despite the general perception that the two Koreas should form a single nation-state because the two Koreas are from a single nation (C. S. Chun 2009; P. Kim 2015; S. Kim, H. Kim, and S. Lim 2017; B. S. Lee 2015; S. Lee and Kang 2017; W. Y. Lee 2002), there is little empirical attention on how ethnic identification influences attitude toward unification (*cf.* N. Y. Lee 2014). Research on South Korean identification is even rarer. The separation of the two Koreas that has persisted for more than 70 years is now recognized as a settled system, consistently reproducing the idea that it would be better for the two Koreas to live as two separate nations (N. C. Paik 1992). In the same vein, those generations born and raised after the separation of the two Koreas already tend to recognize the two Koreas as different nations with different ethnicities (Jeong 2017). Consequently, the prolonged separation could have strengthened South Korean identification. However, there has been no practical research conducted on whether South Koreans distinguish ethnic identification from South Korean identification, or, if they do, how identifications influence their attitude toward unification.

Second, this research ventures toward the variables that relate identification with unification by means of a structural equation model. There has been preceding research on variables that affect attitude toward unification, such as ethnic identification, perception toward North Korea, perception of the benefits coming from unification, and demographic variables. Such research has a strong tendency to conduct a regression analysis by setting the attitudes toward unification as dependent variables while setting those related to attitudes toward unification as independent variables. Regression analysis presumes that independent variables are at play independently from one another. In other words, vertical or causal relationships among independent variables are not of interest in a regression analysis. Structural equation models could investigate causal relationships not only between independent variables and a dependent variable but also among independent variables. In this reason, structural equation models are commonly used to analyze public opinion data in psychological science and business but are seldom found in the area of politics (*cf.* N. Y. Lee

2014).

Our research reveals that ethnic identification and South Korean identification influence unification in a different manner. Ethnic identification influences attitude toward unification directly and also indirectly through cooperative perception. On the other hand, those showing a strong affection for, pride in, and identification with South Korea are found to consider North Korea neither as in-group nor as out-group. According to the social identification theory, it is possible for those with high South Korean identification to perceive unification as an event against their will for self-esteem. That means they are more likely to think unification as something negative to themselves. It is necessary to conduct follow-up research to verify such a hypothesis.

Third, this research shows that the perception toward North Korea and identification is not one-dimensional or zero-sum relation but at least a two-dimensional perception. It means that increase in cooperative attitude does not necessarily lead to the weakening of a confrontational attitude. Such a two-dimensional perception toward North Korea was confirmed by the attitude toward unification elaborated in this research: cooperative perception toward North Korea positively influences an attitude toward unification while confrontational perception does not influence an attitude toward unification.

It also needs to be noted that this research verifies that South Korean identification and ethnic identification are distinct from one another; the strengthening of South Korean identification should not be perceived as weakening of ethnic identification. In the research on identification of a nation with internal conflict, identification is divided into the superordinate group identification and subordinate group identification. For example, in Northern Ireland, Catholic and Protestant identification constituted low-level identification while Irish identification played as high-level identification (Ferguson and McKeown 2016). The relationship between high-level group identification and low-level group identification can be different depending on the context and level of identification. For Northern Ireland, identification on religion constituted high-group identification and identification on nation, low-group identification. Jung et al. (2015) showed that in South Korea, ethnic identification constitutes the superordinate category while South Korean identification, the subordinate category. At least, this research shows South Korean identification is clearly distinguishable from ethnic identification. The relationship between the two identifications needs to be examined further in follow-up research.

These research results deliver meaningful implications especially at a time when more people point out that ethnic identification alone is not enough to be a valid cause for unification. Above all, it shows ethnic identification has strong influence on an attitude toward unification. Perhaps, ethnic identification is still a strong variable to predict an attitude toward unification, although having been relatively weakened over time.

Single nation-unification discourse seems to be besieged by skepticism composed of two-dimensional arguments; first, South Koreans, especially young generations, have low ethnic identification; and second, ethnic identification cannot predict an attitude toward unification. The argument that people would no longer take the single ethnic identification as an acceptable cause for unification is corresponding to the latter of the two. However, this research demonstrates, if anything, that such intuitive arguments are not yet empirically verified.

Building a shared identification for reconciliation of conflicting groups is the first step to achieve the mind for unity (Adelman et al. 2016; Monroe, Hankin, and Van Vechten 2000; Reysen and Katzarska-Miller 2007). To be sure, if the Northern Ireland conflict and Cypress conflict can be any indication, having a shared identification does not necessarily play positively in building a mind for unity. However, it is too hasty to focus on limitations of the ethnic identification without thorough analysis despite the importance of a shared identification.

Naturally, follow-up research is required for ethnic identification and South Korean identification. Research topics can be whether ethnic identification and single ethnic identification can play in a different manner. Due to the long separation of the two Koreas, the ethnic identification for South Koreans could have narrowed down to South Korean identification. In addition, it is possible that ethnic identification that reflects one's affection for, pride in, and identification with the nation could have become a separate concept from the single the ethnic identification that binds South Korea and North Korea as a single nation. The weakening of ethnic identification could be due to the fact that the two Koreas have had little chance to realize their shared ethnic identification. Conducting various research on identification can be a good way to expand the envelope for unification discourse.

References

Adelman, Levi, Bernhard Leidner, Helin Ünal, Eman Nahhas, and Nurit Shnabel. 2016. "A Whole Other Story: Inclusive Victimhood Narratives Reduce Competitive Victimhood and Intergroup Hostility." *Personality and Social Psychology Bulletin* 42 (10): 1416–1430.

Bae, ByungRyeol. 2011. *Structural equation modeling with Amos 19: Principles and practice.* Seoul: Chungram.

Baek, Seung-Dae, and Tae-Jun An. 2013. "A comparative study on the national identity and multicultural receptivity of adolescents living in Daegu and Gyeongbuk regions." *Journal of Regional Studies* 21 (3): 29–51.

Baek, Seung-Dae, and Tae-Jun An. 2016. "The Influence of Adolescents' National Identity on Their Unification." *The Journal of Yeolin Education* 24 (1): 39–58.

Brewer, Marilynn B. 1979. "In-group bias in the minimal intergroup situation: A cognitive-motivational analysis." *Psychological Bulletin* 86 (2): 307–324.

Brubaker, Rogers. 2009. "Ethnicity, Race, and Nationalism." *Annual Review of Sociology* 35: 21–42.

Choe, Hyun. 2016. "National Identity and Multicultural Citizenship in South Korea." *Civil Society & NGO* 5: 21–42.

Choi, Young Eun, and Sang Moon Nam. 2014. "A Study on the Impact of Multicultural Socialization Factors on the Formation of National Identity." *Journal of Education & Culture* 20 (4): 241–279.

Chun, Chae Sung. 2009. "A Theoretical Analysis of Reunification of Korea." *Journal of Peace and Unification Studies* 1 (1): 72–109.

Chun, Woo Young, and Eun Kyung Jo. 2000. "Stereotypes of North Korea and Psychological Distance toward Unification." *The Korean Journal of Social and Personality Psychology* 14 (1): 167–184.

Chung, Ki Seon, and Seon Mi Lee. 2011. "Multicultural Society and the Identity of Migrants: Korean National Identity from a Comparative Perspective." *Comparative Korean Studies* 19 (1): 45–73.

Ferguson, Neil, and Shelley McKeown. 2016. "Social Identity Theory and Intergroup Conflict in Northern Ireland." In *Understanding Peace and*

Conflict Through Social Identity Theory, edited by Shelley McKeown, Reeshma Haji, and Neil Ferguson, 215–227. New York, NY: Springer.

Han, JeongHun. 2016. "Korean Voters' Ideological Propensities: A Case Study of the Effect of Ideology on Voters' Perception of Unification in Korea." *Korean Political Science Review* 50 (4): 105–126.

Hong, Se Hee. 2009. "The Criteria for Selecting Appropriate Fit Indices in Structural Equation Modeling and Their Rationales." *Korean Journal of Clinical Psychology* 19 (1): 161–177.

Hwang, Ji Hwan. 2011. "Rethinking South Korea's Perception of the North Korean Issue: In Search of a New Approach." *Journal of Peace and Unification Studies* 3 (2): 3–32.

Hwang, Jung-Mee. 2010. "Analysis of Multicultural Acceptability in Korea: From the perspective of new politics of membership." *The Journal of Asiatic Studies* 53 (4): 152–184.

Jang, Min Su, and Jun Seok Kim. 2015. "The Causes and Consequences of Ambivalent Attitude toward North Koreans: An Empirical Test." *Journal of Korean Politics* 24 (1): 111–139.

Jang, Seung-Jin. 2010. "Multiculturalism among Koreans: Role of Economic Self-Interests and National Identities." *Korean Political Science Review* 44 (3): 97–119.

Jeong, Han-Wool. 2017. "National Identity Change in South Korea: An Empirical Study on the Rise of Two Nations-Two States' Identities." *Peace Studies* 25 (2): 43–86.

Jones, Frank L., and Philip Smith. 2001. "Individual and Societal Bases of National Identity. A Comparative Multi-Level Analysis." *European Sociological Review* 17 (2): 103–118.

Jung, Jiin, Michael A. Hogg, and Hoon-Seok Choi. 2015. "Reaching Across the DMZ: Identity Uncertainty and Reunification on the Korean Peninsula." *Political Psychology* 37 (3): 341–350.

Jung, Se Young, and Yong Ho Kim. 2014. "Continuity and Variation of Perception on North Korea: Regarding Its Stereotypic Tendency." *Korea and World Politics* 30 (2): 30–58.

Kang, Won-Taek, and Nae Young Lee. 2011. "National Identity and Ethnic

Identity in Korea." In *Understanding Korean Identity: Through the Lens of Opinion Survey*. Edited by Won-Taek Kang and Nae Young Lee. Seoul: East Asia Institute, 11–31.

Kim, Gaksik, 2007. "The South-South Conflict in Korea: Origin, Development and Characteristics." *Korea and World Politics* 23 (2): 31–59.

Kim, Hyeon Jeong, Yeongock Park, and Sang Hee Park. 2015. "Basic psychological characteristics, political attitudes, and candidate choice: A path model analysis." *The Korean Journal of Social and Personality Psychology* 29 (4): 103–132.

Kim, Hyun Suk, Songsik Choi, and Hee Jae Kim. 2011. "The Relationship between National Identity and Attitudes towards Immigrants—A Comparison of Korean, Chinese and Japanese University Students." *Journal of International Area Studies* 15 (2): 141–168.

Kim, KyoungEun, and NoAh Yoon. 2012. "Adolescents' Perceptions of National Identity, Unification and Multicultural Acceptability—Implication for Unification Education of Social Studies in Multicultural Society." *Social Studies Education* 51 (1): 123–140.

Kim, Philo 2015. "Planning the future of a unified Korea: Vision, Reality, Alternative." *The Korean Journal of Unification Affairs* 27 (1): 1–30.

Kim, Sun, Heuijeong Kim, and Sujin Lim. 2017. "An analysis of the social demographic characteristics of the South Koreans according to their views on unification with North Korea." *Journal of Education & Culture* 23 (6): 27–48.

Kim, Taehyun, Gon Namkung, and Yooseok Yang. 2003. "Korean People's Foreign Policy Beliefs and National Images of North Korea." *Korean Political Science Review* 37 (3): 151–174.

Kunovich, Robert M. 2009. "The Sources and Consequences of National Identification." *American Sociological Review* 74 (4): 573–593.

Lee, Byung Soo. 2015. "The Antagonistic Relationship between Unification and Peace—Korean Unification Ideology, State Form of the Unified Korea, Nationality and Stateness." *Epoch and Philosophy* 26 (1): 323–352.

Lee, Nae Young. 2011. "Main Source of Ideological Conflict in Korea: Public Polarization or Elite Polarization?" *The Korean Association of Party*

Studies 10 (2): 251–287.

Lee, Nae Young. 2014. "What Determines Korean Perception and Attitude on National Unification?: Searching for the new analytical model." *Peace Studies* 22 (1): 167–206.

Lee, Sang-Kul, and Chae-Wan Lim. 2016. "A Study on Interrelationship between Identity and Unification Consciousness of New Generation in Koreans in Japan." *Journal of North-East Asian Culture* 46: 355–378.

Lee, Sukhee, and Jung In Kang. 2017. "Why Unification? A Critical Review of Three Unification Discourses in South Korea." *Journal of Korean Politics* 26 (2): 1–27.

Lee, Woo Young. 2002. "A New Discourse for Unification." *Comparative Society*, 69–89.

McGarty, Craig, and R. E. C. Penny. 1988. "Categorization, accentuation and social judgement." *British Journal of Social Psychology* 27 (2): 147–157.

Monroe, Kristen Renwick, James Hankin, and Renée Bukovchik Van Vechten. 2000. "The Psychological Foundations of Identity Politics." *Annual Review of Political Science* 3 (1): 419–447.

Paik, Nak-chung. 1992. "Understanding of Division-system theory." *Creation & Criticism* 20 (4): 288–309.

Park, Juhwa, MinKyu Lee, and Wonbin Cho. 2017. *2017 Survey of Inter-Korean Integration*. Seoul: Korea Institute for National Unification.

Park, Myoung Kyu, and Sang Shin Lee. 2011. "Phenomena and Images—the Measurement and Analysis of North Korean Images." *Journal of Peace and Unification Studies* 3 (1): 129–173.

Reber, Arthur S., and Emily Reber. 2011. *The Penguin Dictionary of Psychology*. London: Penguin.

Reysen, Stephen, and Iva Katzarska-Miller. 2017. "Superordinate and Subgroup Identities as Predictors of Peace and Conflict: The Unique Content of Global Citizenship Identity." *Peace and Conflict: Journal of Peace Psychology* 23 (4): 405–415.

Roccas, Sonia, Yechiel Klar, and Ido Liviatan. 2006. "The Paradox of Group-Based Guilt: Modes of National Identification, Conflict Vehemence, and Reactions to the In-Group's Moral Violations." *Journal of Personality and*

Social Psychology 91 (4): 698–711.

Shin, Shang Hui, Tae Kyung Hur, and Yoshihisa Kashima. 2012. "Various Perspectives of National Identification: Research Suggestions for Globalisation and Multi-cultural Society. *The Korean Journal of Psychology: General* 31 (4): 1231–1254.

Shin, Yul. 2010. "Human Needs Theory Seen from the Perspective of Conflicts within South Korea—Lee Myung-bak Administration's Middle Road Pragmatic Policies and Its Potential to Solve Conflicts within South Korea." *Korean Political Science Review* 44 (2): 69–92.

Smith, Anthony D. 1991. *National Identity*. Reno, Las Vegas: University of Nevada Press.

Tajfel, Henri, and John C. Turner. 1979. "An Integrative Theory of Intergroup Conflict." In *The Social Psychology of Group Relations*. Edited by Stephen Worchel and William G. Austin. Monterey, CA: Brooks/Cole, 33–47.

Turner, John C., Michael A. Hogg, Penelope J. Oakes, Stephen D. Reicher, and Margaret S. Wetherell. 1987. *Rediscovering the Social Group: A Self-Categorization Theory*. Oxford, England: Basil Blackwell.

Yang Kye-Min. 2009. "The Influence of Korean Ethnic Identity upon the Multicultural Receptiveness of Adolescents." *Studies on Korean Youth* 20 (4): 387–422.

Yi, Seong Woo. 2015. "The Influence of South Korean Public Opinion and the Possibility of Domestic Conflict on Policies toward North Korea." *Dispute Resolution Studies Review* 13 (3): 225–256.

Yoon, In-Ji, and Youngho Song. 2011. "South Koreans' Perceptions of National Identity and Acceptance of Multiculturalism." *The Korean Journal of Unification Affairs* 23 (1): 143–192.

Yoon, Kwang Il. 2017. "Political Psychology on Korean National Identity." *Culture and Politics* 4 (4): 4–41.

3. Peace through Cooperation or Peace through Strength?
How to Achieve Peace in an Intractable Conflict Society

Young-Mi Kwon (Sungkyunkwan University) and
Ju Hwa Park (Korea Institute for National Unification)

Abstract

Conflict on the Korea Peninsula has more than 70 years of history, and thus the life of the people on the peninsula reveals the typical characteristics of an intractable conflict society (Bar-Tal 2000). We conducted a nationwide survey of South Koreans (N=1,000) to investigate the attitude toward militant and cooperative internationalism. We measured right-wing authoritarianism (Zakrisson 2005), social dominance orientation (Pratto et al. 1994), and security-harmony value orientation (Braithwaite 1997) as individual difference variables. We also measured South Koreans' hostility toward North Korea, the tendency to regard inter-Korean relations as zero-sum relations, and competitive victimhood (Noor et al. 2012) to examine the respondents' perceptions of North Korea as well as inter-Korea relations. Lastly, we measured attitudes toward peace and war on the Korean Peninsula as the factors that directly predict people's attitudes toward the two ways to achieve peace on the Korean Peninsula. The multiple regression analysis indicates that the value of international harmony and equality and attitudes toward peace on the Korean Peninsula are the best predictors of cooperative internationalism, while the value of international harmony and equality and the attitudes toward war on the Korean Peninsula were the strongest predictors of militant internationalism. We also conducted serial mediation analysis (Hayes 2013) to explore the relationships between the individual difference variables, perceptions of inter-Korean relations, attitudes toward peace and war on the Korean Peninsula, and the attitude toward militant and cooperative internationalism to achieve peace between South and North Korea. The analysis indicates that the tendency to regard inter-Korean relations as zero-sum relations and the attitudes toward peace on the Korean Peninsula mediated the relationship between the value of international harmony and cooperative internationalism, while the zero-sum perception and attitudes toward war on the Korean Peninsula mediated the same value factor and cooperative internationalism. Possible implications are discussed.

Keywords

peace on the Korean Peninsula, intractable conflict, peace psychology

Introduction

As the talks between South and North Korea and between North Korea and the United States surrounding the Korean Peninsula are taking a new turn, there is a rising interest in whether the intractable conflict between the two Koreas, which has lasted for 70 years, will finally end. Talks and negotiations among the South Korean, North Korean, and US governments are aimed at bringing about an agreement and systemic change in such matters as the declaration of the end of the Korean War, the denuclearization of North Korea, and the peace treaty. However, even though the agreement and unification on national and systemic levels are necessary conditions and goals for the realization of peace on the Korean Peninsula, they cannot be considered ultimate goals from a long-term point of view. Even if systemic unification is achieved, without resolving the fundamental causes of the conflicts and disputes between the two separated Koreas, hostile feelings and attitudes toward each other are highly likely to cause new forms of social problems. In a similar vein, the peace scholar Galtung (1969) argued that peace should be divided into "negative peace," which means a state without war, and "positive peace," which means a state in which there are positive social values such as harmony, justice, and equality. In particular, given the special circumstances on the Korean Peninsula with intractable conflicts, achieving harmony and unity between the South and North Korean residents after systemic unification is necessary for the realization of true peace on the Korean Peninsula. The purpose of this study is to grasp people's perceptions on peace from a longer-term perspective, unlike previous studies that mainly focused on South Koreans' perceptions on unification. In other words, this study was conducted to explore people's attitudes toward specific methods (military power or cooperation) of achieving peace as an ultimate goal and diverse variables affecting these attitudes.

– Intractable conflict on the Korean Peninsula

Given the purpose of this study, it is necessary to understand the unique situation of the decades-long intractable conflicts between South and North Korea. Intractable conflicts are defined as long-term conflicts in which there is no clear victory or defeat between the conflict parties, or those in which the parties have not actively cooperated for peaceful settlement of the conflicts for a long time (Bar-Tal 2007; Kriesberg 1993). According to Kriesberg (1993), an intractable conflict is (1) a protracted conflict that lasts for at least one generation, (2) causes large and small violent incidents, (3) is perceived as irresolvable peacefully by the conflict parties, and (4) demands they invest extensive physical and psychological resources. In addition, Bar-Tal considered an intractable conflict a total conflict related to existence and survival of the communities and individuals in conflict, who perceive it as a zero-sum ("winner-takes-all") relationship. He also argued that it is a central conflict affecting the communities and lives of their members in diverse ways.

The characteristics of intractable conflicts are well reflected in the relationship between the two Koreas. The Korean War did not end with a one-sided victory but stopped through the ceasefire agreement in 1953. Officially, however, it did not come to an end. Large and small terrorist attacks and local battles occurred between the two sides, and there have been repeated cases where the mood of reconciliation has been disrupted by sudden violent collision. The attitude toward North Korea and reunification has become an important criterion in South Korean society that distinguishes the leftists and rightists and liberals and conservatists, acting as a powerful variable causing conflicts among regions and generations. In addition, as people of a nation in truce, young Korean men must fulfill their military duties, and the debate over this mandatory military service system sometimes causes conflicts between men and women and between various social strata (Chung 2001). By experiencing a seemingly peaceful yet "lack of peace" situation for a long period of time, people are more likely to perceive unification as a big change that disturbs the current familiar situation rather than as a goal that must be achieved. Although considerable resources are consumed by the nation and individuals because of the ceasefire situation, people may perceive the necessary resources and confusion that are expected in the process of stabilizing the system after the unification as a bigger burden. This is because the systemic unification is not an ultimate goal that can solve all current problems, and people exposed to chronic conflicts tend to perceive peace at an abstract level and may not fully understand the specific method and process to achieve peace (Bar-Tal 2000). In this context, it is vital to have a discourse on how to embody people's perceptions on peace on the Korean Peninsula, the definition of practically realizable peace, and the method to achieve it.

Coleman (2012) considered sustainable peace a state where the potential of violence has been lowered and the potential of peace has been enhanced in overall society as well as the lives of individuals. He classified the factors that can affect sustainable peace into micro-level (individual), meso-level (social community), and macro-level (national) factors. In particular, he argued that micro-level factors consist of various individual-level psychological factors that promote the potential for peace as well as factors that prevent the potential for violence. As the factors that can prevent the potential for violence, he suggested the understanding of the causes and consequences of destructive conflicts; the values, attitudes, and behaviors that support non-violence; acceptance of uncertainties; and openness to difference. In addition, as the factors that promote the potential for peace, he suggested people's awareness of interdependent relationships; the values, attitudes, and behaviors that promote cooperation and trust; healthy harmony between openness to change and conservativeness; awareness of equality; and compassion for in-group and out-group members. Coleman (2012) also emphasized that the potential for peace and potential for violence can co-exist, arguing that psychological factors, which can prevent the potential for violence while increasing the potential for peace, should be strengthened. In a similar vein, this study dealt with attitudes toward peace and war independently and explored the variables affecting perceptions and attitudes toward achieving the goal of peace in "peaceful" or "violent" ways, respectively.

– The ways to achieve peace: Through cooperation or strength

Among the different ways of achieving peace including militarism, cooperationalism, and isolationism, this study focused on achieving peace through cooperation and through military strength (Cohrs et al. 2005; Grossman, Manekin, and Miodownik 2015; Johnson 1990; Vail and Motyl 2010). This study assumed that achieving peace through cooperation and achieving peace through military strength are not in opposite positions but can be treated as targets of relatively independent attitudes. Previous research has studied perceptions and attitudes toward the way of achieving peace in the general context, while this study examined attitudes toward the way of achieving peace in the context of the Korean Peninsula, expecting that South Korean people exposed to the intractable conflict for a long time would have different representations of peace from those they experience in the general context.

– Attitudes toward peace and war

First, this study included attitudes toward peace and war as variables that can affect attitudes toward the way of achieving peace. According to attitude researchers, an individual's attitude toward a specific object is not always entirely positive or negative. Attitudes toward one object can have both positive and negative characteristics—in other words, ambivalent characteristics (Cacioppo, Gardner, and Berntson 1997). Likewise, attitudes toward two objects that seemingly have highly contradictory meanings can also have relatively independent relationships, not completely negative correlations that are always located at the extremes of a single dimension. In a study by Bizumic et al. (2013) that showed a negative correlation between the attitudes toward peace and the attitudes toward war, the researchers also found that attitudes toward peace and attitudes toward war were distinct concepts by showing that the leading variables predicting each attitude were not the same. In the current study, since we also regarded the two concepts as related but distinct, we constructed a scale to measure each one respectively. In particular, this study carried out the measurement with the focus on attitudes toward peace and war in the context of the Korean Peninsula, not in the general context.

– Perceptions of North Korea and inter-Korean relations

Based on the assumption that South Koreans' perceptions and emotional responses to North Korea and their perceptions of inter-Korean relations would affect their attitudes toward peace and war on the Korean Peninsula as well as their attitudes toward the way of achieving peace on the Korean Peninsula, we included related variables in this study.

Hostility toward North Korea. According to previous studies on group conflicts that lasted for relatively long periods of time, like the Israeli–Palestinian relationship, people show a psychological tendency to see the opponent group as responsible for the conflict and derogate the morality of the opponent group, and this hostile attitude makes reconciliation between the two groups more difficult (Maoz and McCauley 2005; Shnabel et al. 2009). In this study, we applied the original items used in previous studies to the context of inter-Korean relations and measured South Koreans' tendency to see North Korea as responsible for the start and continuation of inter-Korean conflict and the tendency to disparage the morality of North Korea. We expected that this detailed measurement of attitudes toward North Korea would show greater predictive power than the simple measurement of positivity or negativity.

Tendency to perceive inter-Korean relations as a zero-sum game. This study applied the variable "belief in a zero-sum game (BZSG)" to inter-Korean relations. The original variable refers to a tendency to believe

84

that in a social relationship that shares limited resources, if one side wins, the other side will be surely defeated (Różycka-Tran, Boski, and Wojciszke 2015). According to this concept derived from the game theory of behavioral economics, the higher the tendency of people to see a relationship between two sides as a zero-sum relationship, the less likely the two sides are to try to resolve the conflict in a peaceful way. This is because they believe that for one side to be a winner, the other side must be a loser, rather than considering a possibility for both sides to gain benefits (Von Neumann and Morgenstern 1944). According to a previous study, people high in this tendency showed low trust in others and tended to choose competition instead of cooperation in a social dilemma situation (Różycka-Tran, Boski, and Wojciszke 2015). Those who perceive inter-Korean relations as zero-sum relations may think that if South Korea wants to gain benefits, it has no choice but to defeat North Korea. Then, they may think that South Korea should win in this competition even by using military strength if necessary. On the contrary, those low in this tendency may think that a win-win strategy, which benefits both South and North Korea, is possible and prefer a method that can bring the best results to both sides through cooperation.

Competitive victimhood. This variable is also a concept borrowed from previous studies that dealt with intractable conflicts among groups. It refers to the tendency of each of the two groups to argue competitively that their group experienced more damage and suffering than the opponent group in conflict (Noor et al. 2008; Noor, Brown, and Prentice 2008; Shnabel, Halabi, and Noor, 2013). This phenomenon occurs mainly in relationships in which the two sides have been harming each other due to a long-lasting dispute rather than in conflict relationships wherein one group apparently has harmed the other group unilaterally. According to previous studies, the more strongly group members experience competitive victimhood, the more likely they are to justify the in-group's violence to the out-group and deny in-group responsibility, and the less likely they are to try to forgive or reconcile with the other group (Noor et al. 2008; Noor, Brown, and Prentice 2008; Shnabel, Halabi, and Noor 2013). Applying this result to inter-Korean relations, the more strongly the South Koreans feel competitive victimhood toward North Korea, the more likely they are to think it is justifiable to return to North Korea as much suffering as it gave to South Korea. Then, they may regard defeating North Korea through violence or military strength as a positive method. On the other hand, those who think that both South and North Korea have suffered from the history of conflict might think that they must achieve peace through mutual cooperation, because another war on the Korean Peninsula would surely bring more suffering to the people of both sides.

– Individual values and attitudes

As argued by Coleman (2012), the diverse values, beliefs, and attitudes of individuals can have a significant effect on the occurrence of violence and peace at higher levels, such as in communities and countries. In this study, we included several individual characteristic variables that may influence beliefs in inter-group relationships, attitudes toward war and peace, and political attitudes.

Right-wing authoritarianism. The concept of right-wing authoritarianism begins with personality factors related to dominance and submission (Altemeyer 1998), and it is characterized by conventionalism (i.e., adherence to traditional norms and values), authoritarian aggression (i.e., aggressiveness toward those who violate norms), and authoritarian submission (i.e., subordination to authority and social norms) (Rattazzi, Bobbio, and Canova 2007; Zakrisson 2005). Right-wing authoritarianism can influence attitudes toward various social values, and it is particularly known to have a strong correlation with political orientation (Rattazzi, Bobbio, and Canova 2007). According to the study conducted by Bizumic et al. (2013), right-wing authoritarianism was negatively correlated with attitudes toward peace and positively correlated with attitudes toward war. Likewise, we also expected that right-wing authoritarianism could predict attitudes toward peace and war on the Korean Peninsula. In addition, considering that negative attitudes toward North Korea have been held by those members of South Korean society with traditional perspectives as well as those in politically conservative positions, we expected that people aligned with stronger right-wing authoritarianism would show a more negative attitude toward North Korea and inter-Korean relations.

Social dominance orientation. Social dominance orientation, along with right-wing authoritarianism, has been treated as a factor that directly influences individual attitudes, perceptions, and behaviors toward political ideologies and social structures (Hong and Lee 2010). Social dominance orientation refers to the individual attitude showing a preference for unequal relations among social groups. Those higher in such orientation believe that groups are not equal and prefer the superior group to be above the inferior group, while those lower in such orientation believe that all groups are equal and claim they should be treated equally (Pratto et al. 1994). According to previous studies mainly conducted in the United States, the higher people's social dominance orientation, the more strongly they supported political-economic conservatism, nationalism, patriotism, and anti-Black racism. Those higher in social dominance orientation also supported military program policies but tended to oppose welfare policies for minority groups in society (Pratto, Sidanius, and Levin 2006; Pratto et al. 1994). If social dominance orientation can be applied to inter-Korean relations in the same way, South Koreans with higher social dominance orientation are more likely to perceive South Korea as superior to North Korea, rather than perceiving the inter-Korean relations as equal, and to justify military attacks on North Korea.

Value of international harmony and equality vs. value of national strength and order. Finally, we included Braithwaite's (1997, 1998) value of international harmony and equality and value of national power, in expectation that those individual values would affect attitudes toward peace and war. Braithwaite investigated 14 values that can predict people's political behavior and found two higher-level independent factors in the value of security and value of harmony. By developing the value balance model, he argued that if the value of security and the value of harmony are not balanced but a greater weight is placed on one value, people are likely to take an attitude toward a specific direction. When deciding on a political behavior, those who regard the value of security as important make their decision based on national strength and order, while those who regard the value of harmony as important make their decision based on international harmony and equality. Braithwaite (1998) found that the former prefer conservative policies, while the latter prefer progressive policies. In the current study, we also expected that those who regard international harmony and equality as important would pursue cooperation and equal relations between the two Koreas and prefer peaceful methods over war, as compared to those who regard the value of national power as important. Braithwaite (1997), meanwhile, argued that these two values do not have an "either-or" relationship. In other words, while there are people who act with greater weight in one of the two values, there are also people who consider the two values equally important and pursue balance between them. Therefore, in this study, instead of treating the two values as extreme concepts, we measured and analyzed them as independent variables.

As there are almost no previous studies on attitudes toward peace and war and attitudes toward the way of achieving peace on the Korean Peninsula, this study examined the research problems in a relatively exploratory manner. First, assuming that the individual characteristic variable, perception variable toward North Korean and inter-Korean relations, and attitude variable toward peace and war on the Korean Peninsula would predict each of the attitudes toward the way of achieving peace on the Korean Peninsula (through cooperation and through military strength), we conducted a hierarchical multiple regression analysis. In addition, we tried to test the mediating hypothesis that perceptions of North Korea and inter-Korean relations will differ according to individual values and that attitudes toward war and peace on the Korean Peninsula and attitudes toward the way of achieving peace on the Korean Peninsula will change accordingly.

Method

– Participants

This survey was conducted between May and June in 2018. A quota sampling method was used to select respondents from a population of adult men and women in South Korea, with sex, age, and region as the quota controls. A sample of 1,000 adults participated in the survey. Data was collected via face-to-face interviews with a structured survey. Demographic distribution of the current study is presented in table 2.

– Measures

In this study, we measured respondents' attitudes toward achieving peace through cooperation and attitudes toward achieving peace through strength as criterion variables. As predictor variables, first we included right-wing authoritarianism, social dominance orientation, value of international harmony and equality, and value of national strength and order as individual differences variables. To measure respondents' perception of North Korea, we included hostility toward North Korea, tendency to perceive inter-Korean relations as a zero-sum game, and competitive victimhood. Lastly, as predictor variables that may directly affect the criterion variables, we measured attitudes toward peace and war.

Achieving peace through cooperation. To measure the respondents' attitudes toward a cooperative way of achieving peace on the Korean Peninsula, we used the following six items: "Building up inter-Korean cooperation is the way to realize peace," "For peace on the Korean Peninsula, we should strengthen the role of organizations and institutions that facilitate cooperation between two Korean governments and residents," "Inter-Korean conflicts cannot be solved in the way of guaranteeing the interest of both parties" (reversed item), "It is important to improve the quality of life of North Koreans for peace on the Korean Peninsula," "Inter-Korean conflicts cannot be resolved through improving mutual understandings of social culture and communication" (reversed item), "To achieve an ultimate goal of peace on the Korean Peninsula, it is okay to use somewhat unpeaceful means" (reversed item). We used a 9-point Likert scale to measure the items (1 = Do not agree at all; 9 = Strongly agree).

Achieving peace through strength. To measure the respondents' attitudes toward a way to achieve peace through military strength and force on the Korean Peninsula, we used the following six items: "The most effective way to realize peace on the Korean Peninsula is to maintain a strong military strength," "Keeping a balance between two Koreas' military power does not guarantee peace" (reversed item), "It is unfortunate to apply military power on the Korean Peninsula, but sometimes it is the only way to maintain peace on the Korean Peninsula," "Collective security based on military alliance does not guarantee peace on the Korean Peninsula" (reversed item), "Balance of terror through military threats can be the best way to maintain a peaceful relationship with North Korea," "Peace on the Korean Peninsula cannot be realized by reducing the two Koreas' military strength and installing a joint organization to regulate military power" (reversed item). We used a 9-point Likert scale to measure the items (1 = Do not agree at all; 9 = Strongly agree).

Right-wing authoritarianism. We used the translated Korean version (Nam 2014) of Zakrisson's (2005) short scale after minor revision and included the following 15 items: "Our country needs a powerful leader, in order to destroy the radical and immoral currents prevailing in society today," "Our country needs free thinkers, who will have the courage to stand up against traditional ways, even if this upsets many people" (reversed item), "The 'old-fashioned ways' and 'old-fashioned values' still show the best way to live," "Our society would be better off if we showed tolerance and understanding for untraditional values and opinions" (reversed item), "Our society should guard closely sacred norms about abortion, pornography, and marriage and punish those who violate them before it is too late; violations must be punished," "It would be best if newspapers were censored so that people would not be able to get hold of destructive and disgusting material," "Our society needs people who challenge and criticize the government and ignore 'the normal way of living'" (reversed item), "Our forefathers ought to be honored more for the way they have built our society; at the same time we ought to put an end to those forces destroying it," "People should develop their own moral standards rather than relying on social norms" (reversed item), "There are many radical, immoral people trying to ruin things; society ought to stop them," "It is better to accept bad literature than to censor it" (reversed item), "Facts show that we have to be harder against crime and sexual immorality in order to uphold law and order," "The situation in today's society would be improved if troublemakers were treated with reason and humanity" (reversed item), "If the society so wants, it is the duty of every true citizen to help eliminate the evil that poisons our country from within." We used a 7-point Likert scale to measure the items (1 = Do not agree at all; 7 = Strongly agree).

Social dominance orientation. To measure the respondents' social dominance orientation, we used the scale created by Ho and his colleagues (Ho et al. 2015) and included the following 16 items: "Some groups of people must be kept in their place," "It's probably a good thing that certain groups are at the top and other groups are at the bottom," "An ideal society requires some groups to be on top and others to be on the bottom," "Some groups of people are simply inferior to other groups," "Groups at the bottom are just as deserving as groups at the top" (reversed item), "No one group should dominate in society" (reversed item), "Groups at the bottom should not have to stay in their place" (reversed item), "Group dominance is a poor principle" (reversed item), "We should not push for group equality," "We should not try to guarantee that every group has the same quality of life," "It is unjust to try to make groups equal," "Group equality should not be our primary goal," "We should work to give all groups an equal chance to succeed" (reversed item), "We should do what we can to equalize conditions for different groups" (reversed item), "No matter how much effort it takes, we ought to strive to ensure that all groups have the same chance in life" (reversed item), "Group equality should be our ideal" (reversed item). We used a 7-point Likert scale to measure the items (1 = Do not agree at all; 7 = Strongly agree).

Two values that determine political behaviors: International harmony and equality versus national strength and order. Among the original 14 items created by Braithwaite (1998), we selected and used 10 items that did not overlap with other individual differences measures. We included items such as "a good life for others," "international cooperation," "social progress and social reform," "equal opportunity for all," "greater economic equality," and "preserving the natural environment" to measure value of international harmony and equality, and items such as "national greatness," "national economic development," "the rule of law," and "national security" to measure value of national strength and order. We asked the respondents to report how important they considered each of the 10 values as criteria when they decide political behaviors on a 7-point Likert scale (1 = Not important at all; 7 = I almost entirely rely on this criterion).

Hostility toward North Korea. We measured the respondents' hostility toward North Korea by asking their tendency to attribute the cause of inter-Korean conflict to North Korea and their tendency to disparage the morality of North Korea. We measured the following four questions on a 7-point Likert scale (1 = Do not agree at all; 7 = Strongly agree): "North Korea is mostly responsible for inter-Korean conflict," "The reason for the prolonged inter-Korean conflict is North Korea's act of provocation," "North Korea does not seem to feel shame about its past actions," "North Korea means to harm South Korea."

Tendency to perceive inter-Korean relations as a zero-sum game. We selected four items from the original scale developed by Różycka-Tran, Boski, and Wojciszke (2015) and revised them in the context of inter-Korean relations. The respondents answered the following four items on a 7-point Likert scale (1 = Do not agree at all; 7 = Strongly agree): "In inter-Korean relations, a gain for North Korea is usually a loss for South Korea," "The inter-Korean relationship is like a tennis match—one side wins only when the other side loses," "In inter-Korean relations, when one side does much for the other side, it loses," "In most situations in inter-Korean relations, the interests of the two Koreas are inconsistent."

Competitive victimhood. By applying the content of the original scale developed by Noor et al. (2008) to inter-Korean relations, we created the following four items: "In the history of war and division, South Korea has suffered more than North Korea," "In the history of war and division, both South Korea and North Korea are victims" (reversed item), "Inter-Korean conflict is painful for both South Korea and North Korea" (reversed item), "The proportion of trauma due to the war and division has been more severe in South Korea than North Korea." The respondents answered the items on a 7-point Likert scale (1 = Do not agree at all; 7 = Strongly agree). A higher score on these measures means a perception that South Korea has suffered more than North Korea, while a lower score means a perception that both South Korea and North Korea have suffered.

Attitude toward peace on the Korean Peninsula. To measure the respondents' attitudes toward peace in the context of the Korean Peninsula, we created the following six items on a 9-point Likert scale (1 = Do not agree at all; 9 = Strongly agree): "The top priority of South Korea should be attaining peace on the Korean Peninsula," "Efforts for peace on the Korean Peninsula sometimes obstruct social development" (reversed item), "People who advocate war on the Korean Peninsula are more courageous than those who support peace on the Korean Peninsula" (revised item), "Inter-Korean conflict should be resolved in a peaceful way," "Peace on the Korean Peninsula brings the best quality of life to our society," "There are many other things that are more important than peace on the Korean Peninsula" (reversed item). Higher scores on these measures indicate the respondents' attitudes consider peace on the Korean Peninsula important and support it.

Attitude toward war on the Korean Peninsula. In the same way, we created the following six items to measure the respondents' attitudes toward war on the Korean Peninsula: "There is a time when a war is the best way to resolve inter-Korean conflict," "We have not given adequate attention to the positive results of an inter-Korean war," "War on the

Korean Peninsula cannot be justified under any circumstance" (reversed item), "War on the Korean Peninsula is a self-destructive, meaningless fight" (reversed item), "Any benefits of an inter-Korean war cannot surpass the catastrophes of the war" (reversed item), "There is a time when a war is necessary on the Korean Peninsula to realize justice." We used a 9-point Likert scale (1 = Do not agree at all; 9 = Strongly agree). Higher scores on these measures mean the respondents' attitudes consider war on the Korean Peninsula necessary and support it.

Data Analysis

SPSS 25 and SPSS PROCESS macro ver. 3.2 (Hayes 2013) were used to analyze the data. After conducting a factor analysis for each variable, we found that for the variables including reversed items, there was a structural difference between the reverse-coded questions and ordinarily coded questions. Also, compared to the variables without reversed items, those with reversed items had noticeably lower Cronbach's α reliability coefficients. This result may be due to response errors caused by the employment of reverse coding. Many researchers have argued that unlike the original aim to reduce response bias, reverse coding rather affects respondents' reactions. More specifically, it was found that using reverse-coded items changed factor structures (Cordery and Sevastos 1993; Marsh 1996), mean of scale (Schriesheim and Hill 1981), reliability, and the validity of the result (Hughes 2009). In this study, to reduce potential response errors due to reverse coding, we excluded reverse-coded items and only used ordinarily coded items to calculate a mean score of each variable.

For the 10 items used to measure value of international harmony and quality and value of national strength and order, the "preserving the natural environment" item was, incongruously with a theory, loaded to the value of national strength and order factor. A factor analysis of the other nine items produced two factors (55.08% of variance explained), supporting the theorized structure. Therefore, we aggregated the remaining five items to calculate a mean score of value of international harmony and equality factor and the four items to calculate a mean score of value of national strength and order, respectively. Means, standard deviations, and Cronbach's α reliability coefficients for each variable are presented in table 3. Correlations between variables are presented in table 4.

To examine the relative effect of predictor variables on attitudes toward achieving peace through cooperation and attitudes toward achieving peace through strength respectively, we conducted hierarchical multiple regression analysis. In addition to the predictor variables, we included a few demographic variables such as sex, age, and average monthly household income. Also, to investigate whether individuals' values affect perceptions of North Korea and attitudes toward peace and war on the Korean Peninsula, and eventually influence preference for a specific way to achieve peace on the Korean Peninsula, we conducted serial multiple mediation analysis on the structure of "values → perceptions of North Korea → attitudes toward peace/war on the Korean Peninsula → attitudes toward achieving peace on the Korean Peninsula through cooperation/strength." For serial multiple mediation analysis, we used the model 6 provided by PROCESS macro, and used bootstrapping to assess indirect effects. Five thousand bootstrap samples were generated. If zero was not included between the lower and upper bound of confidence intervals, we interpreted the result as statistically significant. Lastly, since there is very little research on the serial multiple mediation model concerning the current research problem, we selected highly predictable variables (i.e., high R2) based on the results of hierarchical multiple regression analysis and created exploratory mediation models.

Results

– Hierarchical multiple regression analysis

Before conducting hierarchical multiple regression analysis, to examine multi-collinearity among variables, we checked tolerance and VIF. The test for multi-collinearity showed that tolerance for all variables was higher than .01 and VIF was lower than 10, indicating no serious issue of multi-collinearity.

– Achieving peace on the Korean Peninsula through cooperation.

A four-stage hierarchical multiple regression was conducted with attitudes toward achieving peace on the Korean Peninsula through cooperation the dependent variable. Demographic variables (sex, age, average monthly household income) were entered at stage 1. Value variables (right-wing authoritarianism, social dominance orientation, value of international harmony and equality, value of national strength and order) were entered at stage 2, and the variables to measure perceptions of North Korea (hostility toward North Korea, tendency to perceive inter-Korean relations as a zero-sum game, competitive victimhood) were entered at stage 3. Lastly, attitudes toward peace/war on the Korean Peninsula were entered at stage 4.

As presented in table 5, demographic variables in the step 1 did not predict the criterion variable (accounted for .4% of the variance). Among the demographic variables, only the effect of age was significant, implying that the older the respondents were, the more supportive attitudes toward cooperative ways of achieving peace on the Korean Peninsula they showed. Introducing value variables explained an additional 15% of the variance and this change in $R2$ was significant, $F (4, 990) = 42.37, p < .001$. Among the value variables included in step 2, value of international harmony and equality was the only significant predictor, indicating that the more important the respondents thought the value of international harmony and equality, the more supportive attitude toward cooperative ways of achieving peace on the Korean Peninsula they reported. The addition of variables that measure perception of North Korea to the regression model explained an additional 2% of the variation and the change in $R2$ was significant, $F (3, 987) = 7.63, p < .001$. More specifically, the stronger hostility toward North Korea the respondents felt and the more likely they perceived inter-Korean relations as a zero-sum game, the less likely they supported the way of achieving peace through cooperation. Finally, adding attitudes toward peace/war on the Korean Peninsula to the regression model explained a significant additional 22.5% of the variation, $F (2, 985) = 182.50, p < .001$. Attitude toward peace on the Korean Peninsula significantly predicted the criterion variable, $\beta = .49, t = 17.98, p < .001$, while attitude toward war on the Korean Peninsula marginally predicted the criterion variable in a negative way, $\beta = -.06, t = -1.82, p = .068$. In other words, the more positive attitude toward peace and the more negative attitude toward war on the Korean Peninsula the respondents had, the more likely they supported cooperative ways to achieve peace on the Korean Peninsula.

Achieving peace on the Korean Peninsula through strength. In the same way, we included demographic variables, value variables, perception of North Korea, and attitudes toward peace/war on the Korean Peninsula in the regression model and examined which variables predicted an attitude toward achieving peace on the Korean Peninsula through strength. The results are presented in table 6.

First, demographic variables included in step 1 did not predict the criterion variable (accounted for 0.2% of the variance). Value variables added in step 2 explained an additional 19% of the variance and the change in $R2$ was significant, $F (4, 990) = 59.70, p < .001$. Among the value variables, three variables except for value of national strength and order significantly predicted attitude toward achieving peace through strength, $\beta s = .23, .20, -.31, ts = 7.47, 6.72, -8.91, ps < .001$. More specifically, the higher right-wing authoritarianism and social dominance orientation the respondents had and the less important they thought the value of international harmony and equality, the more likely they supported the way of achieving peace on Korean Peninsula through strength. Included in step 2, value of international harmony and equality was the only significant predictor, indicating that the more important the respondents thought the value of international harmony and equality, the more supportive an attitude toward cooperative ways of achieving peace on the Korean Peninsula they reported. Adding the variables that measure perception of North Korea to the regression model explained a significant additional 14% of the variation, $F (3, 987) = 70.46, p < .001$. Three variables all significantly predicted the criterion variable, βs = .23, .13, .14, ts = 6.81, 3.35, 4.38, ps < .01. In other words, the stronger hostility toward North Korea the respondents felt, the more likely they perceived inter-Korean relations as a zero-sum game, and the stronger competitive victimhood they had, the more positive attitude toward the way of achieving peace through strength they showed. Lastly, an addition of attitudes toward peace/war on the Korean Peninsula to the regression model explained a significant additional 10% of the variation, F (2, 985) = 88.53, p < .001. Attitude toward war on the Korean Peninsula significantly predicted the criterion variable, β = .39, t = 13.09, p < .001, while attitude toward peace on the Korean Peninsula did not, p = .367. The result indicated that positive attitude toward war on the Korean Peninsula positively predicted supportive attitude toward using military strength to achieve peace on the Korean Peninsula.

– Serial multiple mediation analysis

We created serial multiple mediation models including "respondents' values → perception of North Korea → attitude toward peace/war on the Korean Peninsula → attitude toward achieving peace on the Korean Peninsula through cooperation/strength" paths. Based on the assumption that attitude toward cooperative way and military way to achieve peace are relatively independent, we examined each model independently. While creating mediation models, we put priority on the variables that significantly predicted the criterion variables in the regression analysis and examined multiple models.

Serial multiple mediation analysis on achieving peace through cooperation. According to the results of hierarchical multiple regression analysis, value of international harmony and equality was the only significant predictor among the value variables, and hostility toward North Korea and zero-sum perception were significant among the variables measuring perception of North Korea, and attitude toward peace on the Korean Peninsula was also a significant predictor. Therefore, we examine the mediation paths "value of international harmony and equality → hostility toward North Korea → attitude toward peace on the Korean Peninsula → achieving peace through cooperation on the Korean Peninsula (model 1)" as well as the mediation paths "value of international harmony and equality → zero-sum perception → attitude toward peace on the Korean Peninsula → achieving peace through cooperation on the Korean Peninsula (model 2)." As a result, for model 1, the path "value of international harmony and equality → hostility toward North Korea" was not significant. On the other hand, paths in model 2 including zero-sum perception were all significant. The result of model 2 is presented in figure 1 and table 7. The direct effect of value of international harmony and equality on attitude toward achieving peace on the Korean Peninsula through cooperation was B = .031, and the indirect effect including mediating variables was B = .24. The total effect of model 2 was B = .55. The result showed that the more important the respondents considered value of international harmony and equality, the less likely they perceived inter-Korean relations as a zero-sum game. Then, their attitude to support peace on the Korean Peninsula became more positive, and as a result, their supportive attitude toward achieving peace on the Korean Peninsula through cooperation became stronger.

Serial multiple mediation analysis on achieving peace through strength. In the same way, based on the result of regression analysis, we selected three individual value variables (right-wing authoritarianism, social dominance orientation, and value of international harmony and equality), three variables measuring perception of North Korea (hostility toward North Korea, zero-sum perception, competitive victimhood), and attitude toward war on the Korean Peninsula. By including each of the value variables and perception of North Korea variables, we created and examined nine serial multiple mediation models.

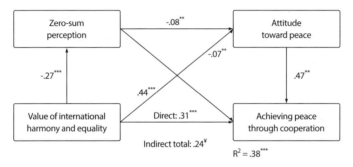

**p < .01, ***p < .001; ¥ indicates that the indirect effect of significant within 95% confidence interval.

Figure 1: Serial Multiple Mediation: Attitude toward Achieving Peace on the Korean Peninsula through Cooperation (Model 2)

The total effect, direct effect, total indirect effect, and insignificant paths of nine models are presented in table 8. For models 1, 4, 7, the direct path from right-wing authoritarianism on achieving peace through strength was not significant. Also, for model 2 and model 3, both social dominance orientation and value of international harmony and equality did not predict hostility toward North Korea, respectively. In the remaining four models (model 5, model 6, model 8, model 9), all paths including direct effect and indirect effects were significant. Especially, model 6 and model 9, which included value of international harmony and equality, produced the biggest direct effect (Bs = -.60). Therefore, we decided to focus on these two models and interpret the mediation effects. The result of model 6 is presented in figure 2 and table 9, and the result of model 9 is presented in figure 3 and table 10. In model 6 (value of international harmony and equality → zero-sum perception → attitude toward war on the Korean Peninsula → achieving peace through strength on the Korean Peninsula), the direct effect was B = -.29, and the total indirect effect was B = -.31. It indicated that the more importance the respondents put on value of international harmony and equality, the less likely they perceived inter-Korean relations as a zero-sum game. The weaker zero-sum perception then predicted the respondents' negative attitude toward war on the Korean Peninsula, leading to a negative attitude toward achieving peace on the Korean Peninsula through strength. In model 9 (value of international harmony and equality → competitive victimhood → attitude toward war on the Korean Peninsula → achieving peace through strength on the Korean Peninsula), the direct effect was B = -.28, and the total indirect effect was B = -.32. According to this model, the more important the respondents considered value of international harmony and equality, the more likely they thought that both South and North Korea are victims of the intractable conflicts. This perception then led to more a negative attitude toward war on the Korean Peninsula, resulting in a negative attitude toward achieving peace through strength.

Discussion

In this study, we tried to understand the perceptions and attitudes

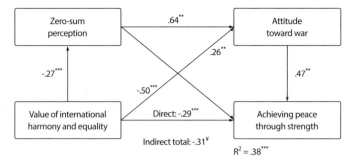

**p < .01, ***p < .001; ¥ indicates that the indirect effect of significant within 95% confidence interval.

Figure 2: Serial Multiple Mediation: Attitude toward Achieving Peace on the Korean Peninsula through Cooperation (Model 6)

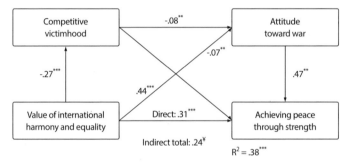

**p < .01, ***p < .001; ¥ indicates that the indirect effect of significant within 95% confidence interval

Figure 3: Serial Multiple Mediation: Attitude toward Achieving Peace on the Korean Peninsula through Cooperation (Model 9)

of the South Korean people toward peace on the Korean Peninsula and explore the variables that can predict attitudes toward the way of achieving peace on the Korean Peninsula. For this purpose, targeting 1,000 adult men and women living in South Korea, we measured individual value variables including right-wing authoritarianism, social dominance orientation, values of international harmony and equality, value of national power, variables to measure perception of North Korea such as hostility toward North Korea, tendency to perceive inter-Korean relations as a zero-sum game, competitive victimhood toward North Korea, and attitudes toward peace and war on the Korean Peninsula and toward the way of achieving peace on the Korean Peninsula.

According to the results of hierarchical multiple regression analysis, stronger positive attitudes toward achieving peace on the Korean Peninsula through cooperation were found when the respondents were older, regarded the value of international harmony and equality as more important, had less hostility toward North Korea, and were less likely to perceive inter-Korean relations as a zero-sum relationship. As expected, those with positive attitudes toward peace on the Korean Peninsula preferred achieving peace through cooperation, while those with positive attitudes toward war showed negative evaluations of this approach. The positive attitudes toward achieving peace on the Korean Peninsula through military force were stronger when right-wing authoritarianism and social dominance orientation were higher, the value of international harmony and equality was seen as less important, hostility toward North Korea was higher, inter-Korean relations were perceived as a zero-sum relationship, and competitive victimhood toward North Korea was higher. In addition, respondents with more positive attitudes toward war on the Korean Peninsula evaluated achieving peace through military power more positively.

As in Bizumic et al. (2013), attitudes toward the two ways of achieving peace on the Korean Peninsula were negatively correlated

(r = -.262; see table 4). However, as the relations between predictive variables were different, they seem to be distinct concepts. Attitudes toward achieving peace on the Korean Peninsula through cooperation were generally positive with an average of 6.45 (standard deviation 1.05), while attitudes toward achieving peace on the Korean Peninsula through military force averaged 5.12, close to the midpoint of the scale (standard deviation 1.44). Interestingly, attitudes toward war on the Korean Peninsula averaged 4.39 (standard deviation 1.76), which is somewhat negative compared to the midpoint, but there seems to be a kind of justification mechanism that even military force may be used to achieve peace on the Korean Peninsula if necessary.

Among the variables that measured individual values, the value of international harmony and equality seems to be the best predictor of both ways of achieving peace. Right-wing authoritarianism reflects the acceptance of authority and tradition within a social system, and social dominance orientation reflects the preference for hierarchical relationships among groups within a society, while the value of international harmony and equality reflects the value of international cooperation and peaceful relations. Therefore, there is a possibility that the value of international harmony and equality was a more sensitive predictor for perceptions and attitudes toward inter-Korean relations. On the other hand, the value of national strength and order did not show any meaningful result. Since the value of national strength and order was measured as importance of "greatness of nation," "economic development of nation," "rule of law," and "national security," it was possible that the respondents' understandings of the potential positive and negative consequences of South-North unification or achievement of peace between the South and North were mixed when they responded to this variable and did not form an attitude in a particular direction.

As expected, negative perceptions of North Korea and inter-Korean relations reduced positive attitudes toward the achievement of peace on the Korean Peninsula through cooperation but supported the achievement of peace through strength. Attitude toward peace did not significantly predict the respondents' attitudes toward achieving peace on the Korean Peninsula through strength, maybe because the dependent variable itself requires support for peace on the Korean Peninsula to some extent. In other words, the more positive attitudes the respondents had toward peace on the Korean Peninsula, the more likely they were to regard creating war or violence using military power as negative. However, at the same time, they were also likely to think that peace should be achieved by any means because they regarded peace on the Korean Peninsula as an important goal. In actuality, attitudes toward peace on the Korean Peninsula and attitudes toward achieving peace on the Korean Peninsula through strength showed a significant but weak negative correlation of $r = -.187$, implying the possibility that the conflicting forces of positive as well as negative relationships between the two variables are commingled.

Finally, according to the results of the serial multiple mediating analysis, the more the respondents regarded the value of the international harmony and equality as important, the less they tended to perceive inter-Korean relations as a zero-sum relationship, and the more positive their attitudes were toward peace on the Korean Peninsula, resulting in a more positive attitude toward achieving peace through cooperation. Similarly, in the mediating model that predicted attitudes toward achieving peace on the Korean Peninsula through strength, the value of international peace and equality was an important predictive variable. The degree to which respondents perceived inter-Korean relations as a zero-sum relationship and showed competitive victimhood toward North Korea predicted their attitudes of supporting war on the Korean Peninsula with similar effect size, leading positive attitudes toward achieving peace through strength.

As predicted, individual values affected interpretations and perceptions of North Korea and inter-Korean relations, and their attitudes toward how to create inter-Korean relations in the future changed depending on their perceptions of inter-Korean relations. From a theoretical perspective, this study has significance in that it extended the study of the phenomenon of intractable conflicts to the new context of the Korean Peninsula. In particular, this study can suggest new understanding and insight into intractable conflicts by dealing with the case of the conflicts on the Korean Peninsula because, unlike other ongoing studies, the members of both sides share the same ethnic identity but have different national identities with the unique characteristic of having had repeated exchanges and battles for 70 years. Future studies should verify the effect of understanding of the world (value) as well as understanding of oneself (identity) on inter-Korean relations and attitudes toward achieving peace by examining whether perceptions of North Korea and inter-Korean relations differ according to the level of ethnic identity and national identity.

As argued by Coleman (2012), this study assumed that peace is a complex concept and used various variables (individual values, perceptions of North Korea and inter-Korean relations, and attitudes toward peace and war) to grasp people's perceptions and attitudes toward achieving peace through seemingly incompatible means.

Considering the fact that the members of groups who have experienced intractable conflicts have relatively abstract and sometimes inaccurate perceptions of peace, these attempts can contribute to better understanding and predictions of attitudes toward peace not only at present but also in the future by reconfiguring the abstract and complex concept of peace into a concrete one. However, in this study, we included many variables for exploratory purposes due to the limitations of related previous studies. Future studies will need to focus on the variables that can best reflect the research phenomena and supplement the mechanism that can strongly predict and explain the relationship between them.

The variables examined in this study were individuals' psychological variables that exhibit higher variability according to time or context changes than demographic variables or personal difference variables. In other words, the values and perceptions of North Korea and inter-Korean relations have been shaped in a specific direction by individual inborn tendencies and experiences, but these characteristics are likely to change through education and new experiences. Therefore, the results of this study have a practical implication in that they could lead to educational programs, intervention programs, or campaigns that could change individual values and perceptions of North Korea and inter-Korean relations as a way to promote peace and cooperation between the two Koreas. However, because this study found the variables that have a strong impact on attitudes toward achieving peace on the Korean Peninsula at the most general level targeting whole respondents, additional analysis is needed to examine whether the most influential variables can change depending on individual characteristics such as gender, age, and socioeconomic status. If we can identify the differences among groups by dividing them into various subgroups (clusters), it will help us to identify the most effective elements of "peace education" for each group and contribute to forming an integrated social discourse among the groups.

The interest in the unification of the Korean Peninsula is now shifting to discourse on peace and interest in peace education from a longer-term perspective. In this context, this study aimed to explore the attitudes toward peace and toward the way of achieving peace on the Korean Peninsula, considering the characteristics of the intractable conflicts between the two Koreas as well as their historical characteristics. The results of the study showed that individual values— especially values concerning international cooperation—influence present and future perceptions of inter-Korean relations, resulting in a change in attitudes toward peace and war on the Korean Peninsula, and eventually a change in attitudes toward the way of achieving peace between South and North Korea. This implies the complexity of peace that requires a comprehensive study of various variables to increase our understanding at the same time. In the future, the effect of psychological variables, including the variables used in this study, on the multidimensional perceptions and attitudes toward inter-Korean relations and peace needs to be continuously studied, and the mechanism that predicts people's attitudes and behaviors needs to be accurately verified by clearly identifying the relationship between those variables. Even though this study focused particularly on individual psychological factors that affect attitudes toward peace and attitudes toward the way of achieving peace, in order to fully understand the complex concept of peace, a comprehensive study needs to be conducted at various (e.g., individual, group and community, national) levels from various (e.g., social, political, cultural, economic, psychological) perspectives.

References

Altemeyer, Bob. 1998. "The Other 'Authoritarian Personality.'" *Advances in Experimental Social Psychology* 30: 47–92.

Bar-Tal, Daniel. 2000. "From Intractable Conflict through Conflict Resolution to Reconciliation: Psychological Analysis." *Political Psychology* 21 (2): 351–365.

Bar-Tal, Daniel. 2007. "Sociopsychological Foundations of Intractable Conflicts." *American Behavioral Scientist* 50 (11): 1430–1453.

Bizumic, Boris, Rune Stubager, Scott Mellon, Nicolas Van der Linden, Ravi Iyer, and Benjamin M. Jones. 2013. "On the (in)compatibility of attitudes toward peace and war." *Political Psychology* 34 (5): 677–693.

Braithwaite, Valerie. 1997. "Harmony and Security Value Orientation in Political Evaluation." *Personality and Social Psychology Bulletin* 23 (4): 401–414.

Braithwaite, Valerie. 1998. "The value balance model of political evaluations." *British Journal of Psychology* 89 (2): 223–247.

Cacioppo, John T., Wendi L. Gardner, and Gary G. Berntson. 1997. "Beyond Bipolar Conceptualizations and Measures: The Case of Attitudes and Evaluative Space." *Personality and Social Psychology Review* 1 (1): 3–25.

Chung, Chin-Sung. 2001. "Feminist Reconsideration on the Compensation Policy for the Military Service." *Journal of Korean Women's Studies* 17 (1): 5–33.

Cohrs, J. Christopher, Barbara Moschner, Jurgen Maes, and Sven Kielmann. 2005. "Personal Values and Attitudes Toward War." *Peace and Conflict: Journal of Peace Psychology* 11 (3): 293–312.

Coleman, Peter T. 2012. "Conclusion: The Essence of Peace? Toward a Comprehensive and Parsimonious Model of Sustainable Peace." In *Psychological Components of Sustainable Peace.* Edited by Peter T. Coleman and Morton Deutsch, 353–369. New York: Springer.

Cordery, John L., and Peter P. Sevastos. 1993. "Responses to the original and revised Job Diagnostic Survey: Is education a factor in responses to negatively worded items?" *Journal of Applied Psychology* 78 (1): 141–143.

Galtung, Johan. 1969. "Violence, Peace, and Peace Research." *Journal of Peace*

Research 6 (3): 167–191.

Grossman, Guy, Devorah Manekin, and Dan Miodownik. 2015. "The Political Legacies of Combat: Attitudes Toward War and Peace Among Israeli Ex-Combatants." *International Organization* 69 (4): 981–1009.

Hayes, Andrew F. 2013. *Introduction to Mediation, Moderation, and Conditional Process Analysis: A Regression-Based Approach.* New York: Guilford Press.

Ho, Arnold K., Jim Sidanius, Nour Kteily, Jennifer Sheehy-Skeffington, Felicia Pratto, Kristen E. Henkel, Rob Foels, and Andrew L. Stewart. 2015. "The nature of social dominance orientation: Theorizing and measuring preferences for intergroup inequality using the new SDO7 scale." *Journal of Personality and Social Psychology* 109 (6): 1003–1028.

Hong, Kiwon, and Jong Taek Lee. 2010. "A Study on the Relations of Ideological Topology and Psychological Bases in South Korean Adults." *Korean Journal of Social and Personality Psychology* 24 (2): 1–25.

Hughes, Gail D. 2009. "The Impact of Incorrect Responses to Reverse-Coded Survey Items." *Research in the Schools* 16 (2): 76–88.

Johnson, M. J. 1990. "Attitudes toward Achieving Peace: A Measure of 'Peace through Strength' and 'Peace through Cooperation' and the Relationship of These Attitudes with Affective, Coping, Personality, and Gender Correlates." Doctoral dissertation, University of Southern California.

Kriesberg, Louis. 1993. "Intractable conflicts." *Peace Review* 5 (4): 417–421.

Maoz, Ifat, and Clark McCauley. 2005. "Psychological Correlates of Support for Compromise: A Polling Study of Jewish-Israeli Attitudes toward Solutions to the Israeli-Palestinian Conflict." *Political Psychology* 26 (5): 791–807.

Marsh, H. W. 1996. "Positive and negative global self-esteem: A substantively meaningful distinction or artifactors?" *Journal of Personality and Social Psychology* 70 (4): 810–819.

Nam, S. 2014. "Generation Gap in Political Orientation." Master's thesis, Seoul National University.

Noor, Masi, Nurit Shnabel, Samer Halabi, and Arie Nadler. 2012. "When Suffering Begets Suffering: The Psychology of Competitive Victimhood Between Adversarial Groups in Violent Conflicts." *Personality and Social*

Psychology Review 16 (4): 351–374.

Noor, Masi, Rupert Brown, Roberto Gonzalez, Jorge Manzi, and Christopher Alan Lewis. 2008. "On Positive Psychological Outcomes: What Helps Groups with a History of Conflict to Forgive and Reconcile with Each Other?" *Personality and Social Psychology Bulletin* 34 (6): 819–832.

Noor, Masi, Rupert Brown, and Garry Prentice. 2008. "Precursors and mediators of intergroup reconciliation in Northern Ireland: A new model." *British Journal of Social Psychology* 47: 481–495.

Pratto, Felicia, Jim Sidanius, and Shana Levin. 2006. "Social dominance theory and the dynamics of intergroup relations: Taking stock and looking forward." *European Review of Social Psychology* 17: 271–320.

Pratto, Felicia, James Sadinus, Lisa M. Stallworth, and Bertram F. Malle. 1994. "Social Dominance Orientation: A Personality Variable Predicting Social and Political Attitudes." *Journal of Personality and Social Psychology* 67(4): 741–763.

Rattazzi, Anna Maria Manganelli, Andrea Bobbio, and Luigina Canova. 2007. "A short version of the Right-Wing Authoritarianism (RWA) Scale." *Personality and Individual Differences* 43: 1223–1234.

Różycka-Tran, Joanna, Paweł Boski, and Bogdan Wojciszke. 2015. "Belief in a Zero-Sum Game as a Social Axiom: A 37-Nation Study." *Journal of Cross-Cultural Psychology* 46 (4): 525–548.

Schriesheim, Chester A., and Kenneth D. Hill. 1981. "Controlling Acquiescence Response Bias by Item Reversals: The Effect on Questionnaire Validity." *Educational and Psychological Measurement* 41 (4): 1101–1114.

Shnabel, Nurit, Samer Halabi, and Masi Noor. 2013. "Overcoming competitive victimhood and facilitating forgiveness through re-categorization into a common victim or perpetrator identity." *Journal of Experimental Social Psychology* 49 (5): 867–877.

Shnabel, Nurit, Arie Nadler, Johannes Ullrich, John F. Dovidio, and Dganit Carmi. 2009. "Promoting Reconciliation Through the Satisfaction of the Emotional Needs of Victimized and Perpetrating Group Members: The Needs-Based Model of Reconciliation." *Personality and Social Psychology Bulletin* 35 (8): 1021–1030.

Vail III, Kenneth E., and Matt Motyl. 2010. "Support for Diplomacy: Peacemaking and Militarism as a Unidimensional Correlate of Social, Environmental, and Political Attitudes." *Peace and Conflict: Journal of Peace Psychology* 16 (1): 29–57.

Von Neumann, John, and Oskar Morgenstern. 1944. *Theory of Games and Economic Behavior.* Princeton, NJ: Princeton University Press.

Zakrisson, Ingrid. 2005. Construction of a short version of the Right-Wing Authoritarianism (RWA) scale. *Personality and Individual Differenes* 39 (5): 863–872.

4. Division and Unification:
Seen through the Eyes of Korean Migrants in Berlin

Eun-jeung Lee (Freie Universität Berlin)
and Jin-heon Jung (Freie Universität Berlin)

Introduction

The year 2019 marks the 30th anniversary of the Berlin Wall's collapse. Koreans walking along the remains of the Berlin Wall can't help but to think of the metal fence that stretches across the waist of the Korean Peninsula. Koreans, still enduring the pain of division, look to Germany as an example of realizing the dream of unification. As a result, Germany has a special place in Korean people's hearts, and it is home for around 30,000 Korean immigrants.[1] While the number of Korean immigrants pales in comparison to the number of Turkish or Vietnamese immigrants, they are considered a migrant group that has settled relatively successfully into German society. What do Korean migrants think about "division and unification," given that they came to West Germany when it was divided and then experienced both German unification and 30 years of German integration? Has their experience of knowing that division can be overcome impacted how they view the division and unification of the Korean Peninsula? How do their perspectives on unification differ from Koreans who live in South Korea? This study sought to find answers to these questions through in-depth interviews conducted with first-generation Korean immigrants living in Berlin, Germany.

This study's researchers wanted to ask such questions because discourse about German unification in South Korea has been characterized by the concept of "the other" as discussed in cultural

---

1   There are almost no North Korean migrants living in Germany. There are only a few North Korean defectors who have been recognized as refugees along with a small number of North Korean foreign exchange students who came to East Germany in the 1960s and escaped to West Germany.

theory. This discourse focuses on German unification, but ultimately the participants in this discourse are projecting their own concept of unification into the discussion. German unification was a symbol of hope to Koreans that unification could be achieved. Up until the 1997 Asian financial crisis, most South Koreans expected that North Korea would collapse as quickly as East Germany did. The South Korean government and various institutes that conducted research on unification created a range of North Korean collapse scenarios and began to research responses to each of these scenarios as part of their efforts to comprehensively learn about Germany's unification experience. It soon become very clear, however, that reunified Germany was paying astronomically high costs because of the collapse of the East German economy, and, consequently, fears that unification could be an economic burden became widespread in South Korea. South Korean experts competed with each other to announce "unification costs" they had calculated the South Korean government would have to pay based on the German government's unification costs. The estimated economic burden that emerged from these specific figures led many South Koreans to ask whether the Korean Peninsula really needed to be unified. Ultimately, South Koreans transitioned from having vague fears toward unification to skepticism about it altogether. Thirty years have passed since Germany has reunified, and South Korean discourse on Germany's experience with unification continuous to shift back and forth between hope and fear. German unification is still an important topic within discussions on unification in South Korea. Most South Korean politicians, social scientists, and members of the media share their own opinions on German unification. It is not an overstatement to say that the South Korean government still aims to learn all it can from Germany's unification experience.[2]

South Korea's discourse on German unification, however, is very different from the unification discourse that occurred in Germany. Rai Kollmorgen and Thomas Koch discovered through a systematic analysis of the unification discourse in Germany that there were critical keywords used by different discourse participants. According to their research, the keywords that appeared in Germany's social science sphere included the terms "late modernization" and "the two sides of drastic change." Meanwhile, the predominant keyword in Germany's political sphere was "the construction of a modern and socialist state." The discourse in Germany's media, moreover, was dominated by four frameworks that defined East Germany and East Germans by "origin, characteristics or differences, weakness, and burden." On the other hand, the discourse on German unification in South Korea after the mid-1990s was defined by keywords such as "unification by absorption, unification costs, unification's aftereffects, and internal integration" (Kollmorgen, Koch, and Dienel 2011)

The focus of South Korean discourse on German unification was clearly German unification itself; however, what took on the central role in the formation of this discourse was Korea's historical experiences, realities, political hopes, and needs (Lee 2014). Of course, Germany's experience did have a role in this discourse. Many South

---

2   A great deal of research on German unification has taken place in South Korea. More than 5,000 pieces of research focused on German unification have been presented from the 1990s to the present, and major dailies in the country have reported ceaselessly on Germany's unification and integration. The records of South Korea's National Assembly have collected 5,000 mentions of German unification across a range of contexts since the 1990s. All of these different outlets of information have created South Korea's own discourse on Germany unification.

Korean politicians, scholars, and journalists visited Germany to learn about Germany's unification experience, and many German experts were invited to South Korea to talk about German unification. The exchange of all this information likely had some impact on South Korea's discourse on German unification. Nonetheless, the focus of the discourse on German unification in South Korea was less on Germany than on unification, and it has always been with the unification of the Korean Peninsula in mind. The discourse on German unification in South Korea, therefore, has directly reflected the range of South Korean perspectives toward unification of the Korean Peninsula. As such, present in South Korea's discourse on German unification are the characteristics of "the other" as discussed in Orientalism and Occidentalism.

The perspectives toward unification held by South Korean migrants living in Germany are connected to the perspectives of "the other" inherent in South Korea's discourse on German unification; however, this study's researchers have assumed that migrants have an understanding of unification that is different from Koreans living in South Korea. This broad assumption has long provided the basis for research on the Korean diaspora. Existing research has found that migrants continue to maintain connections with their places of origin and emphasizes that migrants even have nostalgia for their home countries. As research on Koreans who reside in Japan shows, migrants create their own idea of the future for their home country using the perspectives and opinions they form through their experiences abroad; moreover, this research has even confirmed that migrants tend to place their own identities in a home country that exists in the future.[3] This study has a foundation in the assumptions reflected in existing research on the Korean diaspora. This study's researchers found that, regardless of where they stood on the political spectrum, Korean migrants in Germany believed that the division of the Korean Peninsula must be overcome. The researchers also found that the migrants thought of themselves as citizens of a future united Korean Peninsula. Before moving to explain the results of this study, the following section will describe this study's processes, methodologies, and, lastly, the characteristics of the Korean diaspora in Germany, which form the social and cultural backgrounds of interviewees who participated in the study.

Research Subjects and Methodology

The main interviewees of this study were first-generation South Koreans who live in Berlin. Most of the female interviewees were sent to West Berlin as nurses or nursing assistants in their early to mid-20s between 1966 and 1976 and experienced both the division of Berlin, the process of German unification, and Germany's post-unification period. The male interviewees were sent to West Germany as miners beginning in 1963 and migrated to West Berlin for various reasons, including for marriage and for work. The interviewees all experienced Germany before and after unification, and their ages ranged from the late 60s to

---

3   Sonia Ryang (2009) argues that the General Association of Korean Residents in Japan (Chongryon) National School students she studied place their own national identity not in North Korea but in a unified Korean Peninsula.

the early to mid-70s at the time of the interviews. All the interviewees had lived in Germany for more than 40 years and had spent at least two-thirds of their lives residing in a foreign country, meaning that, culturally at least, they had hybrid identities.[4]

The hybrid identity of migrants refers to the mixture or changes in their knowledge, habits, values, religion, the food they enjoy, the languages they speak, emotional sentiments, and other cultural factors they picked up in their home countries with those of their host society and the process of acquiring multifaceted perspectives, attitudes, and value systems. Hybrid identities also include those cases where existing habits and value systems fail to change and instead simply solidify even further. Their home societies may have changed rapidly due to the passage of time, but migrant communities are frequently more conservative in their thinking and habits compared to the societies they left. As such, there is diversity between generations, genders, and individuals within any migrant community. In other words, migrant communities are hybrid, diverse, and dynamic groups.

First-generation Korean migrants in Berlin experienced Western European liberalism, democracy and multiculturalism. However, most of these migrants had similar or enhanced levels of anti-communist sentiment typical of South Koreans in the 1960s in 1970s. Other migrants had transformed their views to correspond with post-ideological, pan-national, or even pro-North Korean perspectives. In the midst of this deeply divided ideological spectrum, there were many

---

4   The concept of hybridity is evolved from the postcolonial theory of Homi Bhabha (1994) to extent that it refers to the cultural hybridities of transnational migrant people in the multiculturalism studies. See also Vertovec (1997) and Safran (1991) for further discussion about the concept of diasporas.

migrants who wanted to become politically detached from the situation on the Korean Peninsula and avoid being placed on the political spectrum.[5]

This study's researchers attempted a life-history approach through participant observation and in-depth interviews that conform with on-site anthropological research methodologies. The researchers created a rapport with the migrants while participating in their community activities in Berlin over a long period of time and made efforts to learn their own points of view. The interviews were conducted on the basis of this rapport with the migrants. Apart from formal interviews, the researchers attempted a comprehensive understanding of the interviewees' unique lives and culture. In-depth interviews were conducted with only those migrants who agreed to participate. The mid- to long-term process of participant observation began in 2016 and is still ongoing. The interview data analyzed for this study were collected from approximately 60 interviews conducted from February to August 2016.

Germany's South Korean Diaspora

Germany and South Korea began official diplomatic ties after signing a

---

5   This may prove that the geopolitical Cold War system of the Korean Peninsula strongly impacts migrant communities, but it is also impossible to ignore the history of state violence perpetrated by South Korea in Germany. The Tongbaengnim Incident (1967–1969) along with European spy ring cases and South Korean agents who, directly and indirectly, incited South Korean migrant communities to move to the political right, among other historical and social factors, have likely led to this kind of political aversion among Korean migrants.

cooperation agreement in 1883. After the end of World War II in 1945 and German division, East Germany formed a special relationship with North Korea right after its establishment by, among other things, accepting North Korean war orphans in the 1950s. Meanwhile, West Germany formed a close relationship with South Korea's government while concluding an agreement to accept South Korean nurses and miners in 1963. From 1966 to 1976, 10,226 nurses and 7,932 miners were sent to Germany. They formed the first overseas Korean community along with small groups of South Korean students who had studied in West Germany since the 1950s.

Some of these first-generation migrants no longer live in Germany. While there are no accurate statistics available, interviews with migrants suggest that around one-third of the original migrants stayed in Germany while another one-third returned to South Korea after the end of their contracts. The rest migrated again to the United States, Canada, and other parts of North America. The all-encompassing characteristics of these first-generation migrants are that they grew up during the Korean War, experienced poverty, and received intense levels of anti-communist education that taught them to hate communist North Korea. The West Germany they came to was similar to South Korea. Unlike the confrontation that existed between North and South Korea, however, a limited degree of travel was allowed between West and East Germany at the time. South Koreans who lived in West Berlin were able to visit East Berlin. Some of them even visited the North Korean embassy in East Berlin and met with North Korean diplomats. This was, of course, a violation of South Korea's anti-communist laws.[6] In 1967, South Korea's military dictatorship, led by Park Chung-hee, abducted South Koreans living in West Germany back to Seoul and put them on trial. Some were sentenced to death.[7] Within these circumstances, the South Korean community in West Germany either actively participated in the democracy movement against the dictatorship and supported the movement[8] or threw their support behind the Park government's developmental authoritarianism. Even following South Korea's transition to democracy in 1987, these two groups are still at odds with each other.[9]

---

6   You Jae Lee (2018) re-examines the East Berlin Incident and points out that the South Korean militant regime failed to consider a different sense of spatiotemporality of the Cold War that the South Korean migrants in Germany came to experience in the context of the transnational migration. It is fair to say that the state power dominated the foreign monetary funding from Germany and controlled the grassroots transnationalism as an excuse derived from the national division. In other words, the East Berlin Incident reveals an anachronistic ignorance of the state power.

7   The Tongbaengnim [East Berlin] Incident emerged through a Korean Central Intelligence Agency (KCIA) announcement on July 8, 1967, that 194 South Koreans, including Lee Ungno, a painter who lived in Paris, and the Berlin-based writer Yoon Yi-sang, along with professors who had studied abroad in Europe and South Korean students who were studying abroad, were part of a North Korean spy ring in East Berlin. Members of West Germany's cultural and media spheres, along with local citizens and students, led the international movement to release the accused. The West German government's strong protests led the accused, who had received execution, life in prison, or 10-year prison sentences, to have their sentences commuted in 1969–1970.

8   In the 1970s, the Committee for Constructing Democratic Society was founded by educated migrants, such as study abroad students and scholars, who contributed to the progressives, or we can say, the democratization movements, in South Korea. See Yi (2016) for detailed information.

9   Recently, North Korean defectors have applied for refugee status in Germany. In the early 2000s, with the enactment of the US North Korean Human Rights Act, England, Germany, the Netherlands, Belgium, France, and other European countries began to accept North Korean refugees for humanitarian reasons. However, the North Korean defectors who headed *en masse* to Europe at this time were either those who had already received citizenship in South Korea or were Chinese Koreans. Following these revelations, European countries have

The Unification Experience and Views Toward Unification Among First-Generation South Koreans in Berlin

– The collapse of borders: The collapse of the Berlin Wall and German unification through the eyes of Korean migrants

The collapse of the Berlin Wall occurred suddenly and was totally unexpected by both Germans and migrants who lived in the country. On the night of November 9, 1989, East Berliners who had crossed over the Berlin Wall were welcomed by West Berliners. The harsh levels of control over the wall had disappeared and the areas around the wall became like a festival. The collapse of the wall became a gateway to a new post-Cold War era. Koreans residing in Berlin expressed their memories of the time in sentimental language and used words like "thrilling" and "joyful"; yet, their feelings were complicated because they were "not sure how to react" to these "surprising" circumstances.

On November 10, the day after the collapse of the wall, a few members of the Korean Women's Association in Germany, which was made up of nurses and had long been engaged in politically progressive activities, "got up the courage" to visit the site of the fallen Berlin Wall. At the site, they hung up a poster that said "Korea is One." They may have been one of the first "flash mobs" to link the collapse of the Berlin

---

drastically reduced the number of North Korean refugees they accept; however, there are North Korean defectors living in a refugee facility in Stuttgart. These defectors either lived in South Korea before moving to Germany for their children's education or, more rarely, came straight to Germany from China. In Berlin, there are North Korean refugees who left South Korea to study abroad. However, there are much fewer North Korean refugees in Germany than the 500 or so North Korean defectors who live in England's New Malden. North Korean defectors did not experience the division and unification of Germany, so this study did not include their perspectives

Wall with their own hopes for the end of Korean division.

The collapse of the Berlin Wall was an important historical moment where migrants from a divided country experienced life in a country that had achieved unification. This is proven by the fact that, almost 30 years afterwards, this study's interviewees vividly remember the night of November 9, 1989. "K," who worked as a nurse in West Berlin in 1972, explained her emotions that night.

> Ah, yes, I still remember that day. I always turned on the television when I came home. I worked with sick people, so I turned on the TV to think about something else. It was Thursday. The TV said that unification had arrived . . . that the wall had fallen. People from East Germany just started coming over [into West Germany]. West Germans took the withered flowers they had in their homes and stood there and even hugged people who weren't their relatives. I was really taken by that scene. Them giving flowers—I don't remember how much I cried while watching that. I wondered how great it'd be if Korea could unify like that. I went out to the city the next day and it was just full of people. There were a lot of people from East Germany and, from what I heard, there were no incidents at all. It was just peaceful unification. How great it'd be if Korea could experience that kind of unification, too. When I began thinking like that, I just started crying. I just sat down and cried.

For Koreans living in Berlin, the end of German division was not something unrelated to them that happened in a faraway country. It was part of their own narrative, and they shared in the emotions felt by regular Germans. They did not turn the realities of Korea's division into someone else's problem, either. While Germans celebrated the collapse of the Berlin Wall, "K" put the situation in the context of Korea's own situation and hoped for the same change to occur on the Korean Peninsula.

The narrative of post-division that "K" shared was not just the physical fall of the wall; rather, it has a double-layered meaning. While adapting to a different culture after migrating abroad, Koreans residing in Berlin experienced layered border-crossing. While experiencing the realities of German society, they had experienced conflict with, the elimination of, and the restructuring of the anti-communist ideology or "Red Complex" they had learned in South Korea.

– The structure of feelings and trans-border narratives

The German unification that Korean migrants in Berlin experienced, the comparisons they made with the situation on the Korean Peninsula, and their hopes for unification can be understood through the concept of Raymond Williams's "structures of feeling." Feelings in this context are slightly different than that of the intellectual exercise of "thinking"; however, they are mutually reinforcing spheres and are not in a confrontational relationship. Antonio Gramsci's concept of hegemony is useful for understanding the ideological discourse formed by dominant classes, while Williams's concept focuses on the sphere of feelings, where diverse change occurs from the bottom up or from non-dominant classes. Williams proposes that the spheres of feeling can be divided into the dominant, residual, and the emergent. This structure of layered emotions originates from people's experiences. While an ideological system may be perceived homogeneously in a logical structure, the structure of feeling adds texture to that system. It becomes the engine for inducing internal change and becomes the concept to understand that change.

The first-generation Koreans that migrated to Germany in the 1960s and 1970s experienced the Korean War while they were young children and received anti-communist education before migrating to the center of the Cold War in Europe—Germany. Most Korean migrants arrived in Germany with ideologies and feelings dominated by anti-communist ideology and anti-North Korean sentiment. "P," a nurse from Daegu who arrived in West Berlin in 1966, told researchers, "We received education meant to refine us before we left for Germany. The course didn't teach us about German culture or society. It was just focused on anti-communist education."

Anti-communist education in South Korea at the time was not aimed at imparting knowledge about Germany. Rather, it was aimed at ensuring Korean migrants were knowledgeable about what was prohibited and was meant to scare them about the punishment and harm they could face if they broke the rules. Their responses were thus based on emotions, not rationality. "C," who arrived in West Berlin in 1966, had a similar experience.

> Everyone was praying to themselves that I wouldn't be sent to Berlin. When it turned out I was going, everyone, even my family, was really concerned. They told me not to go into the Berlin subway station Friedrichstrasse. I was really scared each time I passed that station. . . .

"P" and "C" were from the Korean War generation, but had not witnessed the horrors of the war themselves. "When I was young, I was told to hide under the floors, so I did what everyone older than me was doing. No People's Army [North Korean army] soldiers came to my neighborhood, so I really didn't know what the war was like. I was scared of the 'commies,' and that fear stayed with me for a long time."

"P" and other interviewees found that their anti-communist sentiments stayed with them for a long time, even after moving to Germany. The responses of Korean migrants toward the fall of the Berlin Wall were, compared to regular Germans, quite complicated. The researchers found during informal talks with Korean migrants that quite a few of them had immediately felt fear accompanied by surprise when they heard that the Berlin Wall had fallen.

"I was scared at first. For a long time, I didn't go into the neighborhood where the wall had been." This was one sentiment expressed casually by many Korean migrants during conversations with this study's researchers. Whether the migrants had participated in politically progressive activities or not, they all had similar responses to the fall of the Berlin Wall. One of them, "L," came to West Berlin in 1973 and has two children with her German husband, who is a doctor. She did not participate much in the local Korean community's activities and did not engage in politically progressive activities; however, her husband's brothers and relatives were in East Germany, so she witnessed familial exchanges across the two Germanies. When the Berlin Wall collapsed, however, she was full of fear that a whole wave of East Germans would flow into West Berlin and cause chaos. In short, "L"'s residual anti-communist sentiment emerged as a defense mechanism to the rapid changes in her social environment. The fear that accompanied her initial surprise at the fall of the Berlin Wall withered as she accepted the broader sentiments of West Germans, who had pursued change in the division system through contact with East Germans.

Koreans in Berlin adapted to and participated in the post-division atmosphere relatively quickly, which was similar to that of a festival. This was because they had experienced Germany's division. This suggests that they had to complete their own "experiential review" of the division situation before applying the experience of Germany's unification to the context on the Korean Peninsula or gain an understanding of it. There was a "wall of steel" that separated West and East Germany, but Germany had allowed considerable levels of exchanges, direct and indirect, that stood in contrast to the uncrossable armistice line that separated the two Koreas. Visits between families, exchanges of letters, listening to each other's broadcasts and other low-level moves toward "unification" that the two Koreas have pursued were, in actuality, the reality of the "division" that existed between East and West Germany. Many Korean migrants experienced something that was impossible on the Korean Peninsula: crossing borders for personal reasons. For example, "P" experienced familial exchanges as her family from West Berlin visited those in East Berlin and vice versa, while "H" went to East Berlin often to participate in picnics hosted by her local Korean church. Finally, "K" visited East Berlin with her German husband as tourists.

"I went to East Berlin two or three times in 1975, 1976, and 1977. . . for picnics. I would receive my visa in the morning—an *ein Tag*, or single-day visa. I would arrive in East Berlin in the morning and have to return in the evenings. I had to change the money I'd use for the day before I left. It was like 20 marks or something those days. After changing my money, I would have to [German: *muss*] bring it with me [to East Berlin]."

"K" crossed a border that she had learned initially never to cross or communicate over, and her experience of going to a picnic in East Berlin likely created emotions that were borderless in nature. Migrants felt feelings of unfamiliarity and exhilaration because they felt they were breaking some kind of rule, and these emotions were clearly seen on their faces as they spoke with the researchers. The migrants remembered their experience because of the new sets of emotions they had felt. These new emotions acted as a mechanism that allowed them to compare their current circumstances with those of their home country or, in other words, allowed them to reflect on the division of the Korean Peninsula.

> I travelled to [East Berlin] in that way. . . . I wondered when I could take a similar holiday on the Korean Peninsula and visit both sides. When can I go there [North Korea] and eat cake? Or drink coffee? . . . I was so envious [of reunified Germany].

Germany and the Korean Peninsula were similar in some respects: both were divided countries and served as the front lines for the Cold War in their respective areas of Europe and Asia. The specific nature of their divisions were, however, different. The two countries were divided in different ways, and only one had endured a horrible civil war. The levels of confrontation that had become embedded through experience and by institutions across the two sides also differed. Most research on German unification points out that comparing Germany and the Korean Peninsula is inappropriate because of their different historical backgrounds—in short, Korea's experience of the Korean

War. However, Koreans who were born during the Korean War period and received anti-communist education before moving to Berlin experienced opportunities to reflect on the fact that remnants of their "learned" anti-communism and its harmful effects were roadblocks to their initial adaptation to life in West Berlin. In other words, their first careful visits to East Berlin or their repeated experience of crossing the land border into East Germany slowly or even drastically lowered the levels of anti-communist sentiment that they had. They also formed hope that the two Koreas would improve their relationship based on the German experience of tearing down borders. Borrowing Williams' concept of the "structures of feeling," Korean migrants formed a trans-border structure of feeling by experiencing life abroad.

The prefix "trans" here does not refer to the words "overcoming," "surpassing," or "after." Rather it should be understood as a transitional experience. This is similar to the "trans" used in the process of change as interpreted in post-socialism research. In other words, the trans-border sentiments formed by Korean migrants who lived in Berlin during the division of Germany could be said to have included the remnants of anti-communist ideology, the history of the Tongbaengnim Incident and other European spy rings that involved their home country's military dictatorship, their fears about the National Security Law (NSL), or that they would be targets of surveillance. As such, their immediate responses to and interpretations of the fall of the Berlin Wall were at once similar to regular Germans yet different, which meant that the meaning of German unification to them was both more complicated and full of richness. They also had unique experiences while meeting with former East Germans after unification.

– The integration process after unification:
Multi-cultural sentiments

The two Germanies reunited just one year after the fall of the Berlin Wall in 1989. During the period of division, West Berlin, which was like an island in East Germany, witnessed an influx of people and capital. Even the hospitals where Korean nurses worked saw the arrival of East German nurses. The hospital was a cultural contact zone where people from East and West Germany, and East Germans and Korean nurses, collided and negotiated their mutual authority and values in daily life. Korean nurses often had relatively high status and authority in West Berlin hospitals.

Korean nurses generally thought that East German nurses had such little experience dealing with other kinds of people that they were unfriendly and looked down on Korean nurses. The former Korean nurses remember that East German nurses thought that the Korean nurses were seated lower on the hierarchy and gave them odd jobs to do and were high-handed in how they spoke to them. East German nurses did not understand why West German nurses received orders from Korean head nurses. East German nurses would frequently try to cause issues between German nurses and doctors and Korean nurses by talking behind their backs. Experienced Korean nurses were confused at the East German nurses' discriminatory way of speaking and the workplace conflict that they were suddenly faced with.

> I spoke slowly and they [East German nurses] understood. It was the first time for them to work with people like us. . . . It was probably because they had developed socialist habits. Talking with them, though, showed that they had an innocent side. They just

didn't know better.

"L" had trouble with some of her East German colleagues, but she understood the difficulties were due to cultural differences, not personal ones, and the hierarchy they had learned in East Germany and their general lack of sentimentality. As a result, she emphasized a "pure" temperament in her personal relationships. This showed the East German nurses that she cared about them. The period of chaos in the early days of unification—including the currency reform, rise in taxes, fall in welfare, increase in population, and fast-paced urban development—put East German people at a socioeconomic level lower than most West Germans. "L" thus tried to understand the difficulties experienced by East German nurses, who likely found it difficult to accept that Korean nurses were considered to be at a higher status than themselves.

While Korean nurses were familiar with West German workplace culture and daily life, East German nurses found everything unfamiliar. "S" told the researchers about East German nurses who had moved to West Berlin then moved back to their original neighborhoods and had to face long commutes. When "S" asked the East German nurses why they did this, she was told that their original neighborhoods felt more like a community and just better to live in.

West German social life divided working and private spaces and their accompanying relationships. Former East Germans, however, tried to maintain their socialist communal culture in response to the liberal culture of West Germany. One interviewee said that in East Germany there was, to borrow a Korean expression, more "*jong*" (affection) and that East Germans were "purer" than those who had become used to competition in the capitalist world.

Korean migrants' direct experience of unification has major implications for the Korean Peninsula. Their experiences provide a criterion for comparing small-scale social phenomena that will emerge in the integration of South Korean society—which, as a neo-liberal system has rapidly transformed into a multicultural, multi-racial society—with North Korean society, which has emphasized the "purity" of the Korean race. In short, North and South Korean people's pursuit of the "integration of their hearts" is not something that just occurs within one people, i.e. the Korean people. Koreans who live in Germany are showing that a country's multicultural and multi-racial circumstances can become a factor in national integration. This should not be overlooked in the context of South Korean society, which has witnessed a great deal of transnational movement. The sphere of the "heart" does not just include emotions and feelings but also encompasses the intellectual activities of perceptions and understanding. Because the concept of the "nation" is not just biological but also historical and cultural in nature, there are limitations to meetings that simply occur between North and South Koreans. Korean migrants' experience of unification in Berlin and their interpretations show the need for discussion on inter-Korean integration that considers the daily exchanges and communication with migrants who are part of Korean culture.

– Hopes for the unification of the divided motherland in a unified Germany

The fall of the Berlin Wall was an historical event that created hope among Korean migrants for the peaceful unification of the Korean Peninsula. After the June 15 North–South Joint Declaration in 2000 between Kim Dae-jung and Kim Jong Il, politically progressive activists tried to actively contribute to inter-Korean unification. From 2008 to 2017, when the logic of the Cold War resurfaced during the Lee Myung-bak and Park Geun-hye administrations, these activists were refused entry into South Korea, among other acts of suppression by these South Korean administrations. The activists nevertheless continued their efforts for peaceful unification through a variety of ways. They have formed a kind of "social remittance" through their solidarity activities abroad and participation in South Korea's unification movement.

Social remittances are different from financial remittances and refer to the intangible assets that migrants contribute to their home countries, such as new knowledge, values, lifestyles, and skills.[10] They are intangible, so it is difficult to measure how much is being contributed from a quantitative perspective. However, there is a need to examine the characteristics of these social remittances through transformations in the perspectives of Korean migrants, the types of perspectives they hold, and their understanding of German unification. This study's participant observation allowed the researchers to summarize specifics about this social remittance phenomenon.

First, activists argue there is a need to resolve confrontation between the two Koreas through inter-Korean communication similar in

---

10 For more on the concept of social remittances, please see P. Levitt, "Social Remittances: Migration Driven Local-Level Forms of Cultural Diffusion," *International Migration Review* 32 (4) (1998): 926–948; P. Levitt, *The Transnational Villagers* (Berkeley and Los Angeles: University of California Press, 2001); P. Levitt and D. Lamba-Nieves, "Social Remittances Revisited," *Journal of Ethnic and Migration Studies* 37 (1) (2011): 1–22.

nature to the sustained exchanges that occurred between East and West Germany during German division. As explained before, Korean migrants in Berlin experienced entering East Germany without restrictions. There are feelings of confrontation between the two Koreas because of the Korean War, but activists argue that fears of North Korea are due to direct and indirect pressure on the migrant community by South Korea's NSL. Using the case of German division, they argue for divided family reunions, freedom of exchanges, and more exchanges through private organizations as possible ways to resolve the fictitious confrontational sentiments that exist between the two Koreas.

Second, activists emphasize that perspectives need to change to become more proactive and subjective toward Korea's relationship with world powers like the US. "M," who is a former miner and now in his 70s, is working in the European office of the Joint Committee to Put the June 15 Agreement into Practice. He says, "There is a need for the South Korean government to actively reduce the tensions on the Korean Peninsula that are controlled by the US." His understanding of international relations is one that believes that "Germany was also under a lot of US influence and still cares about what America thinks, but [nonetheless] was not as severely dependent on the US as Korea is." They also criticize America's sanctions against North Korea, feel sadness about the Arduous March that North Korea suffered, and recognize that negotiations rather than opposition to nuclear weapons is the way to improve the US-North Korean relationship. These opinions are based on the understanding that the Kim Dae-jung government's Sunshine Policy, and its support for independent and tolerant policies toward North Korea, is similar to Willy Brandt's Ostpolitik.

Third, the implications of West Germany's Ostpolitik are not that

Korean migrants in Germany look at unification as the end result, but rather as a process of shifting the paradigm. As described above, the interviewees explained that German unification "was a surprise." In other words, German unification was sudden. Migrants understand that unification is not the end result of efforts to reunify, but rather that the collapse of the socialist bloc and the Berlin Wall came about through policies that continued regardless of changes in government and were aimed at achieving exchanges between West and East Germany. On the other hand, they point out that South Korean society has long placed a priority on results in its socioeconomic development, so it misses the importance of this process. Patience is required to conduct discussions that can lead to agreements. South Korean society has experienced compressed modernity, so it will not be easy to shift the paradigm through a long process. Nonetheless, activists and migrants have made attempts to share this important "value" with South Korean society.

The above discussion ultimately emphasizes that the experience of Korean migrants toward German division and unification is not something in the past but is linked meaningfully to the present and future. These temporal sentiments also prove that the "homeland" or "hometown" imagined abroad continues to exist through the past and into the future.

Conclusion

The objective of this study was to reexamine and analyze the way first-generation Korean migrants in Germany experienced Germany's division and unification. They left a divided Korea for a divided Germany and experienced "another Cold War" in both Asia and Europe. They were then witnesses to the country's rapid post-division process. However, Korea's division is still ongoing. The experience and interpretations of these migrants toward German unification cannot be separated from the current situation of the divided Korean Peninsula. Interestingly, however, the dominant keywords in the discourse on German unification in South Korea are not important in their own narratives about German unification. They place their own identities into a future united Korea. Temporal borders have served to damage its significance.

The changing political situation in Germany and Korea along with Korean migrants' concept of borders, which must be considered, have become the "field" of solidarity and transitional narratives. The trans-border feelings they possess ensure that their life histories will not just remain tragic narratives from the past. With the fall of the Berlin Wall, they began dreaming of inter-Korean unification and are now conducting ceremonies in Berlin's streets focused on Korea's unified future. These ceremonies can demolish the armistice line on the Korean Peninsula just like similar ceremonies did to the Berlin Wall, and they hope Korea's armistice line soon becomes so fluid that it can be crossed. Through these ceremonies, the word in German for "border," *Grenze*, and *Grenzegaenger*, or "those on the border," have the meanings of "crossing," "surpassing," or "compatibility," and also have temporal and spatial meanings. Korean migrants are hoping that a unified Berlin, where physical barriers have been demolished, can become a space that connects Seoul and Pyongyang.

References

Bhabha, Homi K. 1994. *The Location of Culture*. London: Routledge.

Clifford, James. 1994. "Diasporas." *Cultural Anthropology* 9 (3): 302–38.

Jaedokhankukyŏsŏngmoim (Korean Women's Association in Germany). 2014. *Tokil ijuyŏsŏŭi sam: Kŭ hyŏndaesaŭi kirok* (Life of Korean immigrant women in Germany: the record of modern history). (In Korean.) Seoul: Tangdae.

Kaiser, Peter. 2013. Zuwanderung. Der Kumpel aus Fernost. Vor 50 Jahren kamen koreanische Bergmänner nach NRW in: *Deutschlandfunk, Länderreport* on November 22, 2013. https://www.deutschlandfunkkultur.de/zuwanderung-derkumpel-aus-fernost.1001.de.html?dram:article_id=269661.

Kollmorgen, Raj, Frank Thomas Koch, and Hans-Liudger Dienel, eds. 2011. *Diskurse der deutschen Einheit. Kritik und Alternativen*. Wiesbaden: VS Verlag für Sozialwissenschaften.

Lee, Eun-Jeung. 2014. "Deutsche Einheit aus der koreanischen Perspektive." *Neue Gesellschaft, Frankfurter Hefte* 11/12: 9–12.

Lee, You Jae. 2018. "Die Ostberlin-Affäre 1967 und die transnationale Demokratisierung für Südkorea." Paper presented at the 50th Anniversary of the Appeal for Isang Yun: Peace Talk and Concert, Nov. 24, 2018 at Isang Yun Haus, Berlin.

Levitt, Peggy. 1998. "Social Remittances: Migration Driven Local-Level Forms of Cultural Diffusion." *International Migration Review* 32 (4): 926–948.

Levitt, Peggy. 2001. *The Transnational Villagers*. Berkeley and Los Angeles: University of California Press.

Levitt, Peggy, and D. Lamba-Nieves. 2011. "Social Remittances Revisited," *Journal of Ethnic and Migration Studies* 37 (1): 1–22.

Ryang, Sonia. 2009. "Visible and Vulnerable: The Predicament of Koreans in Japan." In *Diaspora without Homeland: Being Korean in Japan*. Edited by Sonia Ryang and John Lie. University of California Press. http://emma-e-cook.net/wpcontent/uploads/2015/09/Ryang-2009-Visible-and-Vulnerable-predicament-ofKoreans-in-Japan-in-Ryang-Lie-eds-

Diaspora-without-Homeland.pdf.

Safran, William. 1991. "Diasporas in modern societies: Myths of homeland and return." *Diaspora* 1: 83–99.

Vertovec, Steven. 1997. "Three Meanings of 'Diaspora,' Exemplified among South Asian Religions." *Diaspora* 6 (3): 277–299.

Williams, Raymond. 1973. *The Country and the City.* London: Chatto & Windus.

Yi, Sam-yul. 2016. *Tokilesŏŭi minjuhwa undong: minjuhwa sahoykŏnsŏlhyŏpŭihoyrŭl chungsimŭro* (Democratization movement in Germany: focusing on the Association of Building Democratic Society). (In Korean.) Korea Democracy Foundation.

5. The Elephant in the Room:
Problems and Potentials of the Workers' Party of Korea in a Korean Unification Scenario

Hannes B. Mosler and Lee Bongki

Abstract

This paper investigates how North Koreans today, after having lived under the rule of a peculiar one-party system, evaluate the role, performance, and potential of the Workers' Party of Korea (WPK) regarding future unification scenarios. In doing so, we analyzed survey data of North Korean migrants (N = 356) residing in South Korea, who serve as the best possible proxy for the North Korean populace. The survey comprises questions on the respondents' general assessment of and trust in the party as well as their opinions on the role and development of the party when they were still in North Korea and now, and it includes questions about possible modes of reform for the party in the case of unification. Normatively speaking, for peaceful reunification it would be desirable for the fate of the WPK to be left to the people and free democratic elections, like in Germany; however, the particular trajectories of Korean contemporary history, including the Korean War (1950–1953), loom over such a worthwhile procedure. This is also reflected in the results that show negative appraisal of and low trust in the party, and high favor for its forced dissolution, thus providing important insights into the state of mind of North Koreans, and an important stimulus for thinking about possible ways to prepare a smooth transition into a post-division era.

Keywords

Workers' Party of Korea, North Korea, unification, North Korean migrants, survey analysis, Germany, Socialist Unity Party of Germany

Introduction

Political parties are central political institutions that aggregate the diverse interests of the people in a given polity and represent them in the institutionalized political arena. Their function is that of a conveyer belt, which translates people's wills into the political system's black box, and, thereby, they not only crucially interlink the system and the lifeworld (Habermas), but also integrate society into a political community. While it is difficult to deny that political parties can have divisive effects too, in ideal terms they would have the effect not only of integrating society but also of legitimizing the (elected) government, and, thus, the political system's stability at large. Despite the obvious fundamental differences, this is, nevertheless, true for multi-party systems in liberal democracies as well as for single-party systems in socialist autocracies. Accordingly, it is reasonable to assume that political parties' function of integration through representation also applies to more extreme cases of domestic conflict, including national division or the overcoming of such a fundamental cleavage. The role of the Socialist Unity Party of Germany (SED; Sozalistische Einheitspartei Deutschlands) in the unification process of Germany is one of the most representative examples regarding the alleviation of the alienation of the outlived system's citizens, and, thus, for integrating people's hearts and minds (i.e., interests, through representation; see W. T. Kang 2011, 72; K. M. Kim 2002, 47; Merkel and Croissant 2012, 310; C. C. Park 2004, 75, 93; K. G. Park 2000, 156; T. S. Song 2006, 275; Vogel and Best 2016, 347; Walter cited in Holzhauser 2018b, 614).[1]

---

1   Of course, at the same time, the authors cited here are well aware of and point out

Against this backdrop, this article empirically explores the facilitative potential of the Workers' Party of Korea (WPK; Chosŏnrodongdang) in a process toward sustainable unification. Besides having served as the vehicle for heredity succession by securing the ruling power of the Kim family, like in many other socialist countries, the WPK represents the fundamental structure of the political system t permeates most areas of public and private life in North Korea (Pak YJ 2017, 263-268). By plication, to understand how the North Korean people perceive this absolute state organization that eaches so deeply into society is crucial to our understanding of the potential role of the WPK in the future. Grasping the mindset of North Koreans regarding the Workers' Party is, in particular, relevant when contemplating possible scenarios for change through reforms, as a precursor for overcoming the division of the Korean Peninsula, if not an eventual reunification of North and South Korea. For at that point, the role of the WPK could be vital for contributing to a smooth and sustainable transition into a ost-division era on the Korean Peninsula.

How do North Koreans make sense of the role of the WPK in the advent of Korean unification? To answer this leading question, we investigated how North Koreans evaluate the role and performance of the party in the past and present, and how they evaluate its potential for the future. In doing so, we surveyed North Korean migrants[2] residing in

---

that the role of the SED or PDS had negative aspects, too, and that an unconditional application to the Korean case is difficult, if not dangerous.

2   There are various ways to name those people who left North Korea and eventually went to South Korea to lead their lives, such as North Korean "defectors" (*kwisunja*), "North Korean refugees" or "North Korean escapees" (*t'albukcha, t'albungmin*), "residents who escaped from North Korea" (*pukhan'it'aljumin*), and "new settlers" (*saetŏmin*), which all carry either some ideologically colored weight (see Y. S. Choi 2016; G. Choi

South Korea (N = 356) who—despite methodological difficulties (Jeong 2005; J. Song and Denney 2019)—serve as the best possible proxy for the North Korean populace. The survey comprises questions on the respondents' general assessment of and trust in the party as well as their opinions on the performance of the party when they were still in North Korea and now, and it includes questions about possible modes of party reforms in the case of unification. Whereas most survey-based studies on North Korean migrants focus on topics such as health, identity, employment, social life in South or North Korea, and attitudes toward the political system of South Korea (see J. H. An et al. 2018; J. An and S. Kim 2015; Cho and Y. T. Kim 2011; Denney and Green 2018; Go 2014; Grzelczyk 2014; Hur 2018; Jeon et al. 2003; P. Kim 2012; Lankov 2006), rather seldom research investigates their attitudes regarding North Korean political institutions, such as the WPK.[3] This is where the present study comes in by addressing the elephant in the room, and, thereby, starting the difficult but necessary conversation on possible unification scenarios involving the WPK.

The remainder of this chapter is organized as follows. We begin

---

2018, 88; Chung 2008, 3–4; S. K. Kim 2012, 95–96) and/or are not sufficient in precisely denoting the particular group of people in mind. Others use "defector-migrant" as a compromise to encompass the notion of having turned one's back on a place negatively perceived by many belonging to this group, and who thus identify themselves by that fact (Denney and Green 2018, 1 [FN]). We decided to use the term "North Korean migrants" (*pukhan'ijumin*), because we think that it is the best possible objective, neutral, and precise way—at least in the English language, for an international audience, and regarding the research focus of this article—for describing this particular group of people.

3   Of course, there are studies on North Korean society, culture, food supply, education, economy, and many more topics (Jeong 2005, 151–152), but attempts to shed light on North Koreans' perspectives of the WPK and its possible role in the process of unification have not yet been presented.

by introducing the genesis, change, and characteristics of the WPK to provide a general overview of the party and its function in North Korea's overall political system and society and to understand its potential role in transition scenarios. Following this, we discuss the role of the SED and its successors in the German unification process, and then critically examine the feasibility of considering it as a reference for drawing lessons for the Korean case. In the next section, we explain the survey sample and its limits as well as introduce the selected survey questions that serve as a guiding grid for the subsequent main section, in which we present the results of the analysis. We conclude the article by cautiously interpreting the findings, shedding light on the role of the WPK in the case of transition to a post-authoritarian state.

The SED Germany as a Reference Case for the WPK in Korea

The ideal core functions of political parties in liberal democracies are to represent the interests of the people, provide participation opportunities for the people, and, thereby, contribute to legitimating the political system as well as integrating a pluralist society. In other words, political parties are crucial for practically realizing as well as maintaining the stability and coherence of a democratic system and its society. This is why the role of political parties in the process of transition to democracy is a key element, for it promises to facilitate a positive outcome if the transformation of political parties is successful. The transformation of the political parties during and after the unification process in Germany is a case in point, despite some fundamental differences between the two cases of division (see Maretzki 1994). Accordingly, this section, first, provides an overview of the WPK and its particularities, and, second, briefly discusses the case of the SED as a reference case, including commonalities and differences between the two parties and cases.

– The Workers' Party of Korea (WPK)

In general terms, the Workers' Party of Korea (WPK) resembles, to a large degree, regime parties of any other socialist political system, such as the former Union of Soviet Socialist Republics (USSR), the former German Democratic Republic (GDR), or the People's Republic of China (PRC), while at the same time featuring particular North Korean characteristics (see T. G. Yi 2007). The WPK was founded shortly after the establishment of North Korea's Government in 1948. The WPK was an amalgam of various communist and leftist factions and parties that have existed since the 1920s as early communist movements on the Korean Peninsula. In 1925, the Communist Party of Korea (CPK; Chosŏn'gongsandang) was formed, and after the country was liberated from Japanese occupation in 1945, various communist factions continuously split and merged. At that time, the northern part of the peninsula was under Soviet military occupation, while the southern part was occupied by the United States Army Military Government in Korea (USAMGIK). The CPK's headquarters was located in Seoul, and in September 1945, it was officially reinstated with Pak Hŏn-yŏng being elected as its chairperson (T. S. Sŏ 1995, 276–277). In October, a CPK northern Korean branch office was established in Pyŏngyang; however, it soon began acting independently from its southern headquarters, and it was only a matter of time before it became a completely independent entity officially, too. In early 1946, communist forces, which had been serving in the Communist Army of China, returned to northern Korea, and established the New People's Party of Korea (NPK; Chosŏnsinmindang), which shortly afterwards, was merged with the CPK, that, in turn, was renamed the Workers' Party of Northern Korea (WPNK; Pukchosŏnnodongdang; Sŏ 1995, 276–277).[4] In late 1946, the People's Party of Korea (PPK; Chosŏninmindang) and the New People's Party of South Korea (NPP; Namjosŏnsinmindang) merged into the Communist Party of South Korea (CPSK; Namjosŏnnodongdang), only to be merged three years later, in June 1949, with the Communist Party of North Korea (CPNK; Pukchosŏnnodongdang) to form today's WPK. While officially proclaimed as an equal merger, in actual fact, the CPSK was absorbed by the CPNK (Yi 2007, 209–210). Formally, the organization and its operations are based on the principles of democratic centralism, meaning a pyramid-like organization reaching from party cells, consisting of a few members, all the way up to the Party Congress (PCS), with more than 3,000 members. Lower organizational units are strictly subordinated under the higher organizational units, which have a decisional prerogative over the former. At the same time, all directing units are formally accountable toward the electorate, and, overall, the principle of majoritarian decision-making abides. Nominally, the PCS is the highest body,

---

4 These developments that have occurred under the occupation of the Soviet Union and in the name of the People's Democratic Revolution can be understood in the same context as the forced merger of the Communist Party of Germany (KPD; Kommunistische Partei Deutschlands) and the SPD into the SED (Malychay and Winters 2009, 35) in East Germany in April 1946.

with authorities such as electing the Central Committee (CCO) and the Central Auditing Commission (CAC), and selecting the party's chairperson (*wiwŏnjang*).[5] However, the PCS is convened very seldom, and, in the meantime, authority rests with the CCO, which holds sessions of its over 230 members at least once a year. The day-to-day operation and decision-making of the party is thus delegated to smaller organizational units, such as the Politburo (PBO) and the State Affairs Committee (SAC). The PBO consists of more than 30 members, out of which the three members of its standing steering committee have the actual authority for party internal decision-making. The SAC organizes and supervises all party undertakings, and, thus, is the actual executive body guaranteeing the implementation of the party's enterprises. The SAC has fewer than 20 members who deliberate and decide on all internal and external issues related to the party. The National Defense Commission (NDC) is another core organ of the party because it supervises all policies and undertakings regarding the country's military forces. It consists of fewer than 20 members, most of whom are selected from among PBO members. Beneath these high-level decision-making bodies, the party operates 19 departments responsible for diverse tasks relating to state affairs, such as industry, education, finance, economy, agriculture, and international relations. These are in charge of making sure that all respective units in government, society, the military, and industry follow the policies decided on by the party. To this end, the party is organized in committees operating at the levels of provinces, cities and counties, districts and villages, and party cells. At each level,

5   Other responsibilities include examining the reports of the outgoing Central Committee as well as Central Auditing Committee, deliberating and enacting party policies, and revising the party's statute.

party functionaries are dispatched to the respective decision-making units of government departments, social organizations, military units, and production facilities.

Besides some negligible satellite parties, the WPK possesses uncontested hegemony in the political and social system. Its organization permeates almost all levels of government and administration as well as production, to ensure foremost control of the whole country. The WPK decides on policies, mobilizes resources, and keeps watch on all social organizations, while the government organization has the function of implementing the party's policies as an executing body. To this end, the WPK provides four pillars to guarantee the North Korean regime's stability—legitimation, repression, co-optation, and funding (Pak 2017, 263–268). De facto, the WPK functions strictly top-down with the undisputed power concentrated in the position of the party's chairperson—presently Kim Jong Un. Chairman Kim is also a member of the PBO's standing committee as well as chairman of the SAC and—besides being the Supreme Commander of North Korea's armed forces—the chairman of the NDC. In this way, by occupying the most crucial nodal points of the WPK's power structure, the Supreme Leader (*widaehan suyrŏng*) is in control of any other organization in government, military, society, and the economy. In other words, the WPK is an organizational system solely for the purpose of realizing the will of the Supreme Leader through a party organization that is excessively centralized and bureaucratized, and permeating all parts of society from top to bottom (see Paik et al. 2007, 213–217).

While the overall adoption of the typical Leninist style resembles most other known socialist single-party designs and operations, its particularities become evident regarding its function for enabling North Korea's peculiar leadership style: the sole leadership system (SLP; *yuiljŏk'ryŏngdoch'egye*). The SLP system is the essence of the Party's Ten Principles for the Establishment of a Sole Leadership System, proclaimed by Kim Jong Un in 2013 to strengthen his rule, by establishing that the SLP is an "ideological system and leadership system that makes the leader's revolutionary ideology the only instructing principle and advances the revolution and construction under the guidance of the leader" (J. U. Kim 2013).[6] Kim Jong Un is explicit in what that means when he demands:

> *The party's Ten Principles of the establishment of the party's sole leadership system should be put in place at every level of organizations to ensure that all functionaries, party members, and workers make the party's Ten Principles for the establishment of a sole leadership system their own bones and flesh, to their firm belief, and live and struggle according to the Ten Principles, no matter where and what they do.*

Of course, what is meant is that every single person in North Korea has to obey the Ten Principles and live by them. In other words, the sole leadership system idea conceptualizes North Korean society as one organic whole with the leader at the top, and, thus, it demands total submission to and obedience of Kim Jong Un as the absolute

---

6   This was a revision of the hitherto effective Party's Ten Principles for the Establishment of a Sole Ideological System that had been in place since the mid-1970s. See the appendix for the main articles. For an analysis of the changes and their meaning and implications, see Kang and Kim (2015) or O (2013).

and undisputable authority for the whole society. This is corroborated by him continuously idolizing his father Kim Jong Il and grandfather Kim Il Sung, whose "great achievements" regarding the realization of the *chuch'e* (also known by the spelling *juche*) and *sŏn'gun* ideologies the people not only "must pass down," but also with the requirement of "inheriting and completing them to the end" (J. U. Kim 2013). This follows a simple but overwhelming logic that the ongoing revolution can only be continued and completed successfully if everyone adheres to the central ideologies and follows the orders and instructions of the central leadership figures, dead or alive (see C. S. Yi 2011, 221–233). The Ten Principles hold the strongest regulatory authority in the North Korean political system, and they even stand above the WPK's party statutes, the constitution, and ordinary laws and regulations. Only the leader's teachings (*suryŏng-ŭi kyosi*) can override the Ten Principles (S. S. Yi 2012, 92).

– The SED in the German unification process

At the time of the East German revolution in October 1989, many people in East and West Germany were worried that the East German government would follow the Chinese government's way of violent suppression as seen in the case of the student demonstrations at Tiananmen Square in June 1989. Egon Krenz, who had visited China after the Tiananmen incident, defended the Chinese armed forces' brutal actions against the demonstrators in a statement. If the East German government had indeed resorted to suppression by force involving severe casualties, the SED (Sozialistische Einheitspartei Deutschlands) would not have been free from responsibility, and, thus, it would have been likely that in the process of reunification the people would have demanded its dissolution irrespective of legal regulations, which, however, eventually did not happen.[7]

There was controversy over how to deal with the SED, which had been the state party of the GDR for 40 years, but this never became a major issue, mainly for two reasons. First, after unification, experts judged that the SED's successor, the Party of Democratic Socialism (PDS; Partei des Demokratischen Sozialismus), would merely become a local, anti-capitalist protest party that maladjusted in the transition process, or a deficit party only supported by past communist bureaucrats, and, thus, once economic reconstruction of the former East German region was achieved, it would soon disappear without the support of the people due to its political activities in the GDR, or be absorbed by the Socialist Party of Germany (SPD; Sozialistische Partei Deutschlands) or the Greens. And indeed, in the first general election after unification in December 1990, the PDS did not reach the minimum rate of 5% of the proportional representation distribution, and only due to an exemption clause, was able to receive seats in parliament according to its respective vote share (see Breuer 2007). Second, the SED procedurally accepted the new regime of liberal democracy, for example, when they decided to take part in the general elections, and when they agreed to the unification process. In early December 1989, the People's Parliament (Volkskammer) deleted the formally ascribed supremacy of the SED from the Constitution, and shortly afterwards, on the occasion of two consecutive party conferences, the party was renamed the SED-PDS, and this included

---

7   See Pfennig (2011).

158

the declaration that the party irrevocably broke with Stalinism as a system. During this period, the party started to reform itself regarding personnel, organization, and programmatic contents. After, in early 1990, the party once again renamed itself, but this time as the PDS only, and 15 years later, in the run-up to the general elections in 2005, it cooperated with the West Germany-based left wing party, Labour and Social Justice—The Electoral Alternative (WASG; Arbeit und soziale Gerechtigkeit—Die Wahlalternative), including heavyweight former SPD politician Oskar Lafontaine—and changed its name to Die Linke PDS. After finally merging with the WASG in 2007, the newly formed party adopted the name The Left (Die Linke), which continues to exist today.

It is reasonable to assume that a forced dissolution of the SED, which had been garnering the support of about 2.5 million party members during the 40 years of East Germany's existence, would have led to protests, so it was appropriate to leave its fate to its own and the electorate's will for reforms. In this way, over time, the SED transformed itself into a political party that represented the interests of many people in the former GDR, and, thereby, contributed to the quick and smooth operation of a democratic parliamentary system in a completely new Germany (see K. N. Kim and Hŏ 2014, 93). As is shown in table 5.1 below, the support rate at elections started relatively weak right after unification, and so far, has only once topped the 10 percent line in 2009, but the overall trend is clearly of increasing support. For obvious reasons, this trend is more accentuated in the former East German regions, but, nonetheless, in the former West German regions the tendency is similar, and, thus, reflects steady support even if only by a small share of voters. At the regional level of the Länder, the party's political and social relevance is even more pronounced, though it is less successful in the former West German regions compared to in the East German ones. In the latter, Die Linke is represented in all local assemblies; the party is part of the governing coalition in three cases, and even provides the governor in Thüringen.

Table 5.1. Polling Rates of the East German Socialist Unity Party of Germany's Successor Parties after Unification

Year	Polling Rate (%)			Seats in Parliament (of ca. 598)
	Nationwide	Former East German Region	Former West German Region	
1990	2.4	11.1	0.3	17
1994	4.4	17.7	0.9	30
1998	5.1	19.5	1.1	35
2002	4	16.8	1.1	2
2005	8.7	25.4	4.9	54
2009	11.9	27.2	10.3	76
2013	8.6	21.2	5.3	64
2017	9.2	17.4	7.4	69

Source: Bundeswahlleiter (www.bundeswahlleiter.de)

While the roles of the SED or its successor parties in the German unification process are not without their flaws and mistakes, the party's transformation and its effects have positively contributed to the overall process (see the section 2.3 below).[8] It contributed to a relatively smooth unification process and a relatively sound post-unification development of party politics and political stability in Germany in general. Not only

---

8   See Kim and Hŏ (2014, 94–107) for likewise obvious shortcomings of this development.

did the process involve democratic procedures, and, thus, let the people decide on the fate of the party, but also the fact that the interests of many people in former East Germany were acknowledged and given representation is important, because this promoted the integration of hearts and minds.

– Utility and Commensurability of the German Case for Future Korean Scenarios

There is a wide array of literature on German unification and what lessons Korea can possibly draw from it, including the role the SED and its successor parties played in the process. The above discussion of the characteristics and development of the WPK and the SED showed basic parallels that suggest potential for relating the two cases. At the same time, caution is warranted for two reasons. First, it is not undisputed that the German case is a successful example of a political party playing a facilitative role in a process of social and political integration in the context of a national unification process, and, thus, worth emulating in the first place. Second, even if the German case can be evaluated as having been helpful rather than harmful for German unification, doubts remain as to whether it represents a reasonable reference case in respect to its commensurability with future Korean scenarios. Regarding the assessment of the SED's role in the German unification process, the majority of research holds that the party's activities and effects were hampering and helpful at the same time (Best and Vogel 2011; 2012 cited in Vogel and Best 2016; W. T. Kang 2011, 72; K. M. Kim 2002, 47; C. C. Park, 75, 93; K. G. Park 2000, 156; T. S. Song 2006, 275; Vogel and Best 2016, 347–348; Walter cited in Holzhauser 2018b,

614). For quite some time, the successor organizations of the SED continued with the former socialist autocracy's ideology, methods, and personnel, while now being democratically legitimized by free and fair elections within a new political system. The problem with this, it is pointed out, is that it counters—if not contradicts—the democratic revolution, and, thereby, the overcoming of the authoritarian regime. In addition, in the early years and having only sufficient support to enter the institutionalized arena in the area of the former GDR, the PDS developed into a regionalist party that would have a divisive effect rather than one that would integrate the country. At the same time, however, many studies also acknowledge that besides potentially negative repercussions, the representation of these now partial interests is not only a necessary way of dealing with diversity and plurality in a truly liberal democratic society, but also helpful for integrating society by having a party that speaks and acts on behalf of a part of that society.[9] In other words, by giving this minority a voice in the institutionalized political arena makes those people feel less alienated from the new mainstream, and, thus, they are potentially prevented from resorting to other more extreme forms of protest, or complete exit strategies, which would have destabilized the unification regime far more than a forced dissolution of the SED would have. And, last but not least, over the decades, the party has developed into a critical leftist party with support in most of the regions of Germany and plays an important role as one of the strong minor parties.

Regarding the appropriateness of the German case for drawing

---

9   Analyzing the cases of the German Greens and Die Linke, Holzhauser (2018a) demonstrates that this "domestication" of extreme or even anti-system parties can work well for a democracy.

lessons for Korean scenarios, the literature, again, is somewhat inconclusive. It is by now well-known that some fundamental differences exist between the cases, which demands caution when referring to the German example (Kim and Hŏ 2014; S. S. YI 2012). First of all, the conditions of the South Korean political party system are much worse compared to those in former West Germany regarding the lack of institutionalization of political parties, strong regional sentiments, corruption culture, weak consolidated democracy, and political parties' extreme organizational egoism, which make it far more challenging to support a unification process from a sound basis on the side of South Korea (see Merkel and Croissant, 304–305). In addition, economic conditions in North Korea are far worse than in East Germany at the time of unification. North Korea does not have the same degree of experience of democracy as East Germany either, and while East Germany enjoyed support from the USSR to the end of its existence, North Korea has been making every effort to make itself as autonomous as possible from the USSR and China (S. S. Yi 2012, 87–88). What is more, different from the East German bloc parties, no comparable parties exist in North Korea that could function as docking stations for South Korean parties in the transition process, which is also true regarding any other autonomous social or political organizations in North Korea that could possibly support building a new democratic political parties system (Merkel and Croissant 2003, 306). In addition, it is not only the experience and implications of the Korean War as a war between the divided parts of a nation that is yet another often-cited fundamental difference that has to be taken into account, but also cross-time differences—the fact that German unification has already taken place and exists as precedence as well as the different international constellations then and now—which can be instanced as discriminative indicators. Last but not least, the above discussion showed considerable differences between the WPK and the SED regarding their characteristics and political reach. However, despite these differences, German unification and the SED remain a viable case for cautiously drawing lessons regarding future scenarios on the Korean Peninsula, even if it is only to realize that there is hardly any other precedence one could think of as a constructive exemplar.[10]

Sampling North Korean Migrants in South Korea

As of December 2018, more than 30,000 North Korean refugees reside in South Korea (Ministry of Unification 2019b). North Koreans usually leave their country by crossing the northern border into China, after which they spend several months or even some years in countries such as Cambodia, China, Mongolia, or Thailand before entering South Korea (see figure 5.1 below). Before North Korean migrants receive one-time settlement funds from the government and can begin their lives as newly naturalized citizens, they are thoroughly investigated by the National Intelligence Service for espionage and other crimes and have to undergo an obligatory three months of training at a designated government facility.

An opinion survey on North Korean migrants residing in South Korea was conducted in 2016, and returned a total of 356 filled-out

---

10 For a different opinion, see S. S. Yi (2012) who argues that due to the larger differences between Korea and Germany, a comparison with the case of Albania would be more helpful.

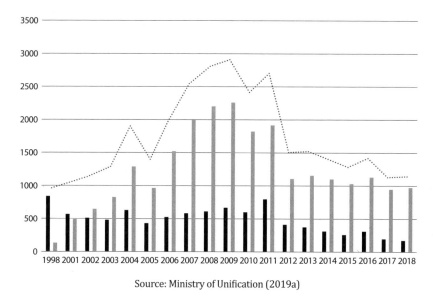

Source: Ministry of Unification (2019a)

Figure 5.1. Yearly Numbers of North Korean Migrants Entering South Korea (Persons)

survey sheets, which represent the basis for our analysis. The survey included 25 questions that asked for basic personal and socioeconomic information as well as for the reasons for leaving North Korea and coming to South Korea. It also asked questions regarding membership of and opinions on, as well as trust in, the WPK, when in North Korea as well as in the present, and concerning an assessment of future developments of the WPK in the case of post-authoritarian transition.

Most of the respondents arrived in South Korea in the second half of 2016, the majority of whom were women (n = 282; 79.2%), and with men being in the minority (n = 74; 20.8%). Regarding age, 14% were younger than 20 years of age, while those in their 20s to 40s represented the largest share of 84.5%, and respondents who were 50 years and older accounted for 10.4% of the sample. As is typical for North

Korean refugees, most of the respondents (81.5%) stemmed from the four North Korean border regions of Hamgyongbuk-do, Ryanggang-do, Chagang-do, and Phyŏnganbuk-do (see Hur 2018, 102–103; Denney and Green 2018). Former residents of Hamgyongbuk-do and Ryanggang-do alone accounted for more than three-quarters (78.1%) of the respondents. In North Korea, most of them had been workers (34.6%), followed by farmers (13.7%), and housekeepers (9%). Some were businesspeople (7.2%), and a share of 19.1% were unemployed. Put differently, almost half of the respondents (workers and farmers) belonged to the working class, and only 6% were professionals, employees, or teachers. Most of them received education until middle school (74%), while only 16.9% had attended a (vocational) college or higher educational institution. Similar to other North Korean migrant samples (see Haggard and Noland 2011, 30; Hur 2018, 103), the largest share of the respondents (56.4%) said that their reasons for leaving North Korea and coming to South Korea were economic, while 23% quoted political freedom as an explanation. Receiving better education (8.4%) was another rationale for coming to South Korea. As for the time that had passed between leaving North Korea and entering South Korea, 27.0% of migrants spent less than one year in a third country such as China, whereas about the same share, 28.4%, spent 10 or more years in another country before they came to South Korea.

Against the backdrop of the above explanations of the sample, several limitations have to be pointed out. First, the sample's proportionate distribution regarding age, class, residency, education, and gender is not representative of the whole North Korean population. The most obvious difference is the origin of a major share of the respondents, almost all of whom came from the border regions. Even more obvious

166

is the fact that these persons left North Korea because they were unsatisfied with their livelihood there to a high degree, which possibly distorts the sample regarding the questions on evaluating the WPK. Despite these shortcomings, this sample still remains the best proxy for exploring North Koreans' opinions on the WPK.

For the present case study, we selected the answers to the following questions for analyzing the sample's (1) evaluation of the WPK's past, (2) its present performance, and (3) the forecast of its future potential:

Evaluation of the WPK in the past

1-1. When you were living your everyday life at school or at your workplace in North Korea, what did you think about the WPK, which claims to be a party for the people's concerns?

1-2. When you were living in North Korea, how much did you trust the WPK?

1-3. When you were living in North Korea, who did you think the WPK was for?

Present evaluation of the WPK

2-1. When you think about it now, how do you evaluate the WPK?

2-2. When you think about it now, who do you think the WPK is for?

Projecting the future of the WPK

3-1. If North and South Korea unite, what do you think is the most desirable way to deal with the WPK?

3-2. If North and South Korea unite, what do you think is the most likely way the WPK will be dealt with?

Making Sense of the WPK's Past, Present, and Future

– Evaluation of the WPK in the past

The first set of questions is designed to find out how the respondents evaluate the WPK's basic trustworthiness, actual performance, and organizational purpose. Their assessment of the WPK can be understood as the basis on which the respondents form their judgment regarding the party's possible role in the future, which is discussed in subsection 4.2 below.

The first question (Q 1-1) asked how they rated the WPK's own claim of that they exist for the people and to facilitate harmony in social life at school and the workplace (see figure 5.2). This question relates directly to concrete living circumstances, and, thus, judgment criteria are less abstract, assuming that answers can be given with less self-censorship. Only a small fraction of the respondents thought, when living in North Korea, that the WPK did fulfill its promise well (5.1%), whereas almost five times more respondents (27.8%) thought that the party was not living up to its own claim. Another 23.6% gave a neutral answer, saying that the WPK sometimes lived up to its promises, and sometimes not. More than one-quarter of the respondents (27.2%) abstained from providing an evaluation by saying that they did not judge the party at all, and just accepted it as it was. In other words, the North Korean migrants were clearly critical in their basic evaluation of the WPK party when they were living in North Korea.

The second question (Q 1-2) asked about how much the respondents trusted the WPK when they were still living in North Korea (figure 5.2). Slightly more than half of the respondents (54.7%) said that they trusted the WPK, while 40.7% did not, reflecting a slight tendency

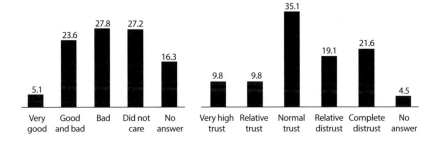

Figure 5.2.
**The WPK's Performance as Judged
While in North Korea (in %)**

Figure 5.3.
**The WPK's Trustworthiness as Judged While in
North Korea (in %)**

to distrust over trust. A more detailed look at the distribution of the frequency of individual answers, excluding the rather neutral answer "normal," reveals distrust in the WPK ("did not trust at all" + "mostly did not trust"; 40.7%), accounting for twice as many respondents' evaluations than trust ("trusted very much" + "mostly trusted"; 19.1%). So, again, when living in North Korea, a large share of the respondents did not have much faith (or none at all) in the WPK.

The third question (Q 1-3) was put to the respondents to find out what they thought about the actual purpose of the WPK when they were living in North Korea. In other words, the question aimed at finding out what were possibly the main reasons behind the positive or negative evaluation of the WPK. Again, a minority of not even one-quarter (23.9%) of the respondents thought that the WPK existed for all or the majority of North Koreans. Meanwhile, the vast majority (69.6%) believed that the WPK's purpose was for a part of the elite or the Kim family only.

To summarize, all three variants asked about the respondents' evaluations of the WPK when they were living in North Korea, and the answers were all quite critical about the party regarding its performance, trustworthiness, and how it lived up to its claims.

– Present evaluation of the WPK

The second set of questions was on trustworthiness and the purpose of the WPK, but now asking the migrants for their present evaluation when they were living in South Korea. This way of rephrasing the question was to make the respondents consider possible changes in their assessments due to the differences in time and context. This is related to a possible future scenario in which North Koreans will have open access to information about the WPK, and the freedom to form opinions on the party. And, indeed, the answers reveal an even more critical judgment (figure 5.4). "Complete" (21.6%) and "relative" (19.1%) distrust in the WPK (Q 2-1) almost doubled from 40.7% to 72.7%,[11] while "very high" (9.8%) and "relative" (9.8%) trust in the WPK shrunk

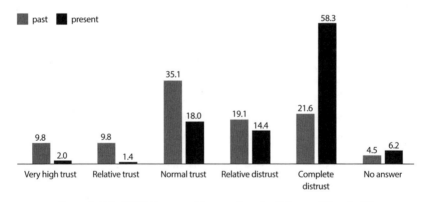

Figure 5.4. The WPK's Trustworthiness as Perceived Then and Now (in %)

11 Here "complete" and "relative" distrust accounted for 58.3% and 14.4%, respectively.

by over 80%, from 19.6% to 3.4%; also, the relatively neutral answer of a "normal" level of trust almost halved from 35.1% to 18%.

An even stronger trend can be observed with the answers to the question about whose party the WPK was (Q 2-2), where the total share of those who answered with "Kim Jong Un or the Kim family" (40.4% → 64.9%) and "parts of the elite" (29.2% → 25.8%) increased from 69.7% to as much as 90.7% (figure 5.5).[12] Meanwhile, relatively positive answers, such as "most North Koreans" (5.6% → 0.8%) and "all North Koreans" (18.3% → 2.5%), dropped from 20.9% to 3.3%.

Taken as a whole, the hitherto answers from the sample regarding the respondents' present opinion clearly point to a very critical evaluation of the WPK, and do not leave much room for ideological illusions of the WPK by the respondents. At the same time, some of the

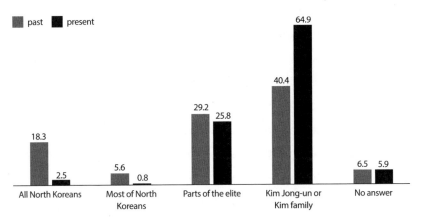

Figure 5.5. Thoughts on Who the WPK Is For as Perceived in the Past and Present (in %)

---

12 Against this backdrop, it is not surprising that 86.8% of the respondents also said that they thought the WPK was "very" (47.5%) or "quite" (20.8%) corrupt.

respondents do not completely reject the WPK and still seem to stand by the party. For example, no less than 20.4% said that they presently trusted the WPK.[13] Admittedly, regarding opinions on the WPK's actual purpose, only 3.3% agreed that the party is for "all North Koreans" or "most North Koreans." But, even in so-called liberal democratic polities, there will be many who would rather answer that political parties are for "parts of the elite." In other words, while these results are telling in their clear critical tendency toward the WPK, there remains a small part of the sample that obviously still feels close to the party.

– Assessing the future potential of the WPK

The third set of questions is designed to find out how the respondents assess the potential and capacity of the WPK to play a facilitative role in the transition to or under a post-division regime. Their view on the matter can be assumed to be somewhat similar to the positions of other North Koreans, and, thus, can help to grasp to what extent it is important to deal with the WPK and in what way, once the present division is to be overcome. Respondents were asked how they thought that the WPK should be and will be handled in the case of unification. While the former question (Q 3-1) asks for a personal normative judgment, the latter (Q 3-2) asks for a personal forecast.

A relative majority of the respondents (46.8%) voted for unconditionally forcing the WPK to dissolve as a way of taking responsibility for its dictatorship (see figure 5.6). Meanwhile, 21.4% wanted the WPK to be handled not by extralegal government

---

13 This includes "very high" (2%), "relative" (1.4%), and "normal" (18%) trust.

intervention but solely on the basis of legal procedures. Another 20.3% opted for accepting the WPK as a legitimate political party and leaving the decision up to the people through elections. Put differently, while those in favor of dissolving the WPK forcefully accounted for about one-half of the sample (46.8%), the other half argued for a process based on legal regulation and/or natural selection through elections (41.7%).

Relating to these answers, the second question asked what will be likely to happen to the WPK in the case that the party is not dissolved by force and its fate is put to the people. Most of the respondents (75.6%) predicted that the WPK will disappear due to loss of support from the people, either because the party will not reform (46.1%) or despite reforming (29.5%). Only 8.7% of the respondents thought that

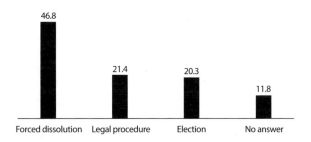

Figure 5.6. Desirable Handling of the WPK in the Case of Unification (in %)

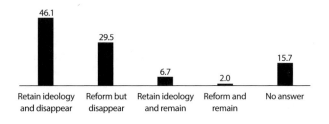

Figure 5.7. Likely Handling of the WPK in the Case of Unification (in %)

the WPK will continue to exist by sticking to their ideology (6.7%) or reforming (2%).

So, the large majority of the respondents do not believe that the WPK will survive in a unified Korea, regardless of whether the party does or does not reform. Regarding the way in which it will disappear, the sample is somewhat divided, while the largest share, in line with the overall negative evaluation of the WPK, advocates an unconditional dissolution of the party followed by legal procedure and selection by election. Again, these results present quite a clear picture of disapproval for the WPK; at the same time, however, even here a residual of at least 11.8% ("no answer") in regard to the appropriate procedure,[14] and 24.4%[15] for the likely handling, do not straightforwardly join in the rejection of the WPK.

Conclusion

The main aim of this explorative study was to understand how North Koreans reflect on the past, present, and future of the WPK in order to project its possible role in future unification scenarios. The results of the sampled North Korean migrants residing in South Korea indicated that the large majority of the respondents were critical toward the

---

14   While many of the respondents ticking the answer "election" (20.3%) may indeed have thought that the WPK would not survive free and fair elections anyway, it is reasonable to assume that at least some of these respondents may have been of the opinion that the WPK should be given a fair opportunity to prove itself in a liberal democratic system.

15   This includes "retain ideology and remain" (6.7%), "reform and remain" (2%), and "no answer" (15.7%).

WPK's performance, trustworthiness, and fulfillment of its promises as a party for the people when they were still living in North Korea. This largely negative assessment by North Korean migrants increased even more when they were asked to judge the WPK from their present perspective, living in South Korea. Only a minority of the respondents answered the questions positively, and this, thus, confirmed various other studies' results as well as commonsensically held expectations in regard to North Korean migrants' opinions on issues related to the North Korean regime.

An important reference for our investigation was the role and development of the SED's successor parties in the case of Germany, which had been facilitative to unification in the sense of integrating hearts and minds of an otherwise neglected and alienated part of society—those who felt and feel attached to the former regime and/ or ideas related to it. Despite the apparent differences between the circumstances in the Korean and the German contexts, the basic ambivalent perception among the populace toward the former regime party's successors is very unlikely to differ much. While a large majority of Koreans will denounce and reject the WPK because of its dictatorial past and potential continuities in personnel and ideology, some will come to perceive it as one of the only ways to represent their interests in the new liberal democracy. The survey results indicated that even though the sample comprised people who deliberately left North Korea behind, not all of them completely rejected the WPK. A share of between 15% and 25% of the respondents does not completely reject the regime party, which is in line with surveys on how North Korean migrants accommodate to life in South Korea regarding norms and ideas of a capitalist liberal democracy (see, for example,

T. J. Chung 2016, 130). Put differently, in a unified Korea, too, there will be a strong, if minor, demand for representing interests closer to the former regime, which will have to be supplied in order to foster the overall integration of hearts and minds in a unified Korea (see Merkel and Croissant 2003, 310). Thus, it does not seem to be too far-fetched that, in a best case scenario of reforming the WPK in a Korean unification process—somewhat similar to the case of the SED in Germany—such a party could contribute to fostering the integration of people's hearts and minds as an important basis for and complement to integrating generations (Hofmann and Martens 2016) and the elites (Vogel and Best 2016). There are a myriad of preparations that are necessary to make for as sustainable a unification as possible, some more indirectly (see, for example, Mosler 2017), others more directly (Merkel and Croissant 2003, 307–313), which are related to institutionalizing and consolidating representative democracy. The issue of the WPK, too, should not remain the elephant in the room: an obvious and acute challenge that everybody hesitates to address because it seems so uncomfortably unresolvable. Against this backdrop, this article—despite its limitations—intended to contribute to starting the conversation necessary for considering future scenarios and possibilities before simply stumbling into history because nobody dared to break the silence.

References

An, Ji-hyun, Kyoung Eun Lee, Hyo Chul Lee, Hae Soo Kim, Jin Yong Jun, Hye In Chang, Suk Sun Kim, Su Yeon Lee-Tauler, and Jin Pyo Hong. 2018. "Prevalence and Correlates of Suicidal Thoughts and Behaviors among North Korean Defectors." *Psychiatry Investigation* 15 (5): 445–451.

An, Jiyeon, and Seokho Kim. 2015. "Pukhan it'alchŏngsonyŏn-ui pukhan-esŏ-ŭi munhwagyo'yuk kyŏnghom-gwa han'kung-nae sahoemunhwa-jŏk jŏgŭng kan kwan'ge-e taehan kŭn'gŏ'iron yŏn'gu" [Study on the relation between cultural education in North Korea and socio-cultural adaptation of North Korean adolescents]. *Governance and Management Studies* 10 (2): 217–241.

Breuer, Marten. 2007. "Die erste gesamtdeutsche Bundestagswahl 1990 und die Folgen für das Parteiensystem," In *Das Parteienspektrum im wiedervereinigten Deutschland*. Edited by Eckhard Jesse and Eckart Klein. Duncker & Humblot: Berlin, 13–32.

Cho, Dong Wun, and Yong Tae Kim. 2011. "A Study on Settlement Service for North Korean Defectors." *Journal of Korean Public Police and Security Studies* 8 (2): 25–50.

Choi, Gyubin. 2018. "North Korean Refugees in South Korea: Change and Challenge in Settlement Support Policy." *The Korean Journal of International Studies* 16 (1): 77–98.

Choi, Yu-sook. 2016. "Sinmungisa-e nat'anan pukhan'it'aljumin chich'ingŏ punsŏk" [Reference terms for North Korean defectors seen in newspaper articles]. *The Journal of Language & Literature* 67: 33–66.

Chŏng, Tong-jun. 2016. "Pukhanjumin-ŭi namhan munhwa kyŏnghŏm-i t'ongilŭisik-e mich'inŭn yŏnghyang" [Survey analysis of the effects of North Koreans' exposure to South Korean culture on their attitudes toward unification]. *Unification and Peace* 8 (2): 111–148.

Chung, Byung-Ho. 2008. "Between Defector and Migrant: Identities and Strategies of North Koreans in South Korea." *Korean Studies* 32: 1–27.

Denney, Steven, and Christoher Green. 2018. "Unification in Action? The National Identity of North Korean Defector-Migrants: Insights and

Implications," Academic Paper Series. Korea Economic Institute of America. Washington, DC: KEIA.

Go, Myong-Hyun. 2014. "Resettling in South Korea: Challenges for Young North Korean Refugees." The Asian Institute for Policy Studies. http://en.asaninst.org/contents/resettling-in-south-korea-challenges-foryoung-north-korean-refugees (accessed: March 2, 2019).

Grzelczyk, Virginie. 2014. "New Approaches to North Korean Politics after Reunification: The Search for a Common Korean Identity." *Communist and Post-Communist Studies* 47: 179–190.

Haggard, Stephan, and Marcus Noland. 2011. *Witness to Transformation. Refugee Insights into North Korea*. Washington DC: PIIE.

Hofmann, Michael, and Bernd Martens. 2016. "Generations and Social Structures in Socialist Countries: The German Democratic Republic and East Germany in Comparison with North Korea," *Historical Social Research* 41(3): 318–335.

Holzhauser, Thorsten. 2018a. "Extremisten von gestern—Demokraten von heute? Zum Umgang mit systemfeindlichen Parteien am Beispiel von Grünen und Linkspartei." *Mitteilungen des Instituts für deutsches und internationales Parteienrecht und Parteienforschung*, 24. Jahrgang, 5–13.

Holzhauser, Thorsten. 2018b. "Neoliberalismus und Nostalgie Politische Re-Formationen und die Entstehung der Linkspartei im vereinten Deutschland." *Geschichte und Gesellschaft* 44: 586–618.

Hur, Aram. 2018. "Adopting to Democracy: Identity and the Political Development of North Korean Defectors," *Journal of East Asian Studies* 18: 97–115. DOI: 10.1017/jea.2017.30.

Jeong, Eun-Mee. 2005. "Yŏn'gubangbŏp-ŭrosŏ t'albukcha chosa-ŭi hwaryong-gwa yŏn'gu tonghyang" [Application and trends of research on North Korean refugees as a method of North Korea studies]. *Review of North Korean Studies* 8 (3): 139–176.

Jeon, Woo Taek, Chang Hyung Hong, and Jin Sup Eom. 2003. "T'albukchadŭl ŭl t'onghayŏ pon Pukhan chumin ŭisik chosa" [Survey of the North Korean people's social consciousness: study on North Korean defectors in South Korea]. *Journal of Korean Neuropsychiatric Association* 42 (5): 631–643.

Jeon, Woo-Taek, Chang Hyung Hong, Chang Ho Lee, Dong Kee Kim, Mooyoung Han, and Sung Kil Min. 2005. "Correlation between traumatic events and post-traumatic stress disorder among North Korean defectors in South Korea." *Journal of Traumatic Stress* 19 (2): 147–154.

Kang, Dongwan, and Hyunjung Kim. 2015. "Pukhan-ŭi 'tang-ŭi yuiljŏkryŏngdoch'ogye hwangnip-ŭi 10-tae wŏnch'ik' kaejŏng ŭimi-wa pukhanjumindŭr-ŭi insik" [A study on the establishment of "Ten Principles of the Sole Guidance System" in North Korea and North Koreans' consciousness: Through North Korean literature survey]," *Pukhanyŏn'guhakhoebo* 19 (1): 339–365.

Kang, Won-taek. 2011. *T'ongil ihu-ŭi han'guk minjujuŭi* [Democracy after unification]. Seoul: Nanam.

Kim, Jong-un. 2013. "Hyŏngmyŏngbaljŏn-ŭi yogu-e matke tang-ŭi yuiljŏkryŏngdoch'egye-rŭl tŏuk ch'ŏljŏhi seulde taehyŏ" [On thorough establishment of the party's sole leadership system consistent with the demands of the revolution's development]. In Ishimaru Jiro. *Pukhan naebu yŏngsang-munsŏjaryojip* [Video and document collection from inside North Korea]. Tokyo: ASIAPRESS, 27–30.

Kim, Kyŏng-nae, and Chun-yŏng Hŏ. 2014. *Chŏngdangbunya. T'onghap kwallyŏn chŏngch'aekmunsŏ* [Political parties section. Policy documents related to integration]. Seoul: Ministry of Unification.

Kim, Kyung-mi. "Togil t'ongil-gwa chŏngdangch'eje-ŭi pyŏnhwa: minjusahoejuŭidang(PDS)-ŭl chungsim-ŭro" [The PDS within the party system of the united Germany]. *Sahoegwahak Yŏn'gu* 10: 31–50.

Kim, Philo. 2012. "T'albukcha myŏnjŏpchosa-rŭl t'onghae pon pukhansahoe-ŭi pyŏnhwa 2008–2011" [Social changes in North Korea, 2008–2011: Based on North Korean refugees survey]. *Review of North Korean Studies* 15 (1): 39–84.

Kim, Sung Kyung. 2012. "'Defector,' 'Refugee,' or 'Migrant'? North Korean Settlers in South Korea's Changing Social Discourse." *North Korean Review* 8 (2): 94–110.

Lankov, Andrei. 2006. "Bitter Taste of Paradise: North Korean Refugees in South

Korea." *Journal of East Asian Studies* 6 (1): 105–137.

Lee, Sang-sin. 2012. "Pukhan-ŭi chŏngdangch'egye-wa t'ongil" [The North Korean party system and unification]. In *Pukhan ch'ejejŏnhwan'gi minjuhwa yudo mit chŏngdang yŏkhal* [Regime change in North Korea, inducing democracy, and the role of political parties]. Edited by Yi Hyŏn-ch'il. Seoul: Han'gukchŏngch'ihakhoe, 87–115.

Malychay, Andreas, and Peter Jochen Winters. 2009. *Die SED: Geschichte einer deutschen Partei*. Munich: C.H. Beck.

Maretzki, Hans. 1994. "Probleme koreanischer Wiedervereinigung aus deutscher Sicht." *Welt Trends* 5: 123–139.

Merkel, Wolfgang, and Aurel Croissant. 2003. "Chŏngdang mit chŏngdangjedo-ga han'guk-ŭi t'ongil-gwa minjuhwa-e mich'inŭn yŏnghyang" [The influence of political parties and the political party system on Korea's unification and democratization]. *T'ongil Haendŭbuk*, 257–325.

Ministry of Unification. 2019a. "Ch'oegŭn hyŏnhwang" [Recent situation]. Ministry of Unification. www.unikorea.go.kr/unikorea/business/ NKDefectorsPolicy/status/lately/ (accessed: May 8, 2019).

Ministry of Unification. 2019b. "T'ongilbu pukhanit'aljumin t'onggye" [North Korean Migrants statistics by the Ministry of Unification]. Public Data Portal, www.data.go.kr/dataset/fileDownload.do?atchFileId=FILE_000 000001507449&fileDetailSn=1&publicDataDetailPk=uddi:6ab39d11-ae6f-4e7e-8d2d-d3aedad8edd7_201903151903 (accessed: May 8, 2019).

Mosler, Hannes B. 2017. "Decoding the 'Free Democratic Basic Order' for the Unification of Korea." *Korea Journal* 57 (2): 5–34.

O, Kyŏng-sŏp. 2013. "10-taewonch'ik kaejŏngan-ŭi chuyo naeyong-gwa chŏngch'i-jŏk ŭimi" [Main contents and political meaning of the revision proposal of the Ten Principles]. *Chŏngse-wa Chŏngch'aek* (September): 12–14.

Oh, Won Hwan. 2011. T'albuk chŏngnyon-ŭi chŏngch'esŏng yon'gu: t'albuk-esŏ t'llamggaji [Study on identity among adolescent North Korean defectors]. PhD dissertation. Department of the Media, Korea University.

Paik, Hak-soon, Jeong Seong-jang, Lee Dae-geun, Kim Dong-han, Lee Mu-cheol, Park Yeong-ja, Jeong Seong-im, and Jeong Chang-hyeon. *Pukhan-*

ŭi tang-kukkagigu-gundae [Party, government organizations and the military in North Korea]. Sejong Research Institute. Seoul: Hanul Academy.

Pak, Yŏng-ja. 2017. Kim Jong Un sidae chosŏnnodongdang-ŭi chojik-kwa kinŭng. Chŏnggwŏn anjŏnghwa chŏllyak-ŭl chungsim-ŭro [Organization and functions of the Workers' Party of Korea in the Kim Jong Un era]. KINU Yŏn'guch'ongsŏ. Seoul: KINU.

Park, Chong-chol et al. 2004. *T'ongil ihu t'onhap-ŭl wihan kaldŭnghaeso pangan: saryeyŏn'gu mit punyabyŏl kaldŭnghaeso-ŭi kibonbanghyang* [Proposal for solving conflicts for integration after unification]. Seoul: KINU.

Park, Kwang-gi. 2000. *Nambukhan chŏngdangt'onghap-ŭl wihan chŏnje-dŭl: tongsŏdok chŏngdangt'onghap-ŭl chungsim-ŭro* [Precondition for the integration of political parties]. *Taehan Political Science Association Journal* 8 (1): 149–170.

Pfennig, Werner. 2011. "Wandlungen der Sozialistischen Einheitspartei Deutschlands." In 20 Jahre Deutsche Wiedervereinigung Band 23. Edited by Eun-Jeung Lee and Werner Pfennig. Berlin: Institut für Koreastudien.

Sŏ, Tae-suk. 1995. *Han'guk kongsanjuŭi undongsa yŏn'gu* [Research on the South Korean communist movement]. Seoul: Iron-gwa Silch'ŏn.

Song, Jay, and Steven Denney. 2019. "Studying North Korea through North Korean migrants: lessons from the field." *Critical Asian Studies*. https://doi.org/10.1080/14672715.2019.1611462.

Song, Tae-Soo. 2006. "Togilt'ongil-esŏ chŏngdang-ŭi yŏkhal" [The role of political parties in the German unification process]. *Sahoegwahak Yŏn'gu* 14 (1): 246–283.

Sung, Jiyoung, and Myong-Hyun Go. 2014. "Resettling in South Korea: Challenges for Young North Korean Refugees." The Asan Institute for Policy Studies. https://www.jstor.org/stable/resrep08152.

Vogel, Lars, and Heinrich Best. 2016. "Political Elites in Transition and Unification: German Lessons for the Korean Peninsula?" *Historical Social Research* 41 (3): 336–367.

Yi, Chong-sŏk. 2011. *Hyŏndaebukhan-ŭi ihae* [Understanding modern North Korea]. Seoul: Yŏksabip'yŏngsa.

Yi, Sang-sin. 2012. "Pukhan ŭi chŏngdangch'egye wa t'ongil" [North Korea's party system and unification]. In *Pukhan ch'ejejŏnhwan'gi: minjuhwa yudo mit chŏngdang ŭi yŏkhal.* Edited by Han'guk chŏngdang hakhoe.

Yi, Tae-gŭn. 2007. "Chosŏnnodongdang-ŭi chojikch'egye" [The organizational structure of the WPK]. In *Pukhan-ŭi tang.gukkagigu-gundae.* Edited by the Sejong Research Institute. Seoul: Hanul Academy, 162–226.

Yoon, In-Jin. 2001. "North Korean Diaspora: North Korean Defectors Abroad and in South Korea." *Development and Society* 30 (1): 1–26.

Appendix. The Party's Ten Principles for the Establishment of a Sole Leadership System (excerpt; 2013)

1. We must give our all in the struggle to model the whole society on Kimilsungism-Kimjongilism.

2. We must honor the Great Comrades Kim Il Sung and Kim Jong Il with all our loyalty as the eternal leaders of our party and the people and as the sun of *chuch'e*.

3. We must make absolute the authority of the Great Comrades Kim Il Sung and Kim Jong Il and the authority of the party, and defend it with our lives.

4. We must arm ourselves firmly with the revolutionary ideas of the Great Comrades Kim Il Sung and Kim Jong Il and with the party lines and policies, which are the manifestation of these ideas.

5. We must adhere strictly to the unconditional principle of obedience in carrying out the Great Comrades Kim Il Sung's and Kim Jong Il's teachings, and accomplishing the party lines and policies.

6. We must strengthen from all sides the entire party's ideology and willpower and revolutionary unity, centering on the Leader.

7. We must follow the example of Great Comrades Kim Il Sung and Kim Jong Il, and adopt a dignified spiritual and moral look, revolutionary work methods, and people-oriented work style.

8. We must hold dearly the political life we were given by the party and the Leader, and repay the party's political trust and thoughtfulness with heightened political awareness and work results.

9. We must establish strong organizational discipline so that the entire party, nation, and military move as one under the sole leadership of the party.

10. We must pass down the great achievements of the *chuch'e* revolution and *sŏn'gun* revolution pioneered by Great Comrade Kim Il Sung and led by Comrades Kim Il Sung and Kim Jong Il, inheriting and completing it to the end.

6. The Making of the "Reader-People" in the 1950–1960s North Korean Socialist Literature

Tae-Kyung Kim

Abstract

This paper focuses on the making of the "reader-people" in post-Korean War North Korean literature, which constitutes the "trinity" of socialist literature: party censorship, party-directed "red" writers, and the people as readers. During the 1950–1960s, the reader-people was defined and organized as a prerequisite of new socialist literature, which emerged through the adaptation process of the Soviet socialist realism to the North Korean context. The making of the reader-people can be understood as the adaptation of the Soviet category of "people-mindedness" (*narodnost'*), which accompanied both discourses and practices concerning the readers or people. First, the discourses on the concept of readers as well as on their talent for the literary productions show how the category of "people-mindedness" was received. Second, practices such as promoting people's cultural activities and cultivating popular art forms contributed to the organization of the reader-people as the agency of socialist literature. By illustrating the making of the reader-people in both theoretical and organizational aspects, this study explains that the indigenization efforts of socialist realism in North Korea were found not only in the ideological framework on literary productions, but also in the organization of the literary community.

Keywords

reader-people, people-mindedness (*narodnost'*), Soviet socialist realism, North Korean socialist literature, post-Korean War socialist system-building

Introduction

This paper examines the making of the "reader-people" in 1950–1960s North Korea, which as one key pillar, constitutes the "trinity" of organizational structure of socialist literature: party censorship, party-directed "red" writers, and readers who are the people as well. The readers-*cum*-people were defined and organized in the process of socialist literature-building: the essence of the post-Korean War socialist system-building was transforming not only the national economy but also its culture.[1] The "modern" sense of a culture whose ideological characteristic was "socialist" emerged as a result of various discourses and related practices on what socialist literature should be, the methods on how to make them, and the prerequisites or conditions for their making.[2] This paper focuses on the component of reader-people among

---

1   On the importance of socialist transformation in the dimension of culture, Soviet "revisionist" studies provide significant comparative insight (Fitzpatrick 2007, 1992). As for North Korean studies, after a few pioneers such as Wada (2002) or Armstrong (2003)'s historical survey on the 1945–1950 North Korean revolution including the changes in culture as well as politics and economy, recent studies show increasing concerns about the cultural changes in analyzing North Korean system-making (see Ryang 2012; S. Y. Kim 2010; Kwon and Chung 2013; and S. Kim 2013, on the field of literature and Gabroussenko 2010; E. Kim 2014; I. Kim 2012; and Myers 1994).

2   The main argument of this paper on the receptive dimension of North Korean literature is connected to a broader thesis on the overall characteristic of North Korean literature as an indigenized socialist realism. The explanation on the historical formation of the domain of people-reader is incorporated with the building of other poles of literature, the writer and the censor, thereby completing the whole organizational structure of socialist literature. My claims on post-Korean War North Korean literature as the making of socialist realism in the North Korean context counter the previous studies such as Myers (1994) or Gabroussenko (2010). In opposition to their argument on the failure of socialist realism in North Korea, I shed light on the historical discourses/practices designed for constructing an indigenous socialist literature. Underscoring the efforts for making North Korean literature as a socialist literature, this study focused on

the organizational "trinity," highlighting the aspect of reception and education of socialist realism in North Korea. It explains the making of the reader-people in light of the North Korean adaptation of the Soviet concept of "people-mindedness" (*narodnost*').[3]

One of the key assumptions is that a better understanding of post-Korean War socialist literature-building is possible only if we arm ourselves with a comparative perspective of 1920–1930s Soviet socialist realism-building. By considering North Korean socialist literature construction as an effort of importing and indigenizing the Soviet model of socialist realism, we would be closer to what was on the minds of the participants in the North Korean literary community at the time and what their ambitions were in building their own version of socialist literature. Through the 1920s to the early 1930s, the Soviet literary communities had undergone fierce debates and power struggles that ended in the forceful unification of various literary groups or sects into the state union of writers (Robin 1992; Fast 1999). Diverse aesthetic discourses on creative methods to socialist literature, entangled with conflicts to achieve hegemony in the literary field, were

---

what was intended and implemented in the inchoate North Korean literature, not on whether the project was successful nor in terms of what the researcher evaluated as the socialist realism.

3   Of the basic principles of Soviet socialist realism, the study of the making of the reader-people is connected with the concept of "people-mindedness" (*narodnost*'). The fundamental aesthetic categories consisting in the Soviet socialist realism include party-mindedness (*partiinost*'), ideological committedness (*ideinost*'), people-mindedness (*narodnost*'), class-mindedness (*klassovost*') (Smorodinskaya et al. 2007, 576–577; Petrov 2015, 127). *Narodnost*', which is translated as "people-mindedness" or "popular spirit," has an especially broad range of connotations when compared to other principles. The main usages are related with accessibility, comprehensibility of a work to people, the contents profitable for people's "enlightenment" of mind, and the elevation of people's participation in the aesthetic process as critic or writer (Dobrenko 2011, 1997b).

subject to the unification and collectivization of literature from the top down (Dobrenko 1997a; Dobrenko and Tikhanov 2011). The process was situated in the context of industrialization and social mobility, where the idea of "modern" transformation of the whole society held sway, while the remaining goal of utopian revolutionary vision went dormant. The societal scale of economic and cultural transformations occurred in the name of socialist construction from the top down, under the direction of Stalin. Parallel with economic transformations including collectivization and industrialization, the literary communites underwent a "cultural revolution," where the same rhetorics of "class struggle" and conflicts of "new versus old" dominated as they did in the economy. Both in economic and cultural changes, what was significant was the emergence of a new generation and the transition of leadership from the previous militant but diverse intelligentsia groups to the army of standardized loyal "red" professionals (Fitzpatrick 1979, 1992; Dobrenko 1997a, 2001).

My point is that we need much more explanation on the making of the organizational structure of socialist literature in order to comprehend what socialist realism was about, particularly from the perspective of its social impacts. This is true not only for the 1920–1930s Soviets but also in the 1950–1960s North Korean literary communities. I emphasize the organizational structure because the process of turning literary spaces into state institutions via organizing the "trinity" of writers, critics/censors, and readers, not just *reflected* but also *constructed* a larger social context of socialist system-building. The building of a socialist system consists of a range of projects for building a new society, which encompass not only the collectivization, industrialization, and the military buildup, but also the making of a new socialist culture whose essence was in making new men for the new era. Literature itself was defined anew, and importantly, literary organizations were reconstructed for the ideological purpose of bringing up the "new man." As noted above, this process was situated in the generational transition in hegemony of overall economic and cultural spaces, which Sheila Fitzpatrick (1979, 1992) termed "cultural revolution." Therefore, bringing light to the organizational changes that occurred in literary spaces in line with the social transformations has great significance.

In what follows, I will examine the North Korean literary discources and practices of readers in the 1950–1960s, focusing on the adaptation of "people-mindedness" criteria. The theme of "people-mindedness" and the making of the reader-people has been hardly discussed in previous studies of North Korean literature and art. Recently, S. S. Kim (2016) offered a good historical review on the reading environments in North Korea, with a special focus on the letters of readers sent to the journal *Choson Munhak*. Kim's sketch on the historically changing socialist literature, particularly on the aspect of readers, is not only valuable as it is, but has significance as a rare reference.[4] Forming the "trinity" of the organizational structure with the other two (the army of "red" writers and the party censorship appratus) the subject of the reader-people is of great importance in understanding the effect of socialist realism. Since socialist realism was an ideological, intentional business for educating and reforming people's "souls,"[5] the interplay

---

4   On the other hand, the theme of making "people" is dealt with comprehensively (Han 2015; S. Kim 2013; Armstrong 2003).

5   The classical Stalinist definition of Soviet writers as "engineers of human souls" summarizes the role of socialist realism. According to Gutkin (1999), this constructive

of intentions and reactions of various agencies should be studied. The reception of socialist realism on the part of people is essential in understanding how the whole structure of socialist realism, in logic and mechanism, was constructed and maintained.

Defining the Reader-People:
The Sophisticated Readers or the Mass Readers

The making of the reader-people is closely associated with the adaptation process of the Soviet concept of "people-mindedness" (*narodnost'*). Soviet socialist realism functioned as a reference model for North Korean socialist literature-building (Yoo 2011; Bae 2012; T. Kim 2018). "People-mindedness," which delineates the people-oriented character of socialist realism creations, is one of the key aesthetic categories in Soviet socialist realism discourses. The concept means that the content of works should not only be about people's lives but have people as their protagonists, thereby representing the people as the masters of both their own lives and of post-revolutionary society. However, it also designates that the forms of socialist realism should be naturally drawn from people's own artistic traditions and adapt those conventions to create new art aligned with people's needs and wants. In other words, the concept of "people-mindedness" does not stop in advancing the agency of people in socialist culture by means of content, but in demanding a new species of art in terms of form and on the basis

---

characteristic of socialist realism via shaping people's minds in the spirit of socialist utopia was inherited from the tradition of the 1920s avant-gardists, whose concerns were also shaping new people in line with a new revolutionary era.

of what people inherited and were familiar with.

On the multifaceted concept of "people-mindedness," Dobrenko (2011, 101) introduced six connotations that Günther (2000, 12) observes: (1) the idea is connected with perceptions of organicity and wholeness, (2) it contains an objective or atemporal ideal that contrasts with the contemporary era of modernist style, (3) it is characterized by simplicity and comprehensibility, (4) it holds an attitude against the morbid and the decadent, (5) it is created in a popular folkloric style, and (6) it has a tendency to exclude any elements that are "'against'" the people or "'foreign'" to them. To grasp this flexible principle of "people-mindedness," it is fundamental to understand the discourses and practices pursued in the name of the reader-people. Here, I focus on the discourses of readers found in *Choson Munhak*. *Choson Munhak* is the official "thick" journal that has published diverse literary genres and criticism, with such additions that offer a good look into the contemporary literary environments as letters from readers and notices from the writers' union. Among the pages of *Choson Munhak*, some of the translated literary criticisms or reports on literary activities and aesthetic discourses from abroad are also worth noting in understanding how the category of readers was debated and received in the 1950–1960s North Korean literary community.

First, letters from readers need special attention since they demonstrate the existence of readers and their influences in new literature. A couple of pages were allocated for the letters several times a year in the 1950–1960s, generally in the latter part of the volumes. Although not every volume published these letters, with an irregular interval, the section for readers continued to show various responses to the journal's published works, even to its overall editing styles.[6] How attentive the journal was to the readers' responses and their rightful place in editing and publishing is well confirmed by the editors' notes that irregularly appended the last page of the volumes. In addition to these editors' notes, the reports on readers' gathering events, which were held to listen to public responses on newly printed works or recent reading trends, also contribute to the understanding of who readers were and how they were interpreted and organized in the process.

In the *Choson Munhak*'s discourses on readers, there appear two distinctive ways of discussing in detail who the readers are: what their roles are in the new literature, and how they nurture their capabilities and promote the literature, guaranteeing their agency. The two different types of readers seem to have coexisted in the 1950–1960s discussions of them. The first type of reader was those with some advanced level of education who were familiar with professional vocabularies for literary traditions and creative processes. They were not only up-to-date on contemporary literature as well as the classics, but also had talent for evaluating works, as well as articulating their own views and demands.

A good illustration of these advanced readers is found in the report on a readers' gathering that occurred at Kim Il Sung University in 1956.

---

6   In the May 1954 issue of *Choson Munhak*, reader's letters first appeared under the title section of "Letters from Readers to the Editing Committee." Three letters, written by Pak Changin, Chong Munsik, and Kim Jongsuk, called for more diverse topics for poetry, more works by new authors, and better quality for translated poetry, respectively. Despite the relatively long break during 1957 and 1959–1962, the section for readers' responses to *Choson Munhak* continued in several-issue intervals throughout the 1960s. The contents consist of readers' requests for their preferred themes, genres, and even styles to writers or poets, critiques on the works they read, demands to the editing board for more spaces (e.g., the Korean classics or the genre of play). On the contents of the readers' letters, see S. S. Kim (2016) and T. Kim (2018), Ch. 5.

The 1956 January issue of *Choson Munhak* covered the event, where university students passionately critiqued recent works and led main discussions. This drew our attention because their comments and demands on current literature were sharp and active, comparable even with professional critiques. They were readers with strong educational backgrounds and professional knowledge on literature as well as the literary community. These readers' responses were met with welcoming reactions from the editing board of the journal, which published a summary of what had been discussed at the event, promising a full effort to answer their requests. This three-page report starts by clarifying the significance of readers' opinions and demands for the literary community.

The readers' demands of the journal *Choson Munhak* and books published by the Choson Writers' Union Publisher are much higher than ever. The readers' opinions and demands—they are just a magnificent contribution to this editing board's and writers' creative activities and give a powerful driving force to their progress. Therefore, the readers' demands are able to offer an indisputable energy to the editors' and writers' business.

The readers' gathering held on December 16, 1955, at Kim Il Sung University, which dealt with the works of the journal *Choson Munhak* editions of no.1–11 of 1955 as well as the poetry collection entitled *Pongsŏnhwa* authored by Sŏ Manil, definitely evidenced this fact.

In the event gathered almost 500 college students, led by comrades of the literary clubs of Kim Il Sung University Humanities College (Anonymous 1956, 197).

It is interesting that the readers presented here as the "powerful driving force" to new literature's progress were well-educated, highly-trained students from the top-class university. At the readers' gathering of the "comrades of literary clubs of Kim Il Sung University Humanities College," Wŏn Sŏnghŭi, Park U., and Cho Jinyong pointed out a wide range of issues in their evaluations on the past works published in *Choson Munhak* from 1954: the lack of diversity of themes studied, the writers' unfulfilled creative plans, the editing problems such as those found in drafts revision process, the problem of generalization in poetry writing, the lack of ideological depth in *ocherk* (the Soviet style of literary sketch) writing,[7] the deficits in clarity when using concepts in the critiques, and the lack of indigenization efforts of advanced theories to North Korean literature. In comments on the recently printed poetry collection *Pongsŏnhwa*, Ch'oe Sŭngch'il and Yun Ch'angju criticized weaknesses in the representation of positive heroes in the work of epic poetry. However, they applauded the poet's use of ordinary people's vocabulary as well as folk song forms in the epic poem "Through the Storm." The report of the event ends with a pledge from the editing board to the readers.

Readers! Don't ever hesitate to send us opinions! We will humbly receive those opinions. With our people's passionate construction

---

7   E. Kim (2014, 77–78) explains that *ocherk* is a Russian prose genre that shares the tradition of western European sketch. The sketch is typically published in newspapers and journals and gives the genre affinity to journalism. In Russia, many renowned prose writers used *ocherk* to critique social problems, and in socialist realism, it established its unique style different from sketch, dealing with "real life and real people" and having a hortatory function for the public.

struggles with the aim of fulfilling and overfulfilling our planned tasks for the year 1956, the last year of the Three-Year People's Economy Plan, we, *Choson Munhak*, affirm with confidence that we too will play a great role in the readers' own hands (Anonymous 1956, 200).

It is worth noting that the above call for readers was based on the readers' gathering at Kim Il Sung University. It is unclear on how inclusive the category of readers can be. At least from the report, we cannot find any sure sign that this category expanded from just readers to the people, who had just managed to achieve literacy after the revolution (S. Kim 2013; Armstrong 2003). However, there was also the second type of readers, widely discussed in the 1950–1960s *Choson Munhak,* which is the group of the reader-people. Discussions concerning readers, exploring what readers want in literature and in society, were not dominated by the upper level of readers or intelligentsia. At the Second Congress of North Korean Writers in October 1956, the role of readers in post-Korean War literature was scarcely neglected. Hwang (1956) explicitly showed how significant the readers' voices were at the time, citing many reader-related events. According to him, from factory laborers to peasant workers, the reader-people did have their own opinions about the present situation of literature and literary community. He insisted that only by listening intently to what people want for their reading, new literature would achieve its tasks of representing people's wishes, and of educating and reforming people's minds in the spirit of socialism.

We have no difficulty finding in the 1950–1960s discourses the perspective of seeing readers as the targets of education and thought reform, rather than "talented readers" capable even of their own literary creations. During the post-Korean War reconstruction, literature and culture were to be reconstructed as the destructed infrastructure and economy were. A series of cultural campaigns such as projects for literacy, hygiene, and prohibition of waste continued, all of which targeted people to effectively mobilize them for faster reconstruction. An illustration for how the reader-people were seen as the object of education and mobilization was in the report on the writer's union's recent activities, printed in the June 1954 issue.

> Through organizing efforts of public addresses on literature, joint seminars, study sessions, while infiltrating deep into the people with full support for post-Korean War reconstruction struggles, (we) are voluntarily mobilized for pushing the struggles by spreading literature among the masses.
>
> For four months this year, 64 writers and poets including Kim Myŏngsu, Sŏ Manil, Yun Sichŏl, Pak Seyŏng, Hong Sunchŏl, Ryu Jongdae, Han Sangun, and Tak Jin were mobilized for activities in institutions totaling 64 times: 17 at factories, 13 in the army, 14 in schools, 20 in others.
>
> They organized comprehensive literary addresses with titles such as what is literature, the creation and reception of poetry, fiction, playwright and stages, scenarios and movies, Korean literature guided by General Kim Il Sung. Moreover, they actively guided literary clubs' activities which took root in each level of production brigades, schools, and militaries, by way of joint seminars or studies on such the long novel *History*, medium-length *Happiness*, long epic poem Ŏrŏribŏl, and translated fiction *Steel and Optical Materials*

(Anonymous 1954, 135–136).

When they discussed readers in the 1950–1960s, they could have meany either the reading masses or the sophisticated readers, or both. Even as the discourses targeting and developing both streams of readers continued, there occurred a gradual shift to the latter, beginning to be visible from 1958 when people's cultural activities boomed nationwide. Without considering people's growing cultural activities and their significance in the new literature, we cannot comprehend the picture of true characteristics of new literature that were established at the end of the 1960s. Before examining the practices of people's cultural activities largely supported by the government, first we should consider what kind of discourses there had been in *Choson Munhak*, particularly on the people's own creativity and its significance in making socialist literature. With the discourses and practices supporting the reader-people combined, the adaptation process of the Soviet concept of "people-mindedness" or the making of the reader-people came into play.

Constructing the Reader-People:
The Translation of Soviet Reader Discourses

The shift from the fewer, more sophisticated readers to the larger, less-educated reading masses was aligned with theoretical, historical discourses on the people as the agency of new culture, mass or talented readers' roles in literature, and the significance of popular art forms. Translated theoretical articles on or criticism about contemporary and classic Soviet socialist realism, printed in *Choson Munhak*, help us to understand what was adapted from the Soviet sources on the concept of "people-mindedness." During the 1950s, a variety of Soviet aesthetic texts, classics, and contemporary literature were translated and widely read via diverse media. The vast translation of Soviet sources was distinct beginning in the liberation and the Soviet occupation period through the 1950s, regardless of field or sector. Until the mid-1960s, foreign influences, especially from the Soviets, were in fact conspicuous, and indigenization efforts were evident, while options for reference and adaptation gradually dwindled. We see competing views and incoherence in the discourse on readers, reading masses, and "people-mindedness" until the establishment of the ideological monolithic rule of the party in 1967.

Here, I examine two distinctive, but not necessarily conflicting, views on readers found in translated Soviet articles published in *Choson Munhak* in 1956 and 1958. The two articles are Chicherov's "Literature and Oral Folk Art" and Marshak's "Opinions on Skills." What both articles are interested in is the "talent" of readers or of people. The theme of talent has particular resonance in considering the category of readers, since it plays an important part in the logic concerning the role of reading masses in literature as well as the method to support them to organize a new literary community.

Chicherov (1956) assumes the reader-people as the basis for all of the flourishing literatures in human history. His argument is that the stratum of reader-people is not only a fertile ground of literary production, but also the main agency for socialist literature. On the place of the reader-people in literature, Chicherov (1956, 165) states that "people give birth to, create, and form geniuses and individual talents; therefore, the force of these geniuses and individual talents comes from their unity with the people." "Under the condition of socialism," he emphasizes, "collective art creations do not conflict with the growth of individual talents; on the contrary, it promotes them to flourish," presenting the organic relations between people and individual geniuses. Chicherov argues that while in capitalist societies, the arts reflect the class struggles under antagonistic social conditions, the arts in socialism are subject to the people, thereby achieving a high level of "people-mindedness." This claim is supported by historical surveys on folklore and its importance vis-a-vis high literature.

> A. M. Gorky stated that under the generalization created by individual talents was people's creations. In other words, he said, "people created Zeus, and the Proletariat formed him in marble. Here it is affirmed that arts of writers, artists, sculptors belong to the people, and that the arts can be completed only when they reflect people's thoughts, emotions, and opinions. What Gorky did is not downgrading the writers' arts, but rather emphasizing the significance of arts that offers special strength and completeness to people's collective creations (Chicherov 1956, 167).

Pointing out the relation between artistic creations and their producers or talents, Chichrov explains the concept of anonymity, which indicates the way people's creative talents are realized and remembered in art history. Chicherov states that in popular art-making, "if only one has an ability to create," one can just "proceed as a co-author of songs or tales of the folk." The characteristic of this collective art-making is "no knowledge of any individual authors, and even the works of individual authors just become a part of the whole collective when they enter into the life of folklores." "Anonymity in collective folklores" is a symbol of "singularity in the creative process of popular art," differentiating its process from that of "bourgeois art." Chicherov argues that the reader-people are the birthplace of both popular art and literature, and their authorial label is nothing else but anonymity, which expands the idea of talent from the possession of the selected few to the originated commons of every artistic production.

Marshak's critiques shed a different light on the readers, who collaborate with authors in the artistic creation. Marshak (1958) discusses two different talents of writers and readers, who constitute the opposite ends of the spectrum of the creative process. Marshak starts his article by saying "every string the writer touches is already inside the heart of the reader. Depending on skills for playing that string, the note might resonate inside people's hearts either softly or brightly, either high or low." He emphasizes the writer's mission to clearly transport one's own messages to "the people who are 'language creators,'" as well as to free their imaginations by one's own works. In Marshak, the reader-people not only provide wide, productive pools of artistic languages, but also act as proactive "participants" in the process of completing the meaning of art.

> A reader does not just remain as the reader. He becomes the participant as he engages in every event the poet experienced and felt.
>
> However, to the contrary, if the author did everything the reader should do for himself, leaving nothing to the reader for activating imagination by explaining his own thinking, theme, images, it

would make the reader uninterested. The reader, too, is an artist. If not, we would not be able to communicate with him in languages of image or color.

For literature we need as many talented writers as talented readers. Only for them, for those talented, sensitive readers possessing creative imaginations, the author exerts all of himself to investigations of the exact images, the exact transitions of event, and the exact languages.

The author as an artist takes up only a part of the work. The other part should be completed by the reader as an artist with his own imagination (Marshak 1958, 118).

Marshak's argument for the "reader as an artist" places readers as an indispensable collaborator for writers in competing aesthetic meaning. Chicherov's readers as originators and creators of oral folk arts are, in the strictest sense, limited to folk traditions. Here, it is unclear how the stratum of readers could engage with individual writers to create literature, even if the former's significance to the latter is recognized and the anonymous characteristic of popular culture intuitively informs the mechanism of collective productions. On the contrary, in Marshak's frame, readers are more clearly defined as equal to writers in literature-making by being labeled as artists. Marshak requires his "talented readers" to master a certain level of knowledge in literature, and to build capabilities for applying "fantasy" in order to construct the artistic meaning in collaboration with the author. In theory, Marshak promotes readers to the equivalent level of writers, matching the "reader as an artist" with the "writer as an artist." In practice, however, he does not give explanation for how the reader could demonstrate one's own qualifications as an artist in completing a work of art's meaning. If Marshak's "talented readers," as was evident in Chicherov, should encompass the reader-people, what is left is to demonstrate ordinary people's talents by their real performances in art-making.

Constructing the Reader-People:
People's Agency in Literature and Folk Arts

The practices concerning the reader-people in 1950–1960s North Korea resulted in the establishment of readers hardly distinguishable from the people. Readers, reader-people, or reading masses became almost undifferentiated during the socialist literature-building. All of them delineate the object of socialist literature or the political-aesthetic project of shaping the "new man." Here, we examine the people's cultural activities in the 1950–1960s, which confirm that the range of what Marshak called "talented readers" became expansive and that they were increasingly encouraged to create literature themselves, regardless of their educational background or social status. This expansion was possible through the nationwide growth of people's cultural activities, covering sports, theater, music, drawing, literature, and dance.

In line with increasing participation of people in various cultural circles, there occurred changes in *Choson Munhak* reflecting the amplifying significance of reader-people. First, the section for readers was listed on the contents page of the journal volume. The section had been in the latter part of the volumes in irregular intervals and not included in the table of contents. In 1958 when the readers' section was edited for three issues (March, October, and November) the section appeared on the contents pages. It appeared under the titles of "In Answering Readers' Letters" (March 1958) and "Readers—Editing Board" (October and November 1958). In the October 1958 issue, even subcategories were included in the table of contents, which mentions contributing readers' names, Sŏ Chŏng and Pak Tosu, and the titles for their letters, "An Opinion of a Reader" and "Focusing on *News for a Son.*"[8]

"Talented readers" in Marshak's terms are not hard to find in 1950s North Korean literary spaces. In the mid-1950s, they had already represented themselves by sending critiques to literary journals in letter form, actively participating in reader-related events, and even starting to publish their own works. In other words, readers demonstrated their capabilities as "talented readers" by making themselves new writers. This corresponds to Marshak's concept of the "reader as artist," even if such labeling might have been figurative speech, depicting the collaborative process of writer and readers' completing the meaning of art. Through the 1950–1960s, *Choson Munhak* shows a steadily increasing trend that readers do not just read but transform themselves into writers.[9] This phenomenon was not limited to readers with an advanced level of education. It also occurred with the reader-people

---

8 This continues in the following November issue. Printed letters were Unt'aek Chŏng's "My Opinion" and Hirim Lee's "Several Requests". On the contents page of the November 1958 issue, the names of readers (Unt'aek Chŏng and Hirim Lee) were aligned with the names of writers who published their works in the same issue, and the titles of their letters were also in the same line with those of literary works. This editing style of the contents made the readers' letters appear to have the same weight as other writers' works.

9 This trend became the norm during the late 1960s. As the procedure of exploring the newcomers from the ordinary masses became routinized, the process became institutionalized for training "red" writers whose social origins were from basic classes of the proletariat, or the peasantry.

with lesser education, constituting a majority of the population and the fundamental target of the state's new literature. Until the declaration of the party's monolithic ideological rule in 1967, there continued a coexistence of sophisticated intelligentsia artists and the reader-people, actively engaged in creating art in collective format. In the late 1960s, the wind reversed and the reader-people established themselves as a main agency as the new generation of workers or peasant-writers that would overtake the old intelligentsia.[10]

The cases of "talented readers" with higher education unintentionally offered a model for the next generation of writers to follow. The readers who successfully transformed themselves as professional writers during the 1950–1960s had achieved their advanced education in the post-Korean War period. For example, Ch'oe Sŭngch'il attended Kim Il Sung University Humanities College at the time of the January readers' gathering event, reported in the January 1956 issue. His letter was printed with other readers' in the June 1956 issue. Before this, Ch'oe Sŭngch'il published his first poem in the October 1955 issue. His successful entry into the literary community was possible through his winning an award at the 10th anniversary of the August 15 national liberation literary contest. Including Ch'oe Sŭngch'il, who was both

---

10   What should be noted is the social background of this emergence of the new generation of worker-author or peasant-worker. During the period of the Chollima mass movement, mobilizing the whole population to the rapid industrialization, there had been a significant rise in graduates from fast-track elementary and middle schools for workers. From the late 1950s to the mid-1960s, these graduates, equipped with a basic level of people's education, played indispensable roles in the Chollima era, both in economic development and in ideological and cultural stance. The North Korean new generation of the 1950–1960s constituted by the young graduates can be compared with the "*vydvizhentsy*" (new generation of proletariat, peasants, and communists during the "cultural revolution") of the 1930s (Fitzpatrick 1979,1992).

a "talented reader" and "new writer" early in his university period, there were more readers making their own debuts as writers beyond publishing letters. The letter of Chin Chaehwan, then a university student at Beijing University, China, was introduced in the August 1956 issue as one of the selected responses to the editing board's survey questionnaire printed in the May 1956 issue. The questionnaire was designed as a special project for deeper investigation of readers' views in *Choson Munhak*, and according to the editing board, drew a number of responses from readers. After this appearance as a reader, Chin Chaehwan was mentioned in the postscript of editors in the 1964 issue as one of the "new writers." His novel *Crowds of Fish Forward to the River* was published in the January 1964 issue, and another work *From the New Mine* was released in a series of three installments beginning from the August 1965 issue.

Following the above readers/writers, the reader-people rose to the level of active authors, reminding of Chicherov's argument for the people's agency in folk culture. Chicherov's analysis of the signature of anonymity in the people's art-making was realized in the 1950s North Korean cultural field in the form of people's collectivity in cultural activities. In 1958, the year of the 10th anniversary of the formation of the republic, the best performances from people's cultural activities were displayed at the venue of the national scale art festival. The people's cultural activities themselves became a new genre in North Korean socialist literature and art, which is worth noting, making its collective author, or the people, a significant agent in literature and art.

Presently, everywhere in the republic, circles numbering in total 79,839 and encompassing 198,323 people are active, covering every field of music, dance, stage, literature, sculpture, science, and so on. In 1958, about 150 artists were sent to factories, firms, or collective farms for supporting the circle activities, for the purpose of advancing the work to a higher level. In addition, each major theater tasked themselves with guiding about 100 circles inside factories, firms, and collective farms near Pyongyang. In 1958, 1,500 circle leaders were trained in the permanent system for raising circle leaders, organized around every city- and province-level artistic theater.

In the field for circles at the national art festival for the 10th anniversary of the republic, 2,306 circle members presented 229 works. The characteristic of presented works was above all the fact that now the workers themselves reflected their own life experiences and struggles to the arts, from the new aesthetic preferences and heights, on the basis of ever-increasing artistic talents and level of life.

At the festival, outstanding works were presented including the plays *Initiator* and *The Water of Life Runs*, the dances *The Reunion at the Highland* and *They Fought and Won*, the chorus *Let Us Persist the Bright Revolutionary Tradition*, and the musical *Song of Mt. Kŭmgang*.

The field of mass culture showed great expansion based on the people's cultural activities at the 1958 national art festival. People's collective culture progressed alongside performances by professional artists, showing off successes in grassroots cultural clubs with huge support from the state. Cho Ryŏngch'ul's report on his own creative experience directing the epic-scale stage production combined with dance and music informs how this collective production process was elevated to a new art form. As director of the huge art performance mobilizing 3,000 people in total, Cho (1958) declared that new changing realities generate new forms, prompting demands to represent this newness. According to him, the collective performance represented the themes of the "great peak of socialist construction" (*sahoejuŭi kŏnsŏrŭi iltae kojogi*) by means of a "huge canvas of music, dance, and narratives." He pointed out that the significance of the performance was in line with the recently increasing demands for long novels or epic-scale poetry and for the imagery of new and magnificent art and literature of "our time."

Contemporary interests in epic-scale performances or larger forms were compatible with the seemingly opposite concerns for modest and simple forms of art. Even though the two tendencies might seem to be in conflict, they share a common ground of representing a new era in which the people had achieved political hegemony, either by the forms mobilizing the majority, or by those easily accessible to them. Along with experiments with bigger artistic forms, other attempts existed for collecting and cultivating short folk songs and lyrics as illustrative popular genres. Serious efforts to preserve and study folklore traditions kindled steadfast interest in the form of songs and lyrics, both classic and contemporary. In the July 1957 issue, seven contemporary sets of lyrics were published, all written by renowned contemporary poets. The titles of the lyrics and their authors were all listed in the table of contents, and after this, *Choson Munhak* steadily published such lyrics. Lyrics from folklore or classic literature also attracted significant concern. As a widely acknowledged popular art form, folklore was intensely covered in the 1960s *Choson Munhak*. After special features on regional folklore were published in three consecutive issues in 1962, the folklore section was established.

The North Korean Adaptation of the Soviet Concept of "People-Mindedness": The Implication on the "National Character" Debates

In the discourse and practices of making the reader-people, we have seen multiple routes to engage with the concept of "people-mindedness" (*narodnost'*). As various attempts developed, practices concerning the reader-people diverged into at least two main streams in the late 1960s: either experimenting with popular forms or promoting the people's own cultural activities. On one hand, the efforts to collect and preserve folk heritage took the form of more academic debates, which were the "national character" debates. In addition, further attempts to create modern genres out of tradition followed, emphasizing new content in newly adapted popular forms such as lyrics or folk songs (*minyo*). On the other hand, the efforts to forward the collective production process, promoting the agency of the people in the new republic's literature, showed greater commitment to expanding authorship.

The two streams of practice, despite the difference in their focus, either on form or on agency, show the serious efforts in North Korean literature toward the formation of its reader-people analogous to the Soviet reader-people. Here, I suggest that the process of making the reader-people contributed to the interpretation of the contemporary literary debates on "national character" during the 1950–1960s (Lee 2002, 2006; Nam 2004; S. S. Kim 1990; Park 1989). According to Kwon and Jeong (1990), the "national character" debates progressed in three phases. The focus of discourse shifted from the issue of content versus form, through the theme of the universal versus the particular, or put differently, the relations between class and nation, to the concrete practices of representation of the "North Korean communists." The debates first touched on the question of what was "national character," in terms of content or form. A consensus formed as a result of the first round of debates, concluding that national character should be understood as an inclusive concept by which national specificities are represented in any socialist literature. In the second phase, the debates built on the problem of what was the specific national character of North Korean socialist literature that differentiated it from other socialist literature. This round of debates contributed to the elaboration of the concepts prerequisite for developing socialist literature in North Korea. As clarifications and detailed explanations were conveyed through arguments, counterarguments, and rebuttals, the second phase opened a space for practice-based critiques and suggestions for actual representations. The final phase centered on the concrete representations of socialist heroes within the national character. On the basis of the previous debates, the literary society focused on produced works of art, "nationalist in form, socialist in content" (Stalin 1925), comparable with those of other socialist literatures.

Situating the "national character" debates in the context of the making of the reader-people, we can better understand what was aimed at in those earnest efforts to preserve and modernize folk art as well as to expand the people's cultural participation. What should be noted in the discourse and practices associated with the reader-people is that they all touched upon the concept of "people-mindedness" in one way or another. All of them contributed to the formative process of the North Korean version of "people-mindedness," participating in the larger process of building the North Korean adaptation of socialist realism. If we reflect on the trajectory of the "national character" debates in comparison with the discourse/practices on the reader-people, it will shed new light on the "national character" debates, which in the previous studies were comprehended as "academic" debates, enjoying relative independence from politics. The previous understanding that the promotion of folk art both in literary history and in literary creation from the late 1950s to the early 1960s was developed in a relatively free academic environment prior to the "ideological monolithic rule of party" does not sufficiently explain why at this particular moment in the making of socialist realism in North Korea, the studies and modernization efforts of tradition flourished. Only when considering the significance of the folk tradition that was accessible and comprehensible to the reader-people and compatible with people's artistic creations was it apparent what fundamental project the "national character" debates served.

In summary, the study highlighted the process in which the reader-people were defined and constructed as a result of the reception of translated Soviet reader discourses as well as diverse cultural practices designed for elevating people's agency in artistic creation. Showing how the reader-people were constructed as ideal readers, or the object of the unifying politico-aesthetic project of socialist realism, the study contributes to a new perspective of organizational structure closely knit with logical structure. By illustrating the case of the making of the reader-people in line with the reception of "people-mindedness," the study emphasizes the historical approach for the organizational aspect of socialist realism as well as the productivity of the discursive process as a method for understanding the historical making of the socialist literature in North Korea. It gives not only a deeper understanding of the historical discourses/practices in the perspective of its broader and unifying project, but also the comparative viewpoint of socialist realism as the indigenization process of both organizational and logical structure of the Soviet system.

References

Anonymous. 1954. "Kunjungdŭlgwa hamkke" [With the masses]. Chakkadongmaengesŏ [From the Writers' Union]. *Choson Munhak* (June).

Anonymous. 1956. "Kimilsŏngjonghaptaehaktokchahoeesŏ" [At the readers' gathering at Kim Il Sung University]. Tokcha/p'yŏnjippu [Readers/ Editing Board]. *Choson Munhak* (January).

Armstrong, Charles. 2003. *The North Korean Revolution, 1945–1950*. Ithaca, NY: Cornell University Press.

Bae, Gaehwa. 2012. "Puk'an munhakchadŭrŭi soryŏn'gihaenggwa chŏnhu soryŏnŭi ishik" [North Korean literati's journey to the Soviet Union and implantation of its policies in the post-war recovery period]. *Journal of Korean Literary History* 50 (December).

Chicherov. 1956. "Munhakkwa kujŏninminch'angjak" [Literature and oral folk art]. *Choson Munhak* (May).

Cho, Ryŏngch'ul. 1958. "Saeroun chip'yŏng" [A new landscape]. *Choson Munhak* (November).

Dobrenko, Evgeny. 1997a. *The Making of the State Reader*. Stanford: Stanford University Press.

Dobrenko, Evgeny. 1997b. "The Disaster of Middlebrow Taste, or, Who 'Invented' Socialist Realism?" In *Socialist Realism Without Shores*. Edited by Thomas Lahusen and Evegeny Dobrenko. Durham, NC: Duke University Press.

Dobrenko, Evgeny. 2001. *The Making of the State Writer*. Stanford: Stanford University Press.

Dobrenko, Evgeny. 2007. *Political Economy of Socialist Realism*. New Haven: Yale University Press.

Dobrenko, Evgeny. 2011. "Socialist Realism." In *The Cambridge Companion to Twentieth-Century Russian Literature*. Edited by Evgeny Dobrenko and Marina Balina. Cambridge: Cambridge University Press.

Dobrenko, Evgenii, and Galin Tikhanov. 2011. *A History of Russian Literary Theory and Criticism: The Soviet Age and Beyond*. Pittsburgh, PA:

University of Pittsburgh Press.

Fast, Piotr. 1999. *Ideology, Aesthetics, Literary History: Socialist Realism and its Others*. Frankfurt am Main: Peter Lang.

Fitzpatrick, Sheila. 1979. *Education and Social Mobility in the Soviet Union, 1932–1934*. London: Cambridge University Press.

Fitzpatrick, Sheila. 1992. *The Cultural Front: Power and Culture in Revolutionary Russia*. Ithaca, NY: Cornell University Press.

Fitzpatrick, Sheila. 2007. "Revisionism in Soviet History." *History and Theory* 46 (4) (December): 77–91.

Gabroussenko, Tatiana. 2010. *Soldiers on the Cultural Front: Developments in the Early History of North Korean Literature and Literary Policy*. Honolulu: University of Hawai'i Press.

Günther, Hans. 2000. "Totalitarnoe gosudarstvo kak sintez iskusstv." In *Sotsrealisticheskii kanon*. Edited by Hans Günther and Evgenii Dobrenko. St. Petersburg: Akademicheskii Proekt.

Gutkin, Iriana. 1999. *The Cultural Origins of the Socialist Realist Aesthetic, 1890–1934*. Evanston, IL: Northwestern University Press.

Han, Sung-hoon. 2015. *Chŏnjaenggwa inmin: Puk'an sahoejuŭi ch'ejeŭi sŏngnipkwa inminŭi t'ansaeng* [War and people: the formation of the North Korean socialist system and the birth of the people]. P'aju: Dolbegae.

Hwang, Kŏn. 1956. "Sanmun punyae chegidoenŭn myŏt kaji munje" [A few issues concerning the field of the prose]. In *Che2ch'a chosŏnjakkadaehoe munhŏnjip* [Documents from the second congress of the North Korean writers]. Pyongyang: North Korean Writers' Union Publisher.

Kim, Elli. 2014. "Rituals of Decolonization: The Role of Inner-Migrant Intellectuals in North Korea, 1948–1967." PhD dissertation, University of California, Los Angeles.

Kim, Immanuel. 2012. "North Korean Literature: Margins of Writing Memory, Gender, and Sexuality." PhD dissertation, University of California, Riverside.

Kim, Seong-su. 1990. "Uri munhagesŏ sahoejuŭijŏng sashilchuŭiŭi palsaeng" [The development of socialist realism in our literature]. *Creation and*

Criticism 18 (1) (September): 245–267.

Kim, Seong-su. 2016. "Sahoejuŭi kyoyangŭrosŏŭi toksŏwa munyeji tokchaŭi wising"[Reading, the socialistic culture, and status of readers of literary magazines]. *Journal of Bangyo Language and Literature* 43 (August): 77–108.

Kim, Suk-Young. 2010. *Illusive Utopia: Theater, Film, and Everyday Performance in North Korea.* Ann Arbor, MI: The University of Michigan Press.

Kim, Suzy. 2013. *Everyday Life in the North Korean Revolution, 1945–1950.* Ithaca, NY: Cornell University Press.

Kim, Taekyung. 2018. "Puk'an 'sahoejuŭi riŏllijŭmŭi chosŏnhwa' munhagesŏŭi tangŭi yuilsasangch'egyeŭi yŏgajŏng hyŏngsŏng" [The "Koreanization of socialist realism" in North Korea: the making of the monolithic ideological system of party in literature]. PhD dissertation, Seoul National University.

Kwon, Heonik, and Byung-ho Chung. 2012. *North Korea: Beyond Charismatic Politics.* Lanham: Rowman & Littlefield Publishers.

Kwon, Soon-keung, and Woo-taek Jeong. 1990. *Urimunhagui minjong hyeongsikgwa minjokjeong teukseong: Bukan munhakgyeui minjokjeong teukseong nonjaeng* [The national culture and national character in our literature: the debates on national character in North Korea]. Seoul: Yŏn'gusa.

Lee, Sang-sook. 2002. "Puk'an munhagŭi chŏnt'ongnon yŏn'gu" [A study on the theory on the tradition in North Korean literature]. *North Korean Studies Review* 6 (2) (December).

Lee, Sang-sook. 2006. "Puk'anmunhagŭi chŏnt'onggwa minjokchŏng t'ŭksŏng" [The argument about "tradition" and "national specificity" of North Korea]. *Journal of Dong-ak Language and Literature* 46 (February).

Marshak. 1958. "Kigyoe taehan sogam" [Opinions on skills]. *Choson Munhak,* (November).

Myers, Brian. 1994. *Han Sŏrya and North Korean Literature: The Failure of Socialist Realism in the DPRK.* Ithaca, NY: Cornell East Asia Series.

Nam, Won-jin. 2004. "Puk'anŭi minjokchŏng t'ŭksŏngnon yŏn'gu" [A study on the "national trait" of North Korea]. *Journal of Literature of Kyŏre* 32

(June): 129–159.

Park, Hee-byeong. 1989. "Puk'an hakkyeŭi sashilchuŭi nonjaengŭi sŏnggwawa munjejŏm" [The strengths and weaknesses of the debates on realism in the North Korean academy]. *Creation and Criticism* 17 (3) (September).

Petrov, Petre M. 2015. *Automatic for the Masses: The Death of the Author and the Birth of Socialist Realism*. Toronto: University of Toronto Press.

Robin, Regine. 1992. *Socialist Realism: An Impossible Aesthetic*. Stanford: Stanford University Press.

Ryang, Sonia. 2010. *Reading North Korea: An Ethnological Inquiry*. Harvard East Asia Monograph 311. Cambridge, MA: Harvard University Press.

Smorodinskaya, Tatiana, Karen Evans-Ramaine, and Helena Goscilo, eds. 2007. *Encyclopedia of Contemporary Russian Culture*. London and New York: Routledge.

Stalin, Josef. 1925. "The Political Tasks of the University of the Peoples of the East." *Pravda*, No. 115, May 22, 1925. https://www.marxists.org/reference/archive/stalin/works/1925/05/18.htm.

Wada, Haruki. 2002. *Puk-Chosŏn: yugyŏktae kukka esŏ chŏng'gyugun kukka ro* [North Korea: from a guerrilla state to a standing military state]. Translated by Sŏ Tongman and Nam Kijŏng. Seoul: Dolbegae.

Yoo, Imha. 2011. "Puk'an ch'ogimunhakkwa soryŏniranŭn ch'amjojŏm" [Early literature of North Korea and the reference of the Soviet Union]. *Journal of Dong-ak Language and Literature* 57 (August): 153–184.

7. The Discursive Origins of Anti-Americanism in the Two Koreas

Kab Woo Koo

Abstract

In this article I explore the discursive origins of anti-Americanism or anti-American sentiments in the two Koreas, where the status of postcolonial states was pursued in different ways. I compare two early examples of stories that embodied anti-Americanism, based on discourse analysis in literary criticism: Jackals, written by the North Korean novelist Han Sorya, and Land of Excrement, written by the South Korean novelist Nam Jung-hyun. I emphasize the differences between the two anti-Americanisms in terms of their respective discursive origins. Land of Excrement was reprinted in a North Korean Communist Party bulletin without the author's permission, and he was arrested in 1965. The incident symbolizes the antagonistic relations of the two Koreas as well as the implicit and unofficial linkage between South Korean civil society and the North Korean state.

Keywords

North Korea, South Korea, postcolonialism, anti-Americanism, civil society

The US flag is burning somewhere today. In modern history, no other national flag has ever been the subject of such antagonism as the Stars and Stripes. Since the end of World War II, people have sought to express their hostility to the hegemonic role of the United States in international politics and economy by burning its flag. As a hegemon, the United States has intervened in many countries in order to maintain a favorable international order, promote security and development, and export democracy and human rights.

Unlike colonial powers during the imperialist era, the United States did not intervene by territorial occupation or other means of colonialization. Political and social forces resisted this nonerritorial imperialism through armed struggle and group protest, during which anti-American sentiments were expressed through incineration of the US flag.

The Korean Peninsula, where two postcolonial states have coexisted as divided nations, was no exception. In particular, anti-Americanism and anti-Sovietism seemed inevitable in the former Japanese colony, for its state of division was caused by these two hegemons that represented, respectively, the capitalist sphere and the socialist bloc. The state of postcolonial division created a social partition, against which Korean unification activists responded with anti-Americanism and anti-Sovietism (Waterman 1989).

It should be noted, however, that World War II ended in Allied victory, during which the United States and the Soviet Union cooperated. Anti-Americanism and anti-Sovietism were not an issue until the Cold War began. Traditionalists and revisionists both agree that the origins of the Cold War can be traced to Secretary of State George C. Marshall's Harvard University commencement speech of June 1947 (Hitchcock 2012). The Marshall Plan provided financial support for the countries that adopted a market economy, and the Soviet Union countered by leading the socialist bloc to establish Cominform (Communist Information Bureau), a coalition of communist parties in the East and the West.

On the Korean Peninsula, the competition and ensuing anti-Americanism versus anti-Sovietism dichotomy arose from a fierce controversy over trusteeship, which was proposed at the Moscow Conference of Foreign Ministers of the United States, the United Kingdom, and the Soviet Union in December 1945.

The Cold War dominated politics at the domestic and international levels. Anti-Sovietism took the form of anticommunism in the Republic of Korea (ROK, South Korea), while anti-Americanism was expressed through anticapitalism in the Democratic People's Republic of Korea (DPRK, North Korea). However, a notable difference exists between the two Koreas. In the North, the state and the civil society set anti-Americanism as the solitary national agenda. In the South, the state promoted anti-communism, but a portion of civil society resisted the government by expressing anti-Americanism, thereby causing an internal asymmetry.

In this article, I explore the discursive origins of anti-Americanism in the two Koreas through an analysis of Korean novels. In both states, anti-American acts existed long before literature portrayed them. However, it was through anti-American novels that the public came to internalize anti-Americanism in the form of a discourse.

Two texts form the centerpieces of my comparative analysis: *Jackals*, a 1951 novel by the North Korean novelist Han Sorya, and *Land of Excrement*, a 1965 novel by a South Korean writer, Nam Jung-hyun. *Jackals* ignited North Korean anti-Americanism to such a degree that in recent years it was adapted to cinema (2001) and theater (2015). The story depicts the brutal acts of a US missionary couple during the Japanese colonial period. On the other hand, *Land of Excrement* depicts a story of violence by the US Forces in Korea (USFK) that were stationed in South Korea following the 1953 Korea-US Mutual Defense Treaty signed in the wake of the Armistice Agreement under the pro-US Rhee Syngman government. If *Jackals* can be described as an abstract of recalled history, *Land of Excrement* is a concrete and allegorical record of the present history. The purpose here is to compare the discursive origins of anti-Americanism in the two postcolonial states of the Korean Peninsula.

Anti-Americanisms as Quasi-postcoloniality

– Postcolonialism

Postcolonialism is a concept that encompasses discourses and theories that critically analyze the history and heritage of colonialism from the perspective of the colonized (Brydon 2000). If the concepts of imperialism and colonialism focus on criticism of the central states, postcolonialism tries to shift the focus to the coloniality of the postcolonial states. However, neocolonialism is maybe a more appropriate concept if the colonial phenomenon continues even after decolonization. For example, Ghana's Kwam Nkrumah argued in *Neo-Colonialism: The Last Stage of Imperialism* (1965) that neocolonialism represents the US stage of colonialism—an empire without colonies. Neocolonialism is colonial rule by other means—the extension of imperialism (Young 2001). Therefore, the concept of postcolonialism must be distinguishable from neocolonialism in order to gain legitimacy.

Postcolonialism differs from neocolonialism in that it criticizes ongoing non-territorial imperialistic hegemony and the history of imperialism and colonialism, while at the same time pursuing a political intervention and a new political identity on the basis of social movements. In other words, postcolonialism is *de*-imperialistic and post-hegemonic, not as a cutoff from the world or international system but as an aspiration for transnational social justice (Young 2001). The prefix *post-* is defined as a historical opportunity to signify the introduction of new forms and strategies in critical analysis and practice.

Postcolonialism can function as a theoretical and practical discourse for overcoming the hegemonic order and coloniality in the real world, provided that we can give meaning to postcolonialism rather than accept it as a mere hybrid between nationalism and postmodernism. The core of the postcolonial agenda is a discourse that tries to overcome nationalism, which sets a dichotomy of "us" versus "them." At the same time, contrary to past notions, postcolonialism seeks an alternative for the postcolonial and post-hegemonic orders that situates it within the historical and political contexts of globalization. Use of the term *postcolonialism* began in the late 1960s and early 1970s and gained institutional consolidation in the 1980s because of the concept of globalization (Brydon 2000).

Those who consider nationalism a device for decolonization say that even if nationalism may be outdated in theory, it still constitutes a revolutionary archive of contemporary postcolonialism (Gandi 2000). However, if nationalism suffices as an alternative, then introduction of postcolonialism as a new concept would not be necessary. Nationalism confronts the West with anti-orientalism; it contains the same logic structure of binary opposition as orientalism, which perceives the West as civilized and the East as savage. Efforts to overcome orientalism will enter a new horizon when it is possible for the inferior that sits on one side of the binary opposition to speak beyond it. Such is the challenge of postcolonialism in a post-hegemonic order. If it were otherwise, we would have no choice but to resort to the old-fashioned "power politics" between imperialism and nationalism

– Postcolonialism and anti-Americanism

Postcolonialism after World War II challenges the United States, the hegemon and the "post-colonial imperial power"—a paradoxical combination of its origins and present existence (Slater 2004,13–17). As a postcolonial state, the United States claims to respect the self-determination of all people, but it also flashes the other face of an interventionist state that imposes US values, suchas a US-based international order, democracy, human rights, security, and development. When intervening, the United States tends to separate people and rulers from target states based on the principle of self-determination. Moreover, the United States establishes a basis for policy choices such as containment or preemptive strikes against "rogue states" by considering itself as an ideal state.

Anti-Americanism or anti-American sentiments can be defined as a psychological tendency to express or maintain a negative attitude toward the United States, which is the postcolonial imperial power and the post–World War II hegemon. The source of such anti-Americanism can be attributed to antipathy toward the United States and rejection of US interventionist foreign policy (Keohane and Katzenstein 2006a). *Postcolonial imperial power* is a paradoxical expression. People may reject the values that the United States promotes, but they might also accept US values but resist the interventionist side of US foreign policy. If anti-Americanism sprouts from different sources, then prescriptions need to differ. If the issue lies with US foreign policy, anti-Americanism can be mitigiated by modification of the policy. However, if the United States is rejected, then anti-Americanism is bound to incur a clash of forces.

Major components of anti-Americanism include specific metaphors, analogies, symbols, cognitive structures that rely on narrative of specific events, and emotions and norms that define intensity and behavioral patterns. Anti-Americanism can be divided into liberal, social, sovereign-nationalist, and radical anti-Americanism, depending on two elements: the degree of fear felt by the states and societies that are the victims of US intervention, and the degree of negative opinion about the United States (Keohane and Katzenstein 2006b). While liberal anti-Americanism and social anti-Americanism are forms of anti-Americanism that emerged in Europe, sovereign-nationalist anti-Americanism and radical anti-Americanism can be grouped as postcoloniality. Moreover, if resistance to postcolonial imperial power is a nationalist anti-Americanism of the third world, anti-Americanism in socialist states and societies that share a war-struggle system and a garrison-state system against imperialism and capitalism often takes a radical form.

If radical anti-Americanism can also be said to contain a nationalistic element, postcolonial anti-Americanism can be classified as quasi-postcolonialism. That is because anti-Americanism is situated on a path toward an alternative to the binary opposition of imperialism versus nationalism. The nationalism that distinguishes "us" from "them" takes a form that reverses the cognitive structure of imperialism, from the perspective of the weak. Nationalism is thus the reversed perception structure of imperialism, which explains why we find that indigenous elites of the postcolonial states who fight against imperialism by mobilizing nationalism often collaborate with the imperial power mainstream—explicitly, implicitly, and cognitively. Only after considering what is to come after anti-Americanism can one go beyond colonialism and finally arrive at the world of postcolonialism—and why anti-Americanism itself should be placed in a quasi-postcolonial category.

Postcolonial Literature and the Discursive Origins of Anti-Americanism

Literature is a tool with which to imagine the impossible. Literature is also equipment for living, a medium that reproduces and constitutes the emotions of the public. It has a strategic character in the sense that it creates different attitudes and choices under specific circumstances (Burke 1998). In other words, if literature has social functions even when it is apolitical, literature as a linguistic practice can be said to perform political acts. To put it still another way, if literature contains strategies for human emotions such as joy, anger, sadness, and happiness and literature is inseparable from politics, literary practice can be a strategy for choosing friends or enemies. The reason why imperialist axiomatic sytems can influence postcolonial literature is also attributed to that political aspect of literature (Spivak 1999).

The novel shows how the novelist understands the historical context in which he or she is placed. Such understanding forms the source of fictional writing (i.e., aesthetic manifestation of imagery). Distortion is therefore inevitable for the writer to reflect what is understood in reality in his or her text. A mere repetition of historical facts is not literature. When the writer appropriates reality in aesthetic form, the relative autonomy of the subject is enhanced. The excess or absence of reality is the outcome of the writer's own understanding. That is why there can be too much or too little politics in literature. However, politics does not guarantee the aesthetic fulfillment of literature. It is the point where literature as aesthetics without purpose conflicts with literature as a purposeful tool.

– *Jackals* as a radical anti-American discourse

Jackals is a novella by North Korean novelist, politician, and international peace activist Han Sorya, published in the April 1951 edition of *Literary Arts* magazine. Han was a member of the Korean Proletariat Artist Federation in the colonial era. His earliest published literary works contributed to shaping the image of North Korea's leader Kim Il Sung after national liberation, and he served as a Central

Committee member of the Workers' Party of North Korea (Myers 1994). In April 1949, Han attended the World Peace Congress in Paris as a representative of North Korea (Wittner 1995).

Han was the representative figure in the North for discourse production, most prominently during the Korean War, which was an internal war between the two Koreas as well as an international war involving the two Koreas, the United States, and China. His wartime novel *Jackals* earned symbolic status as an anti-American novel and was made into a film in 2001 and theater play in 2015.

The spatiotemporal background of *Jackals* is set near Hamhung, Hamgyeong-do, following the March 1 Independence Movement of 1919. Even though it was published during the Korean War, the novel's temporal background is set much earlier in the colonial era. To shape anti-Americanism, the novelist created the US missionary couple and their son Simon as "them" in contrast to "us," the Korean people. The three US citizens conflict with their two hired help at home, Sugil and his middle-aged mother. Sugil's father was arrested by the Japanese police due to an incident involving a peasant union; he died in prison.

The conflict begins when Sugil picks up a rubber ball that has been abandoned in the stall where the missionary raises a milking cow. The ball belonged to Simon. When Sugil plays with the ball, Simon acts violently against him. Eventually, Sugil's condition becomes critical. *Jackals* describes Simon's violence as follows:

> With the bursting vigor of one fattened on milk—the milk brought every day by Sugil's mother—Simon dealt Sugil another blow to the chin that knocked him out entirely. Then he looked around for the others. They had scattered. They had the fixed notion that they

couldn't possibly lay a hand on the fifteen-year-old Simon, although they did not understand who had given him and his kind the right to do such things in Korea. (Han 1994, 164)

Sugil's mother worked day and night to ensure the robust health of Simon, yet Simon acted violently against a Korean child who could not resist. The missionary's son is portrayed as a violent actor in the manner of Japanese imperialism.

The dialogue between the missionary and his son that follows Simon's act of brutality contains the author's criticism of Christanity. The missionary thinks that his son's health is more important than the victim of violence, Sugil: "What, something those children have kicked and handled? Yuck, how filthy! Throw it away at once; there might be germs on it" (Han 1994, 164). The Koreans are portrayed as infectious, and thus the missionary believes that the ball a Korean boy played with may have been contaminated.

Then comes the highlight, which could be read as Christian orientalism. The missionary says, "It is for God to punish thieves. We Americans must not touch filthy people with our sacred hands, is that understood?" (Han 1994, 164). Koreans living in colonies were thieves and filthy people. The missionary's son's response reveals that the way of handling the "other" in the US state-formation period can be imported into Korea: "But, father, we Americans have the right to beat blacks to death, don't we? God forgives us for doing that" (Han 1994,165). The missionary's reply is that "blacks" are not sons of God. Then Simon asks whether Korean people are sons of God. The missionary answers that only the Korean people who are devoted to Christianity are sons of God. "There are some sons of God among Koreans: Reverend Yi,

Reverend Kim, Elder An" (Han 1994, 165). Simon asks again, "Are they really sons of God?" (Han 1994, 165). The missionary says that they are sons of God only because they had sworn to be sons of God. The missionary's son asserts that the thief who stole the ball is not a son of God, just like a black man is not. The missionary replies that he could have a dog bite Sugil to death, just as a white man will use a club but not his hands to punish a black man. It is a scene in which a dichotomy of white and black is replicated as a binary opposition of US citizens and Koreans through Christianity.

Another dramatic scene in *Jackals* is a plot to kill Sugil, the victim of violence. If Sugil recovers, the missionary's son's violence would be revealed. The person who appears as an antagonist in this conspiracy is a female American doctor. The missionary couple asks her why she is in Korea. Her answer is that she is doing her work for the United States. She is working for US citizens, and for the honor of the US people. There follow some extreme statements justifying the US interventionism:

> What is the life of a Korean child when weighed against the glory of the American people? I tell you, why concern yourself any more with a life that even God knows nothing about?. . .
> We have to demand our virtues from others. And if it hasn't got contagious disease, then we must give it an injection of bacilli and make it a contagious disease. . . .
> The victory of the American people and its virtues requires more than just churches. God also gives us bullets, airplanes, and warships. What do you think the Bibles are, that we missionaries carry, or our doctors' syringes? (Han 1994, 176, 177)

Eventually, the doctor injects infectious bacterium into Sugil's body, as if she is using a gun. Subsequently, Sugil passes away. *Jackals* demonstrates that the United States and US interests are behind humanitarian support for the Korean people, and that they can do nothing to protect themselves. When Sugil's mother perceives the truth, she compares the missionary couple and their son who killed Sugil to jackals: "The old jackal's spade eagle's nose hung villainously over his upper lip, while the vixen's teats jutted out like the stomach of a snake that has just swallowed a demon, and the slippery wolf cub gleamed with poison like the head of a venomous snake that has just shed its skin" (Han 1994, 184).

The novel ends with a scene in which the Japanese sergeant picks out Sugil's mother for protesting to the missionary couple. The story develops a plot in which the US elites conspire with the Japanese police to oppress Koreans.

– Nam Jung-hyun's *Land of Excrement* as a sovereign-nationalist anti-American discourse

Land of Excrement is a story by South Korean novelist Nam Jung-hyun, published in March 1965 in *Modern Korean Literature*. Since he made his debut, Nam Jung-hyun has published novels that criticize foreign powers in Korea. The 1961 Dong-in Literary Award–winning novel *Who Are You?* also sharply criticized foreign powers and the Korean people who were on their side. In his representative anthology, Nam matched his criticism of Korea's division with criticism of the United States—to the extent that Nam regarded the "division era" he lived in as the "American era."

Two months after publication, *Land of Excrement* was reprinted in North Korea's May 8 edition of *Reunification of the Fatherland*. Nam Jung-hyun was immediately arrested for violation of anti-communist laws. Charges against Nam included praising, encouraging, and sympathizing with an anti-state organization. *Land of Excrement* was the first novel that brought a South Korean writer to court after national liberation.

The setting of *Land of Excrement* is Mt. Hyangmi. Literally, *Mt. Hyangmi* means "mountain toward the United States," indicating that *Land of Excrement* uses allegorical techniques. The story is composed of monologues of the main character Man-soo, the 10th-generation grandson of Hong Gil-dong as well as a descendant of the founder of Gojoseon (Old Chosun), Dangun, who awaits death on Mt. Hyangmi, encircled by the USFK. Hong Gil-dong was the Robin Hood of the Chosun dynasty, and Man-soo's name means that he will enjoy life for 10,000 years. Through his monologue Man-soo recalls his mother who was raped by a USFK soldier; her life ruined, she died after national liberation. The conflict that leads Man-soo to Mt. Hyangmi is the sexual abuse of his sister, Bun, by a US soldier, Sergeant Speed, and Man-soo's retaliatory rape of Speed's wife, who was visiting South Korea at the time.

The monologue of Man-soo begins with the encirclement of Mt. Hyangmi by the USFK troops. He uses exaggerations laced with fables and sarcasm, describing some 10,000 cannons and missiles. Man-soo argues that the USFK mobilized enormous firepower and the most agile and mobile soldiers from the X Corps to capture him. The Korean residents around Mt. Hyangmi show absolute compliance toward the USFK: "I guess they have no choice but to instantly obey the orders issued by the Pentagon authorities, as I hear that's the only way for them to survive. They're enduring this hardship with the kind of persistence characteristic of 'the white-clad race' as if hanging onto the shoulders of God" (Nam 2013, 15).

The USFK broadcasts a message to Man-soo, who is isolated on the mountain. It is just like President George W. Bush's statement immediately after September 11, 2001, in which he said, "freedom was attacked today" (Woodward 2002). In the novel, the USFK invokes Christianity to contrast freedom with evil. As was the case in *Jackals*, Man-soo is depicted as dirt:

> He is dirt, certainly dirt, mistakenly blessed by God, dirt. He happened to drop onto this world. If he weren't dirt that the devil threw up, how could he dare to trample an American soldier, the purity of the wife of a soldier who's defending freedom under the Star-Spangled Banner? Free people of the world cannot extinguish the fire of their anger right now. (Nam 2013, 17–19)

On the other hand, there are dual aspects to Man-soo's view about the United States. He acknowledges that he was a snob, chewing US-made gum and depending on his sister for his livelihood. But at the same time he acknowledges that the United States eliminated the other during the state-formation period. "I thoroughly believe in the so-called superhuman fighting spirit, zeal, and resourcefulness of the Americans who are known to have reclaimed that vast territory, some nine million square kilometers of paradise that once belonged only to Indians, and to have created paradise on earth" (Nam 2013, 22–23).

Man-soo is claiming that the United States developed into a

postcolonial imperialist state with the formation of the state. Man-soo, the "dirt" that identifies himself with the North American native peoples based on the Indian Wars, sets the meaning of his resistance as follows: "God would be extremely furious at me and would say that a human being must not die in such a silly way whether we refer to either moral principles or Natural Law. . . . I'm now in a sorry situation in which I can't die without ever having been recognized as a human being and having lived a respectable life" (Nam 2013, 25).

In other words, Man-soo believes that his fight is a struggle for recognition as a human being. Man-soo also highlights a conspiracy between the USFK and politicians of South Korea in the age of postcolonialism:

> I know that this is the kind of world in which those who have no experience of fighting for the people or of statesmanship can easily become patriots and politicians, if they keep shouting "anti-communism" and "pro-America." Don't I also know that legislation and the administration seem to run smoothly only for the benefit and prosperity of a few who've contributed to political campaign funds? (Nam 2013, 33–35)

In other words, anti-Americanism is shaping up in South Korea as a resistance to anti-communism and pro-Americanism. South Korean politicians who gave themselves over to the United States are portrayed as a humiliation, which affected two generations of Man-soo's family, his mother and sister:

> Don't be surprised. To make a long story short, your precious

daughter and my sister, Bun, whom you raised so carefully, ah, so absurdly, became the mistress of an American soldier, who might be the very person who raped you: Master Sergeant Speed of the X division of the US Army. Mother, didn't you promise me? Don't ever tremble. It was also inevitable, you know. Now please think about it. (Nam 2013, 63)

In the last scene Man-soo prepares for his end. Just as the "genital part" of his mother is referred to throughout *Land of Excrement*, Man-soo's resolve mobilizes naked sexuality. Man-soo describes the bombing of Mt. Hyangmi: "Maybe another nice high-rise will be built on the site afterwards to serve the overflowing appetites and sexual desires of foreigners" (Nam 2013, 87). Allegorically, Man-soo envisions a nationalistic sexual response.

Only 10 seconds to go. Right. Now I'll make a splendid new flag by tearing up my Taegeuk-patterned undershirt. Then I'll get on a cloud and cross the ocean. I'm planning to carefully stick this rapturous flag into the lustrous navels of women with milky skin, women lying down on that great continent, women that I appreciate. (Nam 2013, 89)

One can see here the extremes of allegorical, anti-feminist imagnation that want to confront the United States and its people withthe same violence.

Conclusion

A particular mindset such as anti-Americanism in literary text appears as a complexity of reason, emotion, will, and imagination at a specific political and economic conjuncture. In other words, anti-Americanism is a mind system that carries intentionality to enable the subjects to act (Dennett 1997). In North Korea, which became a socialist state in the 1950s, we may say that the mind system of anti-Americanism produced by political power brought to life the text of *Jackals*, which was the text of Han Sorya or Han's "embodied mind." On the other hand, in South Korea where a part of civil society resisted the state, Nam Jung-hyun's *Land of Excrement* and other texts were created to counter the political power and can be said to be the embodied mind of Nam's personal experience (Rowlands 2010). These texts convey the mind system of anti-Americanism to the public.

Jackals and *Land of Excrement* are the discursive origins of anti-Americanism on the Korean Peninsula. They share postcolonial text characteristics. However, the materials mobilized for postcolonialism show fundamental differences. If *Jackals* was written to encourage anti-Americanism during the Korean War through the description of a US missionary in the colonial era, *Land of Excrement*'s anti-Americanism is based on the USFK's impositions on South Korea's sovereignty. Therefore, ideas for the next stage of anti-Americanism are bound to differ. *Land of Excrement* shows that anti-Americanism could be resolved if the USFK withdraws; but *Jackals* attacks Christianity, which is seen as underlying US values, resulting in a fundamental denial of the United States.

On the other hand, both works share a similar composition. *Jackals* depicts a binary opposition of white and black people in the United States and subsequently equates black Americans with Koreans. In *Land of Excrement*, the South Korean people are regarded in the same vein as native US peoples, another "other" in US society. The problem of imperialism versus nationalism is also a dichotomist confrontation that can be found in both stories. Anti-Americanism is close to pseudo-postcoloniality in both stories in that it seeks to overcome imperialism through nationalism. In other words, it is a form that confronts orientalism with anti-orientalism.

Another common noteworthy feature is that in both novels, women, the greatest victims of imperialist interventionism, are portrayed as major actors. In *Jackals*, Sugil's mother appears as a victim, while in *Land of Excrement* Man-soo's mother and sister are portrayed as victims. As is the case in postcolonial claims, racialist and imperialist ideology may already be permeating the rhetoric and parables, which are used to mobilize subaltern women in order to strengthen masculinity (Spivak 1999). Although the stories reproduce female victims and allow them to speak, the elite novelists of South and North Korea lack feminist awareness. *Land of Excrement* in particular reinforces masculinity thorugh its naked sexual depiction.

North Korea is continuously reproducing anti-Americanism as a discourse of resistance against the imperialist state, the United States. North Korea's purpose is regime survival, and one of its arguments is that US soldiers committed genocide in Sincheon, Hwanghae-do, during the Korean War in October 1950. There is even a museum to commemorate the massacre. However, the so-called Sincheon Massacre turned out not to be an atrocity by the United States but a violent conflict between right-wing Christians and supporters of the North

Korean regime. This maybe the reason why North Korea still uses the image of *Jackals* as a synonym for what is shrewd, cunning, and cruel. Even North Korea records that its leader Kim Il Sung produced a revolutionary play called *Jackals* in 1934 during the period of anti-Japanese armed struggle. It is a reconstruction of historical memory, and can be interpreted as a postcolonial strategy that identifies Japanese imperialism with US imperialism.

On the other hand, in South Korean society, anti-Americanism heightened before and after the 1987 democratization. But the trend has declined, for two possible reasons. One may be that the Korea-US alliance has shifted to a value alliance, one that accepts US values. The other may be that some institutional arrangements are in place to control the unlawful activities of USFK soldiers. The North Korean media reintroduced *Land of Excrement* in the 1960s and sought to use united front tactics in an effort to create solidarity with anti-US social forces in South Korean civil society. However, the anti-Americanism in the South that North Korea claims seems to have clear limits, in that there is no next stage for anti-Americanism and anti-US sentiments.

References

Brydon, Diana. 2000. "Introduction." In *Postcolonialism: Critical Concepts*. Vol. 1. Edited by Diana Brydon. London: Routledge, 1–26.

Burke, Kenneth. 1998 [1938]. "Literature as Equipment for Living." In *Classic Texts and Contemporary Trends*. Edited by D. Richter. Boston: Bedford Books, 593–598.

Dennett, Daniel. 1997. *Kinds of Minds*. New York: Basic Books.

Gandi, Leela. 2000. *Postcolonial Theory*. London: Allen and Unwin.

Han, Sŏrya. 1994 [1951]. *Jackals*. In *Han Sŏrya and North Korean Literature: The Failure of Socialist Realism in the DPRK*. Edited and translated by Brian Myers. Ithaca, NY: East Asia Program, Cornell University.

Hitchcock, William. 2012. "The Marshall Plan and the Creation of the West." In *The Cambridge History of the Cold War, Volume I: Origins*. Edited by Melvyn Leffler and Odd Ame Westad. Cambridge: Cambridge University Press, 154–174.

Keohane, Robert, and Peter Katzenstein. 2006a. "Introduction: The Politics of Anti-Americanism." In *Anti-Americanism in World Politics*. Edited by R. Keohane and P. Katzenstein. Ithaca, NY: Cornell University Press, 1–6.

Keohane, Robert, and Peter Katzenstein. 2006b. "Varieties of Anti-Americanism: A Framework for Analyis." In *Anti-Americanism in World Politics*. Edited by R. Keohane and P. Katzenstein. Ithaca, NY: Cornell University Press, 9–38.

Myers, Brian. 1994. *Han Sŏrya and North Korean Literature: The Failure of Socialist Realism in the DPRK*. Ithaca, NY: East Asia Program, Cornell University.

Nam, Jung-hyun. 2013 [1963]. *Land of Excrement*. Translated by Jeon Seung-hee. Seoul: Asia Publishers.

Nkrumah, Kwame. 1965. *Neo-Colonialism: The Last Stage of Imperialism*. London: Thomas Nelson and Sons.

Rowlands, Mark. 2010. *The New Science of the Mind: From Extended Mind to Embodied Phenomenology*. Cambridge, MA: MIT Press.

Slater, David. 2004. *Geopolitics and the Post-Colonial: Rethinking North-South*

Relations. Oxford: Blackwell.

Spivak, Gayatri Chakravory. 1999. *A Critique of Postcolonial Reason: Toward a History of the Vanishing Present.* Cambridge, MA: Harvard University Press.

Waterman, Stanley. 1989. "Partition and Modern Nationalism." In *Community Conflict, Partitionand Nationalism.* Edited by Colin Williams and Eleonore Kofman. London: Routledge, 117–132.

Wittner, Lawrence. 1995. *One World or None: A History of the World Nuclear Disarmament Movement Through 1953.* Stanford, CA: Stanford University Press.

Woodward, Kath. 2002. *Understanding Identity.* London: Arnold.

Young, Robert. 2001. *Postcolonialism: An Historical Introduction.* Oxford: Blackwell.

8. Inter-Korean Integration Mirrored in Division Films:

Changing Collective Emotion in South Korea Toward Inter-Korean Integration

Lee Woo-Young and Kim Myoung-Shin

Abstract

Article Type: Research Paper

Purpose: This study aims to examine the changes in collective emotions in South Korea toward inter-Korean integration.

Design, Methodology, Approach: Films reflect the universal emotions in a contemporary society. Given this fact, this study compares four blockbuster films released in the Kim Dae-jung and Lee Myung-bak administrations. This study simplified North-South Korean integration to two axes of integration of institution and mindset, and analyzed the inter-Korean relations and character relationship depicted in the division films as the integration of institution and the integration of mindset.

Findings: Its findings reveal that the collective emotions under the Kim Dae-jung government are oriented toward "peaceful unification" that aims to achieve integration of institution as well as mindset. On the other hand, division films under the Lee Myung-bak administration lean toward "coexistence in division," which pursues the integration of mindset through advancing personal relationships while the unresolved fundamental problem of the divided system remains.

Practical Implications: If the South and the North are not a single divided nation, but an inter-state relationship, achieving only the integration of mindsets that embrace the different perspectives and positions of the other side may be sufficient. However, the collective emotions that justify a divided Korea pose a considerable risk.

Originality, Value: The study is expected to complement existing research in the field of inter-Korean integration and unification in that it provides a new approach in tracing a change of collective emotions via films.

Keywords

collective emotion, division films, inter-Korean integration, relationship

Introduction

When people belong to a specific group, their emotions tend to coincide with the relevant events of that group (Sullivan 2015). For example, the mood of soccer fans can fluctuate depending on their favorite team's game result, and political party members can become elated or disappointed according to changes in approval rating. At the country level, wars, terrorist attacks, or natural disasters, which can affect the entire nation, generate negative feelings such as anger, sadness, and fear among its people, whether they themselves are directly involved or not. Although emotion has traditionally been regarded as an individual phenomenon, it becomes a collective phenomenon when a critical mass of individuals sharing a similar event or experience is reached (Smith, Seger, and Mackie 2007). What matters is that this kind of collective emotion can impact the perceptions and behavior of a social unit or how they interact with different groups.

In the past few decades, there has been growing interest in research on collective emotions in the field of sociology, philosophy, anthropology, and social psychology (Scheve and Ismer 2013). However, collective emotions have been defined in various ways. Bar-Tal and colleagues (2007) argue that collective emotions are "shared by large numbers of people in a society" and a response to "collective or societal experiences." Scheve and Ismer (2013) define collective emotions as "the synchronous convergence in affective responding across individuals towards a specific event or object." Lawler, Thye, and Yoon (2014, 191) propose an understanding of collective emotion as "common feelings by members of a social unit as a result of shared experiences." Here, a common understanding in existing research is that although individual emotions may vary within a shared social context, their emotions caused by a shared experience converge at some point as a group. In this study, a working definition of collective emotion intermingles these key elements as follows: *collective emotions are emotions synchronously converged by large numbers of individuals as a result of shared events and experiences.* Some good examples would be the excitement and ecstasy Brazilians feel in the midst of the Rio Carnival, or the fear and anger that citizens of the US had after 9/11.

In the case of South Korea, the national division and its derived events may be one of the most influential shared events that has directly and indirectly affected the collective emotion of people throughout its history. Not only did the national division divide North and South geographically, but it also built a wall of division in the minds of the Korean people (T. G. Park 2005, 360). The people of South Korea had to live in a divided system, obliged to prove their identity by denying the other. Also, armed provocation and repeated missile and nuclear tests by North Korea, and regular military drills conducted by South Korea and the US locked Koreans in a constant fear of war and deep-rooted hostility toward North Korea (Hamm 1999, 74–78). However, inter-Korean summits, reunions of separated families, and diverse North-South exchange programs in the field of sports and culture allowed Koreans to feel a strong sense of ethnic community and a desire for unification despite the hostile tensions on the Korean Peninsula.

As such, national division has significantly influenced South Korean society and its people. Films are no exception. The division frequently appears as a popular theme in Korean films, and a number of films represent the emotions and sentiments on national division. According to Raymond Williams (1961), although it is only our own time and place that we can fully understand and know, it is possible to grasp a structure of feeling at a particular time and place in history by looking at documentary culture such as films and novels—preferably those that attract the popularity of the public—made in that age.[1] He argues that arts naturally reveal the actual sense of daily life, as they have a present and affective nature. In other words, films that succeed in winning public support rarely deviate from the boundary of the universal sentiment of the public (Jeon 2014). Hence, it is meaningful as well as necessary to examine the changes in the collective emotions of those who have lived in the era of division through South Korean blockbuster films with themes of national division.[2]

Literature Review

According to C. K. Kim (2014), the "division film" refers to a genre of Korean films that adopt the reality and the influence of national division as the main subject and at the same time convey personal and social emotions on national division in the narrative of the film. A variety of studies explore this genre, and the scope of studies centering on the keyword "division" is expanding, as the original characteristic of division films. For example, E. S. Kim (1999), Y. H. Park (2013),

---

1   Structure of feeling does not represent a total emotion in a particular time and place; rather it means either common feelings or the dominant way of thinking. In other words, there is always an inner dynamic in a formation of thought emerge. See Williams (1961, 48).

2   In this article, blockbuster films are defined as films that record large-scale box-office hits. See Neale (2013, 47–60)

C. K. Kim (2014), and H. J. Jeong and H. Cheong (2014) revealed that division films tend to have their own unique characteristics and analyzed the changes in the genre over time. Y. J. Kim and H. J. Lee (2015) and S. E. Han (2014) investigated the meaning of division through narrative analysis of division films, and B. K. Kim (2007) and K. W. Kim (2015) analyzed historical trauma represented in division films.

However, the narrative of division films often contains strong messages and emotions about inter-Korean integration as well. Particularly, as government control over the film industry began to loosen in the 1990s in South Korea, division films were able to escape the boundaries of anti-communism and unveiled people's changing emotions toward North Korea and inter-Korean integration (H. Lee 2014). This change is partially attributable to the expansion of freedom of expression and the post–Cold War atmosphere, but ultimately, it is due to the changing collective emotions of the Korean public towards inter-Korean relations and national division (Jeon 2014, 6–8). Therefore, film analysis must expand to incorporate a new perspective of "integration" in division film analysis that moves beyond "division."

Research on inter-Korean integration expands into the fields of politics, economy, society, and culture. However, most of the studies tend to focus on institutional integration and rarely examine the integration of mindset between the people of the two Koreas (J. H. Park et al. 2016, 3). True integration is achieved only when the North and South constitute a community, where integration of both the institutions and mindsets of the people who make up the community take place. Therefore, a study on the emotions and attitudes of people toward inter-Korean integration is crucial. Although there have been some studies on South Korean attitudes toward Korean unification with

North Korea, most generally utilize direct methods such as interviews and opinion polls (M. K. Park et al. 2013a, 2013b; J. Park et al. 2014).

According to Kahneman and Tversky (1979), however, individuals may not always be aware of their preferences or the changes in their preferences over time. Thus, this study attempts to trace the changes in the collective emotions toward inter-Korean integration through an examination of South Korean division films.[3]

Inter-Korean Integration Compass and New Quadrant

Normally, film analysis examines visual (picture, color, motion, light), cinematic (visual editing), auditory (music, large and small sound effects, intensity and tone of voice) and sentimental (relationship between image and sound) elements (Vanoye and Goliot-Lete 1993, 11–14). This study, however, will not follow the conventional method of film analysis in order to focus on the discovery of changing patterns of inter-Korean relations and character relationship in the films. This study simplifies North-South Korean integration to the two axes of integration of institution and mindset, and analyzes the inter-Korean relations and character relationships depicted in the division films as the integration of institution and the integration of mindset. This approach will indirectly infer South Korea's collective emotions toward inter-Korean integration by interpreting the changing patterns and the orientation of inter-Korean relations and character relationship in the

---

3   There are many studies on the portrayal of North Korea and North Koreans in South Korean television and cinema but most of them focus on identity issues rather than collective emotion. See Epstein (2009), Green and Epstein (2013), M. Lee (2013).

films.

Division films set the spatial, historical, and social background through the inter-Korean relations in the film (B. K. Kim 2007). The narrative of division films is created through the relationships of the main characters and the events that occur between them, symbolizing North Korea and South Korea. In general, the inter-Korean relations described in division films can be categorized into five types: *War, Hostile Tensions, Reconciliation and Cooperation, Korea Union,* and *Unification*. This demonstrates the inter-Korean relations ranging from extreme military conflict between the two Koreas to the ultimate integration of two systems. The human relationships among the characters in the films are often classified into five types: *Devil, Enemy, Others, Friends,* and *Family*. It covers the worst relationship of dehumanizing the opponent to the ideal relationship of unconditional understanding and embracement of the other.

These classifications of inter-Korean relations and character relationships represented in division films are incorporated and illustrated in figure 8.1. The inter-Korean relations in division films are placed on the X-axis, which symbolizes the conflict-integration level of the institution, while the relationships among characters of the two Koreas are placed on the Y-axis, which embodies the conflict-integration of the countries' mindsets. By doing so, four quadrants of the Inter-Korean Integration Compass can be seen. The character relationships can represent the level of conflict-integration of the mind as the nature of the relationships changes according to how each character perceives the other.

Each quadrant of figure 8.1 shows a different approach toward inter-Korean integration. Quadrant 1 represents *Peaceful Unification* in which both the institutions and mindsets of the two Koreas are integrated, while quadrant 2 shows the state of *Coexistence in Division* where people respect and trust each other despite national division. Quadrant 3 can be viewed as *Division System* in which the people living in the divided system are caught in a vicious cycle of mutual mistrust and enmity. Quadrant 4, *Unification by Absorption*, depicts the integration of the system without resolving the deeply rooted hostility

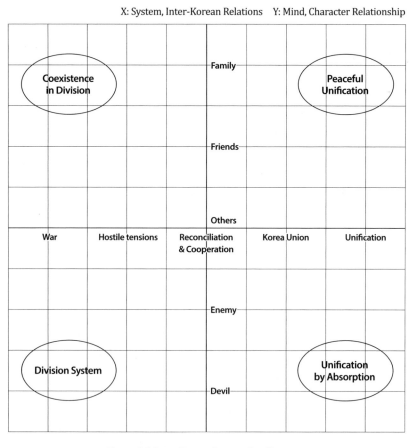

Figure 8.1. Inter-Korean Integration Compass

between people of the two Koreas.

This study will locate where the inter-Korean relations and character relationships representing the North and the South in division films lies in the compass, and what changes take place in each film in terms of the inter-Korean relations and character relationships. Through this reinterpretation process, each film will be relocated on the compass based on its disposition towards *Peaceful Unification, Coexistence in Division, Division System,* or *Unification by Absorption.*

To do so, the level of the inter-Korean relations and character relationships depicted in division films is further classified into 10 levels. Table 8.1 is the Classification Criteria for Inter-Korean Relations and table 8.2 is a Classification Criteria for Character Relationship between North and South Korea. Table 8.1 is rearranged and modified based on the structural integration index from the *Inter-Korean Integration Index* issued by the Institute of Peace and Unification of Seoul National University (M. K. Park et al. 2013). Table 8.2 is a new coding of character relationship in the films according to the context of the relationship between main characters and how they address each other.

Table 8.1. Classification Criteria for Inter-Korean Relations

X-Axis 10 Steps		Inter-Korean Relations in Division Films
War	+	All-out military conflict involving mass killings and destruction
	-	Military conflict in limited areas on the Korean Peninsula
Hostile Tensions	+	Terrorist attacks, gunfire between groups of characters, kidnapping / assassination, imminent military engagements
	-	Terrorism threats, search and reconnaissance activities, missile tests, physical fights and gunfire between major characters
Reconciliation & Cooperation	+	High-level and working-level talks and joint events and cooperation

	-	Preparation and plan for inter-Korean working-level talks and cooperation projects
Korea Union	+	Free exchange of people, freedom of media and broadcasting, regular cooperation projects
	-	Establishment and activities of transitional Korea Union
Unification	+	Establishment and execution of a joint political and military executive organ
	-	Unification of the inter-Korean political system and joint legislation

Table 8.2. Classification Criteria for Character Relationship

Y-Axis 10 Steps The Relationship Context Between the Main Characters of Two Koreas		Character Relationship in Division Films	
		Titles Used to Address the Other	
Family	+	Blood relatives	Mother (mom), son, brother, family, one's name, honey
	-	Sworn brothers, foster parent/child, lover, and close neighbors	
Friends	+	Unconditional commitment and devotion	One's name, friend, comrade
	-	Thoughtful and embracing relationship with the opponent	
Others	+	Recognizing the opponent as an equal human being to oneself without a deep understanding	Northern side, southern side, upper area, one's name
	-	Treating the opponent as a means to achieve a goal	
Enemy	+	Recognizing the opponent as an enemy based on the realities of national division	Enemy, bastard, friend (sarcastic), espionage, one's name
	-	Believing that one should win and suppress the other	
Devil	+	Disdain, contempt and discrimination against opponents	Commie, puppet army, American puppet-state, son of a bitch, rat, dog
	-	Perceiving the opponent as an object of killing, and using profane language	

Most division films present the background of inter-Korean relations and character relationship in the introduction, normally within the first 10 to 20 minutes of the film. Therefore, the change of relationship will be analyzed by comparing the beginning and the end of the story. However, if there is an inflection point between the beginning and the end in which dramatic changes in inter-Korean relations and character relationship occur, it will be addressed separately.

The study will analyze four blockbuster films: *Swiri* (1999), *Joint Security Area* (2000), *Secret Reunion* (2010), and *The Berlin File* (2013) released in the Kim Dae-jung (1998–2003) and Lee Myung-bak (2008–2013) administrations, which pursued different North Korean policies. Amongst division films released in both presidential terms, these four movies attracted the largest number of audience members— more than 5 million—as table 8.3 shows.[4] The fact that an unspecified number of masses living in different social circumstances have watched and responded to the same film means that the film contains the social emotions shared by the people of the same era (H. Cho 2008, 52–58). Of course, individual audience members may have different emotional responses to these films, but it is reasonable to expect that there is a convergence of emotion amongst a large number of viewers as a result of a shared experience of watching the same films and sharing their experiences with others.

From this perspective, it is possible to harness these films as a means of indirectly inferring the collective emotions of each period.

---

4   With the total population of South Korea at less than 50 million, only two-thirds of the population can actually go to the cinema. Considering the distribution of films through various kinds of media such as television, DVD, and internet, the 5-million viewer number does not simply stay at 5 million. Therefore, the fact that the films attracted over 5 million viewers and watched these same films carries great social and cultural significance that goes beyond commercial success. See H. J. Cho (2010, 18–22).

Table 8.3. List of Division Films[5]

Government	Title	Released Year	Genre	No. of Accumulated Viewers
Kim Dae-jung Administration	*Swiri*	Feb. 1999	Action, Drama, Romance, Mystery	5,820,000
	Joint Security Area	Sep. 2000	Drama, Mystery	5,830,000
	Double Agent	Jan. 2003	Thriller	1,025,928
Lee Myung-bak Administration	*Secret Reunion*	Feb. 2010	Drama, Action	5,416,829
	71—Into the Fire	Jun. 2010	Action, War, Drama	3,385,706
	The Front Line	Jul. 2011	War, Drama	2,945,137
	As One	May. 2012	Drama	1,872,681
	Return to Base	Aug. 2012	Action, Drama	1,201,944
	The Spies	Sep. 2012	Drama, Comedy, Action	1,310,895
	The Berlin File	Jan. 2013	Action	7,166,513

Representation of Inter-Korean Relations and Character Relationship in the Division Film

During the first decade of the 2000s, inter-Korean relations shifted from highs to lows. The South Korean administration was not the only cause for this shift as North Korea also played a role. Thus, it is useful to briefly review major inter-Korean events during the Kim Dae-jung and Lee Myung-bak governments in order to understand how those shared events influenced the collective emotions of people in theperiod and are reflected in the films. A timeline of the major events can be summarized as below in table 8.4.

---

5   In the early 2000s, statistics were not accurate, but according to the Korea Film Council (n.d.) and various news media (*Cine 21*, 2001), it is estimated that the number of accumulated viewers of *Swiri* and *JSA* is more than 5.8 million.

In 1998, the newly elected South Korean president Kim Dae-jung (February 1998–February 2003) announced his "Sunshine Policy," a comprehensive engagement policy towards North Korea. This led to the first inter-Korean summit in June 2000 in Pyongyang, and it drastically improved inter–Korea relations followed by active humanitarian assistance projects for North Korea, cultural and economic exchange and cooperation such as reunion of separated families, the opening of the Kaesong Industrial Complex—a special administrative industrial region of North Korea—and the commencement of tourism programs for South Koreans to Mt. Kŭmgang in North Korea. Since the summit, there have been large and small conflicts between the two Koreas, but the Kim Dae-jung government emphasized the consistency of its policy toward North Korea and continuously pursued reconciliation and cooperation between the two Koreas. This policy trend continued in the Roh Moo-hyun administration (February 2003–February 2008) despite the US hardline policy toward North Korea and North Korea's nuclear and missile tests. However, with the inauguration of president Lee Myung-bak (February 2008–February 2013) in 2008, the new government introduced great conditionality for inter-Korean cooperation and took a hardline policy toward the North. Unfortunately, other setbacks occurred in the process. A South Korean tourist at Mt. Kŭmgang was shot and killed by a North Korean soldier in 2008, and a South Korean warship, the *Cheonan*, was fired upon and sank in 2010. In response to North Korea's provocations, the Lee Myung-bak administration announced "May 24 Measures" that suspended all inter-Korean cooperation. As a result, the deteriorating inter-Korean relations became even worse.

Table 8.4. Major Inter-Korean Events, 1998–2012

Government	Year	Events
Kim Dae-jung Administration (1998–2003)	Feb. 1998	New president Kim Dae-jung launches "Sunshine Policy"
	Jun. 2000	First inter-Korean summit in Pyongyang North-South joint declaration
	Aug. 2000	Reunion of 100 members of separated families in Pyongyang and Seoul
	Jun. 2002	North and South Korean navies clash
	Sep. 2002	Connection of Kyŏngŭi Line and Tonghae Line railways and roads
	Jan. 2003	North Korea withdraws from the Non-Proliferation Treaty
Roh Moo-hyun Administration (2003–2008)	Jun. 2004	Pilot complex for Kaesong Industrial Complex completes construction
	May 2007	Pilot operation of inter-Korean train
	Oct. 2006	North Korea's first nuclear test
	Oct. 2007	Second inter-Korean summit in Pyongyang
Lee Myung-bak Administration (2008–2013)	Feb. 2008	New president Lee Myung-bak introduces hardline policy on the North
	Jul. 2008	Tourism in Mt. Kŭmgang is suspended due to attack on a tourist
	May 2009	North Korea's 2nd nuclear test
	May 2010	"May 24 Measures" (suspension of all inter-Korean cooperation) in response to the North Korea's attack on a South Korean warship
	Apr. 2011	North Korea's unilateral announcement of cancellation of Hyundai Asan's exclusive rights to tourism in Mt. Kŭmgang
	Dec. 2011	Death of North Korean leader, Kim Jong Il
	May 2012	North Korea's launch of its 2nd long-range missile

Source: Ministry of Unification (South Korea)

The rapidly changing inter-Korean relations have been reflected in the division films of the 2000s that set this period as the temporal background. Now, this study will reframe and analyze the pattern of change in inter-Korean relations and character relationship in *Swiri* (1999), *Joint Security Area JSA* (2000), *Secret Reunion* (2010), and *The Berlin File* (2013) based on the Inter-Korean Integration Compass.

Division Film #1 (Kim Dae-jung Administration): *Swiri* (1999)

Swiri begins with subtitles that set the spatio-temporal background of "Special 8th Corps in Kaesong" and "1992." Dozens of North Korean Special Forces soldiers are being trained to infiltrate the South, and Lee Bang-hee (the main character representing North Korea), who successfully completed this difficult training, is selected as a spy and sent to South Korea. Some years later, the scene shifts to Yoo Jung-won (the main character representing South Korea), who is a top-secret intelligence agent in South Korea, reporting Lee Bang-hee's various terrorist acts in South Korea from 1993 to 1996.

The beginning of the film sets the inter-Korean relations to a level of *Hostile Tension* (+) where North Korea-trained special spies are sent to South Korea to commit various terrorist attacks. The relationship of the main characters under the inter-Korean relations is situated between the *Devil* (+) *and Enemy* (+) levels as a counterpart that must be put to death or suppressed.

After the introduction scene, Yoo Jung-won and Lee Bang-hee, who appears as Lee Myung-hyun (his alias in South Korea), turn out to be lovers engaged to one another. However, Yoo Jung-won finally learns that Lee Myung-hyun and Lee Bang-hee are the same person after continuous investigation. In the final scene, Yoo Jung-won and Lee Myung-hyun (Lee Bang-hee) meet at the inter-Korean summit where they both take aim at each other as an agent and spy, and Lee Myung-hyun is killed by Yoo Jung-won.

In the film, the human relationship starts at the level of *Devil* (+) of killing opponents, and then it transforms into a *Family* (-) phase of loving one another, and then dramatically reverses to *Enemy* (-) due to the realities of national division in the end. Inter-Korean relations also show great variations as the film progresses. The overall atmosphere of inter-Korean relations is *Reconciliation and Cooperation* (+), centering on the story for the preparation of the inter-Korean summit before the 2002 World Cup. However, terrorist attacks by an anti-peace group of the North Korean Army reverses the improved relations to the stage of *Hostile tensions* (+). In the end, however, the terrorism of the hardline forces is suppressed and the film is concluded in the direction of *Reconciliation and Cooperation* (+) once again. To summarize the above analysis, the changing pattern can be shown in figure 8.2.

Division Film #2 (Kim Dae-jung Administration): *JSA* (2000)

Lee Soo-hyeok (the main character representing South Korea), a South Korean soldier, accidentally gets lost during his daily search and reconnaissance activities in the DMZ and unfortunately steps on a landmine. At this time, a North Korean army officer, Oh Kyung Pil (a main character representing North Korea), and his colleague, Jung Woo Jin, pass by and happen to meet Lee Soo-hyeok. As soon as they recognize each other, they point their rifles at each other. However, once Oh Kyung Pil and Jung Woo Jin realizes that Lee Soo-hyeok stepped on the land mine, they quickly move away. Lee Soo-hyeok shouts, "Son of a bitch, how can you leave me here!" and begs desperately for their help, and eventually Oh Kyung Pil dismantles the landmine and saves Lee's life.

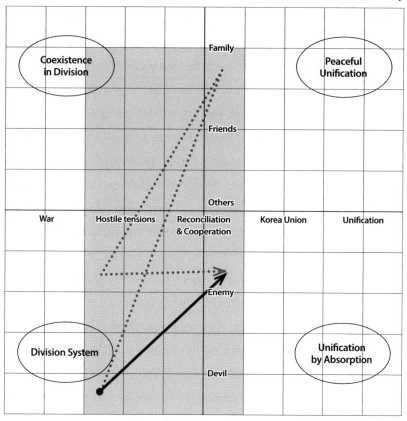

Figure 8.2. *Swiri* **on the Inter-Korean Integration Compass**

At the beginning of the plot, the two Koreas maintain *Hostile Tensions* (-) in which soldiers conduct daily search and reconnaissance activities in the DMZ without direct military conflict, and the main characters of the two Koreas see each other as someone between *Devil* (-) and *Enemy* (+) given the act of pointing rifles at each other and the use of swear words.

From the incident, Lee Soo-hyeok is very grateful to Oh Kyung Pil for saving his life and occasionally takes his subordinate Nam Sung-sik to a North Korean security post late at night. Lee, Nam, Oh, and Jung secretly drink together and chat about their personal lives, and their relationship eventually becomes very close, even calling each other brothers. However, their relationship rapidly changes as Choi Man Soo, a North Korean high-ranking officer, unexpectedly visits the post. Choi questions Oh why South Korean soldiers are in the North Korean security post. In the middle of this commotion, Lee Soo-hyeok screams, "Damn it. I don't care if we are brothers or not. After all, we are all enemies," and points his gun at Choi. Although Oh Kyung Pil tries to settle the situation, they begin to shoot at each other and Jung Woo Jin is killed by Lee Soo-hyeok's bullet. Soon after the gunfight at the post, the South and North troops send support forces, firing at each other. Although both military officials claim that they are victims of the inter-Korean shootings, they soon reach a dramatic agreement on cooperation to have a working-level talk for a joint investigation. However, Lee Soo-hyeok and Oh Kyung Pil, who meet again at the negotiation table, hide their feelings of sympathy and friendship and treat each other as enemy soldiers of South and North Korea.

While the human relationship was advancing towards the level of *Family* (-) after the introduction, the relationship suddenly deteriorated toward *Enemy* (-) with a sudden recognition of their own identity as soldiers under a divided system. Similarly, inter-Korean relations deteriorated from the *Hostile tensions* (-) in the truce to the stage of *War* (-) of military conflicts in the restricted DMZ area. In the end, the inter-Korean relations moved to the *Reconciliation and Cooperation* (+) stage in which inter-Korean working-level talks take place. Figure 8.3 shows their changing patterns.

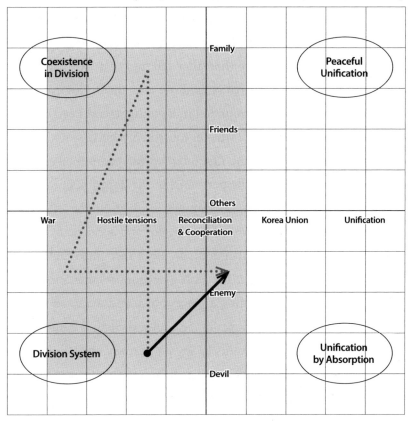

Figure 8.3. *JSA* on the Inter-Korean Integration Compass

Division Film #3 (Lee Myung-bak Administration): *Secret Reunion* (2010)

Secret Reunion begins with a scene of chasing North Korean spies. Song Ji Won (the main character representing North Korea), who is one of a number of undercover North Korean undercover spies living in South

Korea, and his senior spy go to an apartment where a North Korean defectors lives and kill him with a handgun. Lee Han-gyu (the main character representing South Korea) and his colleagues, agents of the National Intelligence Service (hereafter referred to as NIS), arrive at the site right after the assassination and run after them. However, Lee's fellow agents are shot and wounded in a gunfight, and Lee Han-gyu fails to catch them and says, "I will kill you, son of a bitch."

Soon after this incident, the first inter-Korean summit takes place, and NIS decides to reduce the personnel in the department of North Korean affairs. In the process, Lee Han-gyu is fired from the NIS. A few years later, Lee becomes a private investigator and accidentally bumps into Song Ji Won at a construction site. Both recognize each other, but think the other does not. Lee Han-gyu proposes that Song work for him in return for providing a place to live and wages so that he can turn him and his fellow spies in for a reward. Song Ji Won accepts Lee's offer because he also wants to spy on Lee, as Song still believes Lee is an agent. As they work together in a detective agency, the two men who harbored their own agendas and tried to use one another for their own gain, gradually begin to develop a sincere brotherhood after realizing the hardships of the other. Then one day, the senior spy that disappeared reappears with the news of the North Korean nuclear test. He gives one last chance for Song Ji Won to prove that he is not a traitor by killing a North Korean defector living in Seoul. On the other hand, Lee Han-gyu learns of the NIS plans to kill Song Ji Won and tries to save him. While chasing them, the North Korean spies and Korean agents are engaged in a gunfight, and Song and Lee end up saving each other's lives by sacrificing themselves.

Figure 8.4 shows the variation of inter-Korean relations and character relationships. At the beginning of the film, the inter-Korean relations start with *Hostile Tensions* (+) with the gunfight between North Korean spies and South Korean agents and evolve into the *Reconciliation and Cooperation* (+) stage of holding the inter-Korean summit to *Hostile Tensions* (+) symbolized by North Korea's nuclear test and the city shoot out. The human relationship extends from the level of *Devil* (+), wanting to kill each other, to *Family* (-), with devotion and protection of each other like brothers.

X: System, Inter-Korean Relations   Y: Mind, Character Relationship

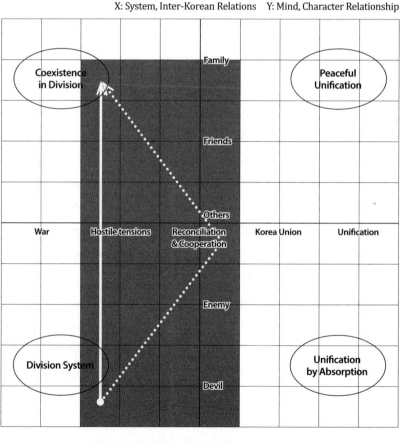

Figure 8.4. *Secret Reunion* on the Inter-Korean Integration Compass

Division Film #4 (Lee Myung-bak Administration): *The Berlin File* (2013)

The Berlin File begins with a scene in which a North Korean spy, Pyo Jong Seong (the main character representing North Korea), is negotiating an arms deal with an Arab terrorist at a hotel in Germany. Negotiations are interrupted by Israeli intelligence agencies, and NIS agents led by Jung Jin-soo (the main character representing South Korea) who was watching this situation with a hidden camera subsequently begin to chase Pyo Jong Seong. However, Pyo knocks out NIS agents and gets away. Jung Jin-soo curses Pyo in the foulest language, shouting "That commie completely destroyed the spine of my colleague."

The core narrative of the film is that Pyo Jong Seong solves the conflict with the help of a South Korean, Jeong Jin-soo. Dong Myung Soo, a newly dispatched surveillance agent from North Korea to Germany, intends to put the North Korean Embassy in Germany in his possession, illegally trading weapons and raising funds for the ruling Worker's Party. To this end, Dong Myung Soo intimidates Pyo Jong Seong by kidnapping Ryun Jung Hee (Pyo's wife). Pyo Jong Seong asks for Jung's help to rescue his wife in an unexpected crisis. Jung Jin-soo decides to help Pyo under the condition that Pyo and his wife both turn themselves over to South Korea. Eventually, the two succeed in rescuing Ryun Jung Hee, but unfortunately she dies from a gunshot wound.

After the incident, the Blue House official informs Jung Jin-soo of the government's plan of a cross-border gas pipeline project through Pyongyang and the handover of Pyo to Pyongyang as a condition to implement the project. Frustrated with politics and internal corruption,

Jung Jin-soo lets Pyo go free as he knows Pyo will end up dead once he is returned to Pyongyang. Jung cautions Pyo to run away and live in hiding for the rest of his life.

The inter-Korean relations in the film encompass *Hostile Tensions* (+) represented by the struggle between the inter-Korean secret agents and the level of *Reconciliation and Cooperation* (-) with plans for the transcontinental gas pipeline project via Pyongyang. The character relationship extends from a *Devil* (-) relationship that despises the opponent to the level of *Others* (+), a transactional relationship providing conditional help, and a relationship between *Friends* (-) who consider and embrace the other's position. These changes can be summarized and shown in figure 8.5.

– Changes in collective emotion toward inter-Korean integration mirrored in division films

Based on the above discussion, this study will compare similarities and differences on the changing pattern of the inter-Korean relations and human relationships depicted in the films of each administration.

– Division films under Kim Dae-jung administration: Unstable peaceful unification

Following the historic inter-Korean summit in 2000, hostile tensions of the Korean Peninsula were transformed into an atmosphere of reconciliation and cooperation. *Swiri* (1999) and *JSA* (2000), which were released during the presidential term of Kim Dae-jung, exhibited the thawing mood in inter-Korean relations to some extent. However,

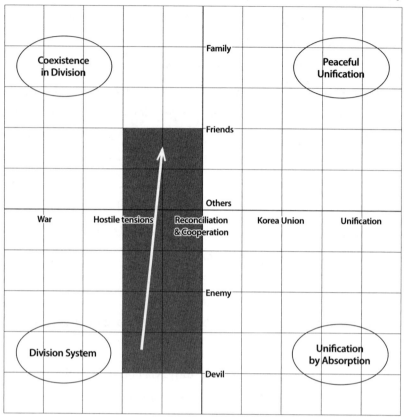

X: System, Inter-Korean Relations   Y: Mind, Character Relationship

Figure 8.5. The Berlin File on the Inter-Korean Integration Compass

inter-Korean relations represented in the introductory part of both films are still set to *Hostile Tensions*, which continue as the main mood of the film throughout the entire plot. Both films repeatedly show inter-Korean relations under the boundary of conflict and integration and fail to bring the inter-Korean relations to an enhanced mood of reconciliation and cooperation. Only towards the end of the movies do the films finally reveal the transition in the inter-Korean relations towards reconciliation and cooperation.

Although the two films differ in that one focuses on the relationship between two lovers while the other focuses on male friendship, both films share a commonality in that the main characters demonstrate a dramatic change in the emotion towards their counterpart. In the beginning of the film, the main figures of North and South Korea view the opponent as a target or enemy, but as the story unfolds, their relationships begin to develop either as lovers or brothers. However, both films reach the inevitable conclusion in which all the characters come to face the cold reality of national division where they can only view one another as an enemy.

Figure 8.6 shows the pattern of change in inter-Korean relations and character relationships represented in the two films. It is interesting to see the pattern in the form of number 4 in the flow of change. This jumbled pattern of movement reflects a sudden change of inter-Korean relations in the early 2000s that promoted reconciliation and cooperation after decades of conflict and hostility. While people accepted and understood the value of unification and the need to improve inter-Korean relations, it is unlikely that hostility that was built up over decades could be readily abandoned, and South Koreans are still suspicious and apprehensive towards North Korea.

Despite these confusing changes, however, there is a commonality when comparing the inter-Korean relations and character relationships described at the beginning and end of the two films. Both reveal that the inter-Korean relations and character relationships are more oriented toward an integrated relationship. Moreover, it is noteworthy that although the level of integration of system and mind is not yet high, it is clear that at least the direction of the two films is headed toward

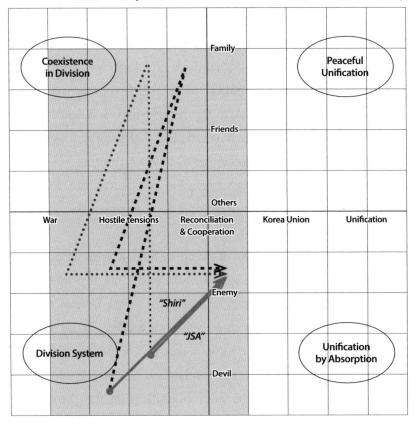

Figure 8.6. Inter-Korean Integration Compass of Division Films in Kim Dae-jung Administration

Peaceful Unification (quadrant 1). This implication can be interpreted as the collective emotions of the public living under the Kim Dae-jung administration, who are confused by the rapidly changing inter-Korean relations, but ultimately support peaceful reunification.

270

– Division films under Lee Myung-bak administration: fixed under division

When President Lee Myung-bak took office in 2008, his hardline North Korea policy began to strain inter-Korean relations. Moreover, North Korea's provocations further exacerbated the situation, quickly turning the existing reconciliation and cooperative relations into a hostile one. The death of a South Korean tourist at North Korea's Mt. Kŭmgang in 2008, the North Korean nuclear test in 2009, and the sinking of the *Cheonan,* a South Korean naval vessel in 2010, had dramatically chilled inter-Korean relations.

The films *Secret Reunion* (2010) and *The Berlin File* (2013), which were released in the presidential term of Lee Myung-bak, featured such a changed reality of inter-Korean relations. First of all, *Secret Reunion* sets the temporal background of the film from the late 1990s to the late 2000s. In doing so, it provided the social and historical background of the film which incorporated the shifting inter-Korean relations of this period that moved from hostile to reconciliation and back to hostile tensions. *The Berlin File* maintains a low level of hostile tensions throughout the film and ends with a story that suggests a shallow level of reconciliation and cooperation. Although there are some differences between the two films, both films do not deviate much from setting the inter-Korean relations as hostile tensions.

Secret Reunion describes the process of a former NIS agent of the South and a secret agent of North Korea that come into contact as enemies at first, but later transform their relationship into a brotherhood. *The Berlin File* is a story of a NIS agent of the South and a spy of North Korea collaborating to rescue a hostage. The main characters of both films have hostility toward each other in the beginning and start collaborating with each other in order to achieve one's own goal later. However, the story encompasses the theme of transformative process of the characters, where they come to the realization that they are after all equal human beings and learn to accept the other by the end.

Based on the above discussion, the changing pattern of the inter-Korean relations and character relationship represented in both films are shown in figure 8.7. The relationship patterns of the two films are similar as they form the shape of the number one. This shape that forms an upward-moving pattern can be explained as both films promote character relationships as *Friends* and *Family*, regardless of hostile inter-Korean relations.

This is an interesting phenomenon as this pattern is witnessed during the South Korean government's hardline policy towards North Korea. Despite worsening inter-Korean relations, it shows the collective emotions of the people of South Korea to live peacefully with those in the North. At the same time, it can also be interpreted that there is a tendency for people to accept the current national division, as long as peace is ensured on the Korean Peninsula, revealing a somewhat regressive attitude toward inter-Korean integration.

– Changes in collective emotions toward inter-Korean integration: from peaceful unification to coexistence in division

Figure 8.8 compares the changes in inter-Korean relations and character relationship depicted in the films of Kim Dae-jung and Lee Myung-bak governments. It is worth noting that all four films show that the starting point of inter-Korean relations and character relationships lies in quadrant 3 of the compass. This implies that a deep-rooted hostility is situated in the collective emotions of Koreans due to the violent trauma of the Korean War accumulated over generations, and this is set as the social and historical background of the films. This reveals that the level of the integration of institution and mindset at present is still very low. However, the direction of the collective emotions toward inter-Korean integration in the films has been changed.

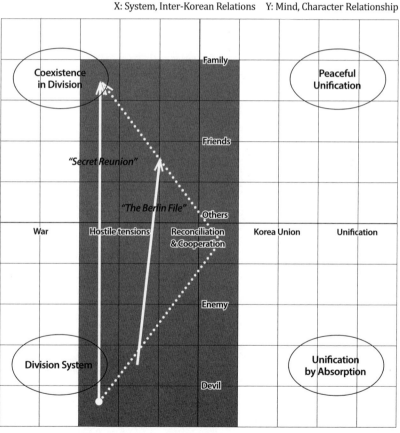

X: System, Inter-Korean Relations   Y: Mind, Character Relationship

Figure 8.7. Inter-Korean Integration Compass of Division Films in Lee Myung-bak Administration

The collective emotions in the division films of the Kim Dae-jung and Lee Myung-bak governments have shifted from *Peaceful Unification* to *Coexistence in Division*. If the South and the North are not a single divided nation, but an interstate relationship, it may be sufficient to achieve only the integration of mindset that embraces the different perspectives and positions of the other side. However, since inter-Korean relations are a unique relationship, as is

X: System, Inter-Korean Relations   Y: Mind, Character Relationship

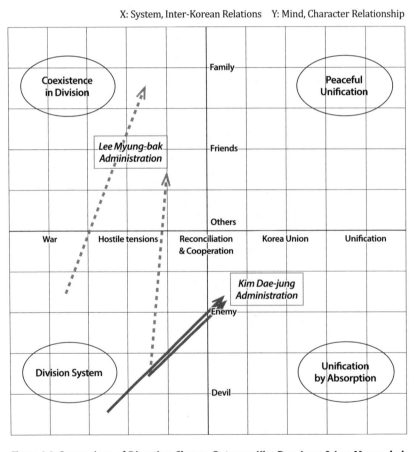

Figure 8.8. Comparison of Direction Change Between Kim Dae-Jung & Lee Myung-bak Administration on the Inter-Korean Integration Compass

understood in conjunction with unification, the collective emotions that justify division of the two countries in peaceful coexistence poses a considerable risk (B. S. Lee 2015). *Unification by Absorption*, which insists only on institutional integration without the integration of the thinking that places "unification first" is problematic. However, *Coexistence in Division* that supports peaceful coexistence between South and North Korea, without resolving the fundamental and structural contradiction of division, also poses risks. Therefore, it is desirable to pursue an inter-Korean integration that achieves the value of peace and the ideal of unification through the integration of the institutions and mindsets of the two Koreas at the same time.

In addition, it is important to realize that the collective emotions toward inter-Korean integration have changed in the face of reality and the growing indifference toward unification (*The Diplomat* 2011; *The Guardian* 2013). According to research by Seoul National University, while 92% of South Koreans perceived unification as "necessary" in 1990s, support has drastically decreased throughout the 2000s: 55.8% in 2009, 53.7% in 2011 (M. K. Park et al. 2013b, 21–22; P. Kim and Choi 2012). In 2012, only 47% of people in their 20s considered it necessary. This means that more people are starting to think that national division is acceptable, as long as peace can be maintained with North Korea without dispute. However, from an oppositional perspective based on this analysis, it can be interpreted that the sense of hostility and rejection toward the North Korean people decreased accordingly. According to a survey of Seoul National University (2012), a decade-long reconciliation and cooperation policy continues to affect people's emotions as well as lessen hostility toward North Korea even under Lee Myung-bak's presidency (M. K. Park et al. 2013b, 46).

Therefore, if inter-Korean relations are restored again, the collective emotions toward inter-Korean integration could be expected to adopt a more advanced form than those in the past. In the end, whether South Korea's collective emotions will lead to peaceful unification or coexistence in division will depend on inter-Korean relations.

Conclusion

This study aims to compare and examine the collective emotions toward inter-Korean integration represented by four blockbuster division films released during the Kim Dae-jung and Lee Myung-bak governments. For this purpose, this study analyzed the changing pattern of the inter-Korean relations and character relationships depicted in the division films as the integration of institution and the integration of mindset. As a result, it was found that the division films of the Kim Dae-jung government tend to lean towards peaceful unification aimed at achieving institutional integration and the integration of mindset at the same time. On the other hand, division films under the Lee Myung-bak administration lean toward coexistence in division, which pursue the integration of mindset through advancing personal relationships between people while the unresolved structural violence of the divided system remains intact.

Most of the existing division film studies have focused on the theme of "division." However, this study is a new attempt in that it sees division films from the perspective of "integration." In addition, the existing studies on attitudes toward inter-Korean integration generally investigate and analyze the quantitative figures through the survey of the public, while this is descriptive research tracing the changes in collective emotions toward inter-Korean integration by analyzing division films.

Nevertheless, it is still too early to generalize that the analysis framework used in this study can be applied to other periods, as it analyzed only the division films of the Kim Dae-jung and Lee Myung-bak administrations. Therefore, for future studies, it would be useful to expand the number and period of division films, and if possible, to extend the research to analyze division films of North Korea using the same analysis framework.

Biographical Statements

Lee Woo Young is a professor at the University of North Korean Studies and a director of the Simyeon Institute for North Korean Studies, South Korea. He has published various books on North Korea such as *Change of North Korea's Perception Toward Capitalism* (2000), *Private Space of City Resident in North Korea* (2008) and *Understanding North Korea Regime and System* (2014).

Kim Myoung Shin is a senior program specialist of the Korean National Commission for UNESCO and a PhD candidate in North Korean studies at the University of North Korean Studies. He has also been working as a policy advisor for the Korean Sharing Movement (KSM). His research interests include inter-Korean integration and peace and sustainable development of the Korean Peninsula.

References

Bar-Tal, Daniel, Eran Halperin, and Joseph De Rivera. 2007. "Collective Emotions in Conflict Situations: Societal Implications." *Journal of Social Issues* 63 (2): 442. https://doi.org/10.1111/j.1540–4560.2007.00518.x.

Cine 21. 2001. "Ch'oegohŭnghaengjang t'ait'ŭrŭl tollyŏjwŏ." April 30, 2001. http://www.cine21.com/news/view/?mag_id=1724. Accessed July 21, 2017.

Cho, Hae Jin. 2010. *The Principle of the Korean Genre Movies*. [In Korean.] Seoul: Koohak.

Cho Heup. 2008. *Yŏnghwa ka chŏngch'i ta: taejung i p'yŏngnon'ga in p'osŭt'ŭsidae munhwa chŏngch'I* [Cinema is politics]. Seoul: Person and Idea.

The Diplomat. 2011. "Unification Indifference." September 12, 2011. http://thediplomat.com/2011/09/unification-indifference/. Accessed July 21, 2017.

Epstein, Stephen. 2009. "The Axis of Vaudeville: Images of North Korea in South Korean Pop Culture." *The Asia-Pacific Journal* 7, No. 2.

Green, Christopher K., and Stephen J. Epstein. 2013. "Now on My Way to Meet Who? South Korean Television, North Korean Refugees, and the Dilemmas of Representation." *The Asia-Pacific Journal* 11, No. 2.

The Guardian. 2017. "Korean Unification: Dreams of Unity Fade into the Past for Young South Koreans." May 27, 2013. https://www.theguardian.com/world/2013/may/27/south-north-korea-unification. Accessed July 21, 2017.

Hamm, Taik-Young. 1999. *Arming the Two Koreas: State, Capital and Military Power*. London: Routledge.

Han, Sang Eon. 2014. "Anxiety on the Korean Peninsula Looked at Through Berlin." [In Korean.] *Journal of Contemporary Cinema Studies* 17.

Jang, Hun, dir. 2010. *Secret Reunion*; South Korea: Showbox/Mediaplex et al. 2012. DVD.

Jeon, Young-Sun. 2014. *Unification Story Through the Films*. [In Korean.] Seoul: Institute for Unification Education. http://116.67.50.138/WebBook_data4/00265294/ebook/media/src.pdf. Accessed April 21, 2017.

Jeong, Hyun ju, and Heesun Chung. 2014. "Representing Political Discourses and Places in South Korean Films About the National Division." [In Korean.] *Journal of Cultural and Historical Geography* 26, No. 2.

Kahneman, Daniel, and Amos Tversky. 1979. "Prospect Theory: An Analysis of Decision Under Risk," *Econometrica* 47(2) (March): 263–291. https://doi.org/10.2307/1914185.

Kang, Chegyu, dir. 1999. *Swiri*; South Korea: Kang Chegyu Films. 2001. DVD.

Kim, Bo Kyung. 2007. "A Study on Meaning Changes in the Division of the Korean Peninsula Represented in the Korean Division Film: Focused on the Latter Half of the 1990s." [In Korean.] Master's thesis, Hanyang University.

Kim, Choong-Kook. 2014. "Cinema and Division—As the Practice of Coexistence Beyond the Illusion of Suture." [In Korean.] *Journal of Koreanology* 53:282–284. https://doi.org/10.15299/jk.2014.11.53.279

Kim, Eui Soo. 1998. "A Study of Korean Division Film: Focusing on the Definition and Evolution Process of Korean Division Films as a Genre." [In Korean.] Master's thesis, Sogang University.

Kim, Kyoung Wook. 2015. "A Study on 'Historical Trauma' Represented in Korean Cinema Since the 1980s." [In Korean.] *Film Review* 63.

Kim, Philo, and Kyung Hui Choi. 2012. "Comparative Analysis of Attitudes Toward the Unification of North and South Korea," *Journal of Peace and Unification Studies* 4 (1): 106.

Kim, Young Jun, and Hyun Jin Lee. 2015. "A Study on the Division Recognition Through the Narrative Analysis of Secret Reunion." [In Korean.] *The Journal of Humanities and Social Science* 6, No. 4.

Korean Film Council. n.d. http://www.kobis.or.kr. Accessed April 21, 2017.

Lawler, Edward J., Shane R. Thye, and Jeongkoo Yoon. 2014. "The Emergence of Collective Emotions in Social Exchange." In *Collective Emotions.* Edited by Christian von Scheve and Mikko Salmela. Oxford: Oxford University Press. https://doi.org/10.1093/acprof:oso/9780199659180.003.0013.

Lee, Byung Soo. 2015 "The Antagonistic Relationship Between Unification and Peace—Korean Unification Ideology, State Form of the Unified Korea, Nationality and Stateness." [In Korean.] *Epoch and Philosophy: Journal of Philosophical Thought in Korea* 26 (1): 330–340.

Lee, Hyunseon. 2016. "The South Korean Blockbuster and a Divided Nation." *International Journal of Korean History* 21 (1): 259–264. https://doi.org/10.22372/ijkh.2016.21.1.259

Lee, Mina, Won Whan Oh, and Kyung Sook Lee. 2013. "North Korean Refugee Women's Consumption of South Korean TV Dramas and Movies." *Asian Women* 29, No. 4.

Ministry of Unification (South Korea). n.d. http://eng.unikorea.go.kr/content.do?cmsid=1795. Accessed July 21, 2017.

Neale, Steve. 2003. "Hollywood Blockbuster: Historical Dimensions." in *Movie Blockbusters*. Edited by Julian Stringer. London: Routledge.

Park, Chan-wook, dir. 2000 *JSA*; South Korea: CJ Entertainment et al. 2002. DVD.

Park, Ju Hwa, ed. 2016. *2016 Survey of Inter-Korea Integration.* [In Korean.] Seoul: Korea Institute for National Unification.

Park, Myoung-Kyu, Byung-Yeon Kim, Philo [Byoung-Ro] Kim, and Eun-Mi Jeong. 2013a. *Inter-Korean Index 2008–2013: Changes and Implication.* [In Korean.] Seoul: Seoul National University Institute of Peace and Unification Studies.

Park, Myoung-Kyu, Won-Taek Kang, Philo [Byoung-Ro] Kim, Young Hoon Song, Soo Jeong Lee, and Yong Suk Jang. 2013b. *Unification Perception Survey 2012.* [In Korean.] Seoul: Seoul National University Institute of Peace and Unification Studies.

Park, Jongchul, ed. 2014. *Inter-Korean Integration Survey: Perceptions and Attitudes.* Seoul: Korea Institute for National Unification.

Park, Tae Gyun. 2005. *The Korean War.* [In Korean.] Seoul: With Books.

Park, Yu Hee. 2013. "Isolated Warriors and Others at the Boundary: The Representations of 'North Korea' in Korean War Films in the Post–Cold War Era." [In Korean.] *Korean Classics Studies* 58.

Ryoo, Seung-wan, dir. 2013. *The Berlin File*; South Korea: Film Base Berlin et al. 2015. DVD.

Scheve, Christian von, and Sven Ismer. 2013. "Towards a Theory of Collective Emotions." *Emotion Review* 5 (4): 407–410. https://doi.org/10.1177/1754073913484170.

Smith, Eliot R., Chrales Seger, and Diane Mackie. 2007. "Can Emotions Be Truly Group Level? Evidence Regarding Four Conceptual Criteria." *Journal of Personality and Social Psychology* 93 (3): 431. https://doi.org/10.1037/0022-3514.93.3.431.

Sullivan, Gavin Brent. 2015. "Collective Emotions," *Social and Personality Psychology Compass* 9 (8): 383–390. https://doi.org/10.1111/spc3.12183.

Vanoye, Francis, and Anne Goliot-Lete. 1993. *Précis d'analyse filmique.* Paris: Laurent.

Williams, Raymond. 1961. *The Long Revolution.* London: Chatto and Windus.

9. Remaking a Transborder Nation in North Korea:
Media Representation in the Korean Peace Process

Sunkyung Choi
(University of North Korean Studies, South Korea)

Abstract

Recently, North Korean media have engendered greater connectedness with the outside world. One important goal of the North Korean regime is to create ties with Koreans living outside the country through its official website. Analyzing media representation of a transborder Korean nation, this article discusses the shifts that have occurred in the recent context of the peace process on the Korean Peninsula. I argue that the transborder nation-building in North Korean official media reveals a hybrid form of patriotism and nationalism that juxtaposes loyalty to the nation and loyalty to the state. North Korean media thus emerges as a critical site where the two loyalties coexist, demonstrating an attempt to provide the impression of a whole—albeit divided and dispersed—Korean nation.

Keywords

North Korea, media, nation(alism), Korean nation, globalization, Uriminzokkiri

Recent scholarly interest in transborder nations has addressed various transborder practices linking states to populations residing in outside territories. The literature has largely focused on the relationship between emigration states and labor migrant populations. Yet what about a transborder nation that is a product of division rather than labor emigration? And how can nationhood be represented by a socialist state media in a world of global communication? This article addresses these two issues by (1) incorporating a territorially divided nation—Korea—into the discussion and (2) exploring the representation of a transborder nation by a socialist regime. This approach offers a deeper understanding of the politics of transborder belonging.

This article examines how North Korean media represent a transborder nation amid current political shifts. By comparing the media representation of the Korean nation in the postsummit period with the presummit period, this article suggests that the North Korean regime's communication practices have an ambivalent character as a state and as a nation with the advent of the peace process in 2018.

This article is organized as follows. The next section elaborates how the article builds on existing interdisciplinary literature. Then I describe the national discourse in North Korea, the context of globalizing North Korean media, and the North Korean media's representation of the Korean nation. The analytical sections critically examine the North Korean media representation of the transborder nation in the periods before and after the summit. The conclusion fleshes out the main arguments and highlights the implications of the article.

The Politics of a Transborder Nation

The ideas that nations and nationalism are best understood as modern creations (Anderson 1991; Gellner 1983; Hobsbawm 1990) rather than as given and that the modern nation as a bounded community is socially "imagined" have been widely applied to the literature of nationalism. Every community based on wider links than face-to-face contact is imagined: people who define themselves as members of a nation "will never know most of their fellow members, meet them, or even hear of them, yet in the minds of each lives the image of their communion" (Anderson 1991, 6). The modern nation is thus imagined in terms of its ideological constructions seeking to forge a link between a cultural group and a state (Anderson 1991; Gellner 1983). Further, the modern nation, as "imagined as both inherently limited and sovereign" (Anderson 1991, 6), is an imagined political community. Nation-states are thus presupposed as active agents of this nation-building process (Anderson 1991; Hobsbawm 1990) and as the "pre-eminent power-container of the modern era" (Giddens 1985, 12). In the case of North Korea, the process of national identity formation has long been performed by the regime's elites.

Identity claims and practices that connect people living outside a national territory are often called "long-distance nationalism" (Anderson 1992a, 1992b, 1998) or "transborder nationalism" (Brubaker 1996). The population of a nation needs to be understood beyond the territorial boundaries of an ancestral land; at the same time, the political focus and center of identity of transborder populations continue to be connected to the territory of their homelands (Anderson 1992a, 1998). In this sense, a transborder nation is expected to maintain some kind of loyalty to the homeland. Cross-border belonging also exists in the realm of the imagination, and nation-states are deeply involved in creating the diasporic imagination. Therefore, this kind of belonging encompasses nationalism as a project that consists of political movements and state policies through which people seek to act on behalf of the nation with which they identify (Calhoun 1997; Wimmer 2019). As Smith (1995) noted, both nationalism and nations "remain indispensable elements of an interdependent world and a mass-communications culture" (160). As it pertains to the process of making North Korean diasporic belonging a national project beyond the territorial border, media transforms into a contested site in the construction of a Korean nation.

Research on transborder nations has been discussed in the context of transnationalism (Anderson 1992a; Fuglerud 1999; Skrbiš 1999). More recent literature has tended to focus on the ties between emigration groups in the South and labor migrant groups in the North (Guarnizo, Portes, and Haller 2008; Østergaard-Nielsen 2003; Waldinger 2015). The adopted framework of current research is embedded in transnational networks, mainly owing to the advent of instantaneous communication and relatively inexpensive air travel, which have spurred new waves of ideas and immigration and increased flows of goods. Many people today seek their identifications and social alignments along different axes such as cross-border mobilization and transnational loyalties, because capitalism and modern communications technology have relativized the human spatial dimension (Appadurai 1996). In this process, technologies have allowed "nationalism" to become "globalized" across national borders, and thus digital media can promote new, alternative forms of national imagination (Conversi 2012).

The reconstruction of distant homelands is not merely an outcome of recent migrations. In the case of Korea, many transborder nation groups are the product of colonial migration and political division born of the global Cold War.[1] Further, the national division was not limited to those on the Korean Peninsula; it also included Koreans who were colonial migrants and their descendants residing in Japan and China. The division has produced deep tension. However, at the same time, its strong legacy of ethnic homogeneity has functioned as a unifying force. North Korea, which creates both interethnic conflict and ethnic unity, defies "the nationalist principle of congruence of state and nation" (Gellner 1983), creating incongruity in both political and ethnic dimensions. This bilevel incongruity, in turn, has produced a new source of identification as political project and has resulted in a contested "politics of representation" between the two Koreas (Shin, Freda, and Yi 1999).

In North Korea, the representation of a transborder nation as identity politics reflects on the failure to form a single nation-state as well as the incongruities in the political and ethnic dimensions of Korean nationhood. The territorial division into two opposing political entities

---

1 Transborder Koreans are regionally concentrated in four countries: China, the United States, Japan, and Russia. Particularly, Chosŏnjok in China, Zainichi Koreans in Japan, and Koryŏin in Russia are colonial-era migrants and their descendants. Meanwhile, the main population of ethnic Koreans in the United States are postwar immigrants from South Korea. For North Korea, people in the South are another type of transborder *tongp'o* (coethnic) that was produced by division.

after 1945 created an additional source of beliefs concerning national identity and the "homeland." Examining the case of North Korea provides a theoretical contribution to our current understanding of the dynamics of transborder nation-building politics. This article illustrates how North Korean media utilizes ethnic and political elements in the construction of transborder belonging amid current political shifts.

National Discourse in North Korea

The term *minjok* in Korea—a translation of the Japanese term *minzoku* (ethnic nation)—used in the early 20th century reveals an overlap of race, ethnicity, and nation (Park 2008; Shin et al. 1999). Historically, various elements, including territorial unity, a shared common language, and culturally unified elites, served as important sources to mobilize ethnic discourses on the Hanminjok (Korean nation) that facilitated anti-colonial struggles when Korea was colonized by Japan over the period 1910–1945 (Duara 2006). Korean nationalism emerged as an ideology of anti-colonial struggle. This fight against the Japanese empire, in turn, reinforced Korean nationalism based on a shared belief of ethnic homogeneity and a desire for an independent Korean nation-state (Koo 1993; Shin 2006). However, national division pushed by the two power blocs of the Cold War thwarted this illusion of ethnic unity and created incongruencies in the political and ethnic dimensions of Korean nationhood. The legacies of anti-colonial nationalism and Cold War ideological confrontation formed two critical pillars in the nation-building project of North Korea.

First, an anti-Japanese armed struggle led by Kim Il Sung became a valuable political touchpoint in North Korea. It allowed Kim to be portrayed as a national liberator and semi-mythical hero and permitted him to lay claim to the legacy of a pure ethnic Korean nationalism (Shin et al. 1999, 478). The establishment of his Democratic People's Republic of Korea (DPRK) thus had its origins in anti-imperialist struggles. In time, this developed into anti-Americanism, as the United States emerged as a new imperialist adversary with the outbreak of the Korean War. Generally, the narrative of nationalism is seldom without an enemy, which traditionally involves either a colonial or imperial power (Barker 2006, 105). Likewise, North Korea has constructed its long-lasting antagonism toward the United States as the cornerstone of its state-building.

Second, North Korea has maintained its legitimacy by negating South Korea and competing with its regime in order to claim sole legitimacy over the entire ethnic Korean nation. The post-1945 division created the problem of who should represent the Korean nation and who has political legitimacy. Both Koreas reconstructed peculiar links between ethnicity and the state, which otherwise would have resulted in a loss of political legitimacy. For example, North Korean citizens are automatically offered citizenship when they step into South Korea. This is not because of the South Korean government's tolerance toward refugees but rather because of the South's negation of the legitimacy of the DPRK regime. Meanwhile, North Korea has branded the South Korean government as a puppet regime, beholden to American imperialists. North and South Korea have also competed to redefine as their nationals the ethnic Koreans in Japan and northeast China and their descendants (J. Kim, 2009) as well as the populations on either side of the 38th parallel.

The legacies of anti-colonialism and the competition over legitimacy based on the belief of homogeneity have entailed interethnic conflicts and the establishment of us-versus-them mindsets that have now lasted over a half century. This situation sits in stark contrast to the conventional wisdom that ethnic unity produces peaceful coexistence. The drive toward homogenization has also created critical others, thereby confirming the integrity of the nation through this contrast. The postcolonial nation-building interwoven with the Cold War constituted the national discourse in North Korea, with confrontations between the Korean nation and its enemies—the United States and conservative groups in South Korea.

However, despite making critical others, North Korea has emphasized the "blood relations" of the Korean people since the 1970s, effacing the original concept of Stalin's theory of nation with the development of Kim Il Sung's *juche* ideology, which promotes self-reliance in politics, economics, culture, and philosophical outlook (Cumings 1993).[2] Since the late 1990s, North Korea has redefined the concept of *minjok*, expanding the imagined scope of the Korean nation by embracing overseas Koreans (Choi and Lee 2017). Even today, unification proposals issued by both Koreas are based on the quasi-primordial belief that the Hanminjok (Korean nation) is a "unitary nation" (*tanil minjok*) and that this premise will inevitably lead to national reunification (*minjok t'ongil*).

Kim Jong Un's regime has used two veins of discourse: *Kim Il Sung*

---

2   In 1970, the law of the North Korean Worker's Party, which was reformed during its Fifth Congress, prescribed that the Worker's Party would follow *juche* ideology, applying Marxist-Leninist thought in a practical way in the DPRK (I. S. Kim, 1983, 232–256).

minjok,[3] an interpellation from the mid-1990s that draws boundaries between the North and the South; and *Chosŏn minjok*,[4] which emphasizes the homogeneity of the two Koreas. The ethnic nationalism was activated in the 2018 Korean peace process as a potentially unifying force. National discourse in North Korea has cemented the political cleavages of division while emphasizing the ideal of unity with the "brethren" in the South. Historically, this paradoxical national discourse raised the question of how a transborder Korea should be represented, which turned out to be complicated by failures to form a nation-state in the peninsula. The new representation of a Korean nation became necessary as a response to the regime's change in outlook and the drastic political shift from provocation in 2017 to dialogue in 2018. Before analyzing North Korean media representations of transborder nationhood, I first discuss how Kim Jong Un's regime transformed mediascapes in pursuit of globality and rebuilt the idea of the Korean nation through media.

Toward a Global Imaginary: Contextualizing North Korean Media

Today, media technologies enable people to imagine themselves as

---

3   The term *Kim Il Sung minjok* emerged at the time of the death of Kim Il Sung in 1994, and it identified Kim Il Sung as the father of the nation (J. I. Kim 1998). This rhetoric was developed to overcome the crisis of legitimacy between two Koreas and the crisis over the survival of the global socialist system by emphasizing the superiority of the late leader as well as the North Korean socialist system.

4   *Chosŏn minjok* (Korean nation) refers to a unitary nation of identical bloodline, language, and culture based around Pyongyang in the Korean Peninsula.

being together despite spatial distance, thereby strengthening the idea of nation and belonging. As Anderson (1991) reasoned, print capitalism is an important condition for modern imagined communities; through the spread of the printed word in cheap publications, potentially unlimited numbers of individuals have access to identical information without having direct contact with the originator. The internet has played a significant role in standardizing and strengthening nationalist sentiment. Television channels, websites, and social networks have become the new forms of print capitalism in our global era.

Communication technologies have made interaction across borders much more viable. These technologies include websites, which are crucial both at the level of identity and as a political tool. For example, the Chilean government has designated a "14th region" in the country to reintegrate Chileans abroad—not by encouraging their return, but by enhancing their sense of "Chileanness." The primary tool for creating an imagined community of diasporic Chileans was the government's official website (Eriksen 2007). The development of the state-sponsored website allowed for the conditions for the continued loyalty and identification of a transborder nation. In the age of deterritorialization, media technologies have made it possible to reterritorialize transborder nations. In North Korea, the regime's efforts to embrace the transborder Korean indicate the intersection of globalizing media and nation-building.

North Korea is known as an extreme case of isolationism and has treated globalization as a new form of colonialism. The North Korean government controls the most powerful sectors of its culture industry, and because of this, North Korean press and news broadcasts directly reflect the character of the regime and its agenda. Historically, the regime's attempt to tighten mass media was closely connected to the aim of blocking the inflow of foreign culture as well as to maintain its national socialist culture against the "invasion" of capitalism and the centrifugal "threat" of globalization. The media strategy of the DPRK in the past is encapsulated in the idea of "the mosquito net,"[5] attributing the collapse of the communist bloc to capitalist powers' ideological "poisoning." Yet, with the rule of Kim Jong Un, North Korean media has recently attempted to engender greater global connectedness with the outside world. For instance, North Korean media is actively using social media to distribute the regime's message to target audiences outside the country.

These changes reflect the regime's strategy of transforming itself toward the global imaginary in pursuit of the global trend (*segyejŏk ch'use*) and world class (*segyejŏk suchun*).[6] Even the Kim regime still fights against globalization, regarding it as an "imperialist force" for "world integration" (*Rodong Sinmun* 2018). However, the regime has been attempting to facilitate rapid contact across the borders. The production of media content in global settings reflects current situations such as the progression of marketization, the inflow of mass foreign media, and the progress of inter-Korean peace.

---

5   Joint editorial for 1999 states that "we should fix a mosquito net against the ideological and cultural penetration" (*Rodong Sinmun* 1999, 1).

6   For example, a series of construction projects such as cultural and leisure facilities in the Kim Jong Un era were often admired as "world first-class" in the national press.

Representation of a Transborder Korean Nation
in North Korean Media

There are many ways to examine the processes that embrace transborder nationhood in reference to media, including broadcasting, websites, and other social media (Ding 2007; Eriksen 2007). In the North Korean context, I propose that an official website can serve as a fitting case. I specifically point to the Uriminzokkiri website, which is part of the global connectedness project aimed at embracing the idea of a unified Korean nation—including South Korean citizens and Koreans living overseas.[7] Importantly, the site operates channels on international platforms and actively posts news, pictures, and video clips that specifically target Koreans outside the DPRK. Throughout its short history, Uriminzokkiri has played a significant role in reshaping the representation of the Korean nation in order to meet the Kim regime's agenda. Recent political shifts, including the series of inter-Korean summits in 2018, led Uriminzokkiri to open up new spaces for the idea of Korean nationalism.

The significant change in North Korean media mentioned above becomes more salient at this particular juncture, which has brought "a swift end to the Cold War relic of longstanding division

---

7   The website for Uriminzokkiri can be found at www.uriminzokkiri.com. The site is controlled by the DPRK's Committee for the Peaceful Reunification of the Fatherland (Choguk P'yŏnghwa Tongil Wiwŏnhoe), which is an organization that promotes Korean reunification. The website posts public statements related to inter-Korean relations and propaganda operations in South Korea and elsewhere abroad (Ministry of Unification, n.d.). Though Uriminzokkiri is currently blocked in South Korea because of the National Security Law, some South Korean audiences connect to the website through alternative routings.

and confrontation," and "to boldly open up a new era of national reconciliation, peace, and prosperity" (Ministry of Foreign Affairs 2018a, para. 3). In its emphasis on a unitary nation, ethnonationalism became valuable as a unifying force in both the North and the South. In fact, the reunification discourse in both the Panmunjeom Declaration and the September Pyongyang Joint Declaration, signed by leaders of both Koreas, is based on "national reconciliation" (*minjok hwahae*)— the premise that a long history of ethnic unity should inevitably lead to reunification. In addition, the "independence of the Korean nation" (*minjok chaju*) is mentioned in both declarations as another principle for reunification.

In the recent dramatic improvement of inter-Korean relations, from the PyeongChang Winter Olympic Games to the third inter-Korean summit, the journey of the Korean peace process in 2018 has allowed cracks in the so-called "division system" (N. C. Paik 2011) and thus has made an impact on the representation of the Korean nation as well. The making of a transborder nation postulates the existence of an imagined community based on shared culture and beliefs. At this new juncture, a need has arisen for representation that is capable of creating cohesion and loyalty among ethnic Koreans. My interest here lies in how North Korea represented the two veins of the premise toward reunification— the principle of independence and the reconciliation of a Korean nation.

Uriminzokkiri

Uriminzokkiri, a website hosted in China, was launched in 2003, and the information posted can be read in Korean, English, Russian, Chinese, and Japanese. The website does not have an English name, but a relatively literal translation is "our people together," or "our nation together." The site carries news from official North Korean sources including *Rodong Sinmun*, the official North Korean newspaper of the Central Committee of the Workers' Party of Korea; the Korean Central News Agency; and Korean Central Television. Some of its own programming focuses on the reunification of the Korean Peninsula. It also maintains social media accounts, including Twitter, Google+, Tumblr, Flickr, Pinterest, Instagram, Youku, and Weibo.[8]

In all, the Uriminzokkiri website consists of 11 sections, three of which are "Revolutionary Leadership" (*Hyŏngmyŏng hwaldong sosik*), "Documentary" (*Kirok yŏnghwa*), and "Important Information" (*Chungyo podo*), which posts selected news from the official North Korean sources. Its own programs and material are uploaded to other sections: "News" (*Sosik*), "Camera Focus" (*K'amera ch'ojŏm*), "Popular Feelings" (*Kyŏreŭi minsim*), "Film Editing" (*Hwamyŏn p'yŏnjimmul*), "Newsletter" (*Sisa haesŏl*), "Film and Poem" (*Hwamyŏnkwa si*), "UCC"

---

8 Until September 2017, Uriminzokkiri had a YouTube channel with more than 18,000 subscribers as a primary distribution network for its propaganda. However, the channel, which had been on YouTube for about seven years, was shut down for violating YouTube's community guidelines. After YouTube blocked its channel, Uriminzokkiri TV started to utilize other platforms, such as Youku in China and VKontakte in Russia. Altogether, Uriminzokkiri TV has archived thousands of videos and other footage.

(user created content), and "Film Music" (*Hwamyŏn ŭmak*) sections. The division of "Popular Feelings" (*Kyŏreŭi minsim*) predominantly covers the voices of overseas Koreans in South Korea, Japan, and China. Here, *kyŏre*, literally meaning the ethnic nation, has been used in kindred image.[9]

I compare the media representation of the Korean nation in the postsummit period with the presummit period, setting the 2018 PyeongChang Winter Olympic Games as a catalyst for talks of peace on the Korean Peninsula. I analyzed video clips posted on Uriminzokkiri TV from 2017 to 2018 and conducted qualitative document analysis— a research method that aims to rigorously and systematically analyze the contexts of written and new documents such as government reports (Altheide 1996; Altheide, Coyle, DeVriese, and Schneider 2010). I follow Altheide's (1996) method, which involves organizing information into categories related to the research questions, articulating key areas of analysis, and analyzing the results. Because the *Kyŏreŭi minsim* section in Uriminzokkiri TV produces content especially for South Koreans and Koreans abroad, I chose to examine these examples. In this analysis, I refer to 15 video clips that provide examples of the representation of the Korean nation and additional sources from the *Sosik* section[10] as well as Panmunjeom and Pyongyang Declarations. In so doing, I highlight how media representation makes

---

9   The use of the word *kyŏre* emphasizes affective attachment, while *minjok* emphasizes a political project.

10   According to the English version of the Uriminzokkiri website, *Kyŏreŭi minsim* and *Sosik* are translated as "popular feelings" and "news," respectively. The full title of *Kyŏreŭi minsim* is "Namnyŏkkwa hae-oeŭi moksori Kyŏreŭi minsim," which means "the voice of the people of the South and abroad, the popular feelings of the nation."

the Korean nation imaginable in the progress of inter-Korean peace.

Video Texts and the Korean Nation

- Struggling against imperialism

In 2017, Uriminzokkiri TV posted 62 videos on its *Kyŏreŭi minsim* page, where most of the content is related to criticism of either the United States or South Korea. One-third of the episodes criticized the United States, particularly expressing strong antagonism toward President Donald Trump, who was mainly portrayed as a madman addicted to war. For example, a video clip uploaded on September 14, 2017, names the United States as the "axis of evil" and proclaims that the Terminal High Altitude Area Defense (THAAD) deployed in South Korea is part of an invasion of the peninsula (*Kyŏreŭi minsim* 2017c). Interestingly, it also claims Seongju, a county where the THAAD missile defense system was deployed, as "our territory" and states that the missile system is "bitter water that should be extracted out of our land" while portraying images of anti-THAAD protests by villagers. The title of another video uploaded on November 8, 2017, during Trump's visit to South Korea is "Anti-war, Anti-America" (*Kyŏreŭi minsim,* 2017a). Here, Trump is demonized as a warmonger trying to colonize at least the southern part of the Korean Peninsula, set against battle scenes. The video asserts that the key strategy for the *minjok* is being anti-American by showing South Koreans protesting Trump's visit and using South Korean protest songs (*minjung kayo*)[11] that express a victory-

---

11   The title of the song is "The Song for Anti-war, Anti-America," which was composed

Figure 9.1. "Anti-War, Anti-America" (*Kyŏreŭi minsim*, 2017a)

over-imperialism narrative as the background music. In addition to the slogan "anti-war, peace practice," it uses the phrase "unification land, national land without war, we will make ourselves" (see figure 9.1).

These two anti-American videos use images of South Korean protests and South Korean colonization in order to construct a "Korean nation" that sits in contrast to the American other. The South Korean protesters embody two contrasting forces: the Korean nation and the American imperialists. The imagined America in North Korea is the Caucasian other, who is invariably a hostile and fixed opponent.

While the South Korean demonstrators against America are depicted as patriots, the opposite group is described as national traitors. The other two-thirds of the 2017 videos cover explicitly blame South Korea, especially targeting the conservative party in South Korea and Park Geun-hye, South Korea's former president. For Kim Jong Un, since all Koreans belong to a single group—despite the fraction of so-called internal traitors who surrendered the nation to imperialist forces and contaminated the purity of the Korean nation—the majority of grassroots forces (*minjung*) can unite behind the imagined idea of a single Korean nation. For example, some videos show support for the "candlelight revolution" that ousted President Park Geun-hye.

---

in South Korea in the 1980s.

Overall, the struggle is depicted as one between patriots and traitors, and between the forces of national liberation and the imperialist forces. Besides criticizing the South Korean "traitors," other video clips covered the domestic and international situation in South Korea.

In the making of the critical others, images of past suffering and injustice are often invoked. For instance, the tragic deaths of two teenage schoolgirls, Mi-sun and Hyo-sun, who were hit by a US military vehicle in 2002, and which inflamed anti-American sentiment (*panmi*) in South Korea, are introduced in one video with the aim of demanding the withdrawal of US forces from South Korea (*Kyŏreŭi minsim* 2017b). Another video clip, commemorating a missile test on August 29, emphasizes the fact that North Korea fired a ballistic missile across Japan on the historical date of the Japanese annexation of Korea, remarking that this day is to be reestablished as a national occasion (*minjokŭi kyŏngsa*) by threatening Japan through citing South Koreans' comments. The upload of this episode was strategically set at a time just after the Japanese annexation day—widely understood as a day of disgrace in Korean history. The temporal shift from a moment in

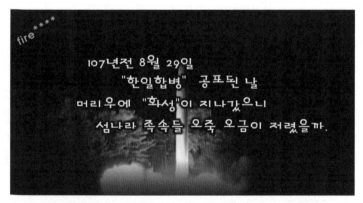

Figure 9.2. "Value of Nation, Hwasŏng" (*Kyŏreŭi minsim*, 2017d).

302

history to the present time stresses the missile test's historical link to the past and its contemporary relevance (see figure 9.2).

I also find North Korean ideologists selecting and reinterpreting historical material to bolster the legitimation of the regime, which has suffered from colonial invasion. Using historical traumas as a resonating chord, they portray that the pain of colonialism and war is necessarily their pain also by dint of their shared "Koreanness." Accordingly, all the North's practices, including its missile tests, which are intended to threaten imperialist powers, can be framed and justified as legitimate revenge with the overarching aim to protect the independence of the Korean nation (*minjok chaju*). The Kim regime's imaginings of a Korean nation are based on a contrast between a unified Korean nation and the enemy (or traitors). This stark contrast was highlighted further during the heightened tension between North Korea and the United States throughout 2017. As a result, the incongruity of the political and ethnic dimensions is seen as a key factor behind the tension on the Korean Peninsula. The imagination of a Korean nation operates in the continuation of their tradition of anti-colonial struggle, cementing the clear boundary between the independent *minjok* in the North and the semicolonial *minjok* in the South, and between the legitimate successors and the illegitimate traitors.

– Representation of the Korean peace process

The escalation of tensions between North Korea and the United States in 2017 dramatically changed; at the turn of the new year, there was a general leaning toward peace. In 2018, three inter-Korean summits took place in the space of fewer than six months, as well as a historic first summit meeting between the leaders of North Korea and the United States, held in Singapore in June 2018. The North and South's move toward peace in 2018 was initiated during the PyeongChang Olympic Games.[12] Since the DPRK agreed to participate in the Winter Olympics in Pyeongchang, *Kyŏreŭi minsim* changed its tune toward peace and reunification and began celebrating the series of summits as core elements of Kim Jong Un's achievements. Since this change of outlook, only one video was uploaded concerning the United States; it condemns Vice President Mike Pence with the comment stating that "during the peace festival, Pence visited the *Chŏnan* vessel with North Korean defectors" (*Kyŏreŭi minsim* 2018e). In addition, although it continues to maintain its negative stance toward the United States as well as conservative forces in the South, the frequency of references to both has been relatively lower compared with the previous year.

The first video *Kyŏreŭi minsim* posted on January 14 proclaims "Let's make 2018 the year of national reconciliation and unity." It also refers to spring being in the air, a bright future for the South and the North, and the idea of reunification, including cooperation, talks, and *minjok kongyŏng* (coprosperity; *Kyŏreŭi minsim* 2018f). These welcome sentiments were provided through the comments of South Koreans.[13] Another video, posted on March 10, right after Kim Jong Un's meeting with a South Korean envoy on March 5, uses a combination of images of the delegations meeting and cherry blossoms, symbolizing that the

---

12 Additionally, prior to the games, in Kim Jong Un's 2018 New Year's Day address, the North Korean leader discussed conditional talks with South Korea and mentioned the potential offer of sending a delegation to the PyeongChang Winter Olympics (J. U. Kim 2018, 1).

13 The source of these quotations collected by Uriminzokkiri TV was not disclosed.

relations between the two Koreas had warmed during the prior month's Olympic Games. Both videos feature an inter-Korean cheering team with Korea Unification flags in the background.

In the aftermath of the first inter-Korean summit in April 2018, about which *Kyŏreŭi minsim* declared that "South and North Korea will reconnect the blood relations of the people at Panmunjeom," *Kyŏreŭi minsim* posted a series of episodes titled "Panmunjeom shock seen from the comments" (*Kyŏreŭi minsim* 2018g, 2018h). The episodes reflect welcoming responses from South Koreans regarding the inter-Korean summit in Panmunjeom, with internet comments stating, "Panmunjeom, from a symbol of division for 70 years to a symbol of peace." The video also depicts the welcome dinner as a national feast, where "it was difficult to tell who is from the North and who is from the South," demonstrating that the Korean nation is racially homogeneous. In the reconstruction of Korean nation, North Korean media is appealing to a sense of primordial bond that derives from the assumed givens of social existence, which provide the congruities of blood, speech, custom, and so on (Geertz 1963).

Interestingly, another way to get the message of the reconciliation of

Figure 9.3. Panmunjeom Shock Seen from the Comments (2; *Kyŏreŭi minsim*, 2018h).

the Korean nation across was by using food metaphors. For example, Pyongyang *naengmyŏn* is shown with the subtitle "Pyongyang *naengmyŏn*, the most searched for word [in South Korea], national pride, world's best food, and now the symbol of peace!" The video uses the image of a South Korean–style cocktail mixed with Pyongyang's Taedonggang beer and Jeju's Hallasan soju to show the expectation for national unity (see figure 9.3). Here, Taedonggang beer and Hallasan soju symbolize the North and the South respectively, thus the mixed cocktail was used as a unifying symbol. Symbols are selected and deployed to resonate within aspects of contemporary culture to invent nationhood (Brown 2000).

After the first North Korea–US summit in June 2018, the third inter-Korean summit took place in Pyongyang in September of the same year. This summit further reaffirmed the principle of independence and the reconciliation of the Korean nation. Again, *Kyŏreŭi minsim* posted an optimistic picture of the Korean Peninsula on September 24. It also uploaded the same clip with English subtitles on October 12, featuring the two Korean leaders and a blueprint of the Pyongyang-Busan train along with a South Korean protest song.[14] The lyrics run:

> Let's unify hand in hand. Let's unify hand in hand. / (Verse one) Right, we wish our unification more than anybody else in the world. Let's not mind other countries. It is our unification to achieve. / (Verse two) Right, there is no reason to fight against each other. We are all one blood. Let's lay down guns and swords aimed at each

---

14 This song was composed in 2000 to celebrate the June 15 Joint Declaration in South Korea.

Figure 9.4. Korean Peninsula Free from War, the Story Just Imagined in a Dream (*Kyŏreŭi minsim*, 2018a).

other. Let's open our hearts and hug each other.

The clip ends with images of symbolic Paektusan Mountain behind a photo of the two leaders holding hands and posing with their wives, with the lake in the background (see figure 9.4).

This episode suggests that it is time to remove the wire fence that divides the Hanminjok (Korean nation), as "through policy measures, the aspiration and hope of all Koreans that the current developments in inter-Korean relations will lead to reunification" (Ministry of Foreign Affairs 2018b, para. 3). In the clip, the image and the sound of a train imply the inter-Korean railway connection project could overcome the division and bring a new future to the Korean Peninsula. It also engages in the ethnogenesis of the Korean nation by inviting the two leaders to be part of the alliance. On the one hand, Paektusan Mountain is understood as the background of both Koreas' mythohistorical derivation from a common ancestor called Tan'gun.[15] On the other hand, the mountain is a centerpiece of the North's idolization and

15   Tan'gun is the mythical, divinely descended founder of the ethnic Korean people.

propaganda campaign to highlight the sacred revolution and bloodline of the ruling Kim family.[16]

It is common in Korean nationalist discourse to represent the myth of a singular ancestry and genealogy from the distant past to the present (Lie 2004). By using cultural symbols like Paektusan Mountain to indicate both shared ancestry and revolutionary work, nationalist ideologists of the regime are engaging Korea in a primordial way, essentially treating myths as historical facts or as having foundations in facts, while also downplaying differences between personal experiences and group history (Kapferer 1988). The selection of symbols used in the nation's representation of itself is highly politically motivated; the use of standard ethnic symbols in nationalism is intended to stimulate reflection on one's own cultural distinctiveness, thereby creating a feeling of nationhood. In this way, the interpenetration of myth and state power suggests that Koreans' primary identities connect the transborder nation to their ancestral land, even if they may have lived their entire lives elsewhere.

Indeed, the embrace of overseas Koreans activates a shared sense of ethnic unity and enhances the imagined scope of the Korean nation beyond the territorial boundary. Uriminzokkiri TV produced several videos that aired articles written by overseas Koreans living in China, Japan, the United States, and Russia in the *Sosik* (news) section of the website. All these episodes are titled "An essay written by coethnics"

---

16   In North Korea, Paektusan Mountain is represented as an important historical site in Korea's arduous, 20-year guerrilla war against the occupying Japanese in the 1930s and 1940s. In this long struggle, Kim Il Sung is depicted as a great leader who played a leading role. North Korea asserts that Kim Jong-il was born at Paektusan Mountain.

(*tongp'oka ssŭngŭl*)[17] and cover the voices of various transborder Koreans. The section's regular reports include a welcoming opinion

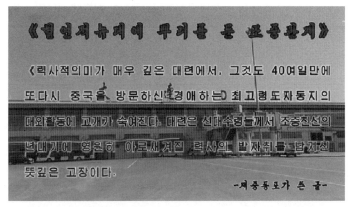

Figure 9.5. DPRK-China Relations Rooted in Blood Ties (*Sosik* 2018a).

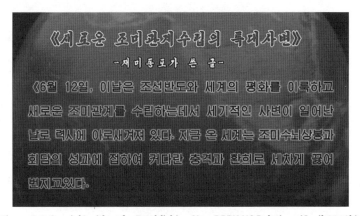

Figure 9.6. Special Incident for Establishing New DPRK-US Relations (*Sosik* 2018b).

of the inter-Korean and DPRK-US summits as well as the joint North Korea–China summits and contain themes that call for peace on the

---

17 *Tongp'o* literally means "sibling." *Tong* in *tongp'o* emphasizes common origin.

Korean Peninsula, independence, and reunification of the Korean nation. After Kim Jong Un visited China in early May 2018, the *Sosik* section introduced articles written by overseas Koreans living in China, stressing friendly relations between the DPRK and China and describing the relationship as "rooted in blood ties" and "brotherhood." Similarly, an essay written by a Korean American uploaded on June 25, 2018, celebrates a new establishment of North Korea–US relations (see figures 9.5 and 9.6).

These videos also offer a view that overseas Koreans belong to the same culture and have shared political interests. The diasporic imagination of Korean nationhood means that Koreans should care about Korea not only while on the peninsula but also while abroad. The key to such transborder nation-building is to maintain loyalty to the nation, even when residing in another country. For example, North Korea is often referred to as the motherland when discussing the idea of unification. In this way, transborder Koreans become connected to the "legitimate" homeland—North Korea—no matter where they currently live or where they were born. North Korean media embraces not only a divided nation (South Korean people) but also colonial-era migrants and their descendants, including Korean Chinese and Korean Japanese as well as ethnic Koreans in the United States. In this sense, nation-building in North Korea is a controlling mechanism that attempts to activate a sense of belonging to the transborder Korean nation.

– Celebrating Kim Jong Un's achievements

North Korean media also constructs nationalism by celebrating Kim Jong Un's achievements in the Korean peace process. *Kyŏreŭi minsim,* which covers the voices of peace mentioned above, presents not only a unified Korean nation but also Kim Jong Un as a national hero. For example, its first video in 2018 placed the North's esteemed leader as a peacemaker, stating, "80 million people! Let's be proud of the hero to which our nation gave birth," and "Kim Jong Un is a guardian for peace on the peninsula." Further, on both May 7 and 9, *Kyŏreŭi minsim* praised Kim's brave, open, confident, and humorous character. Additionally, the video uploaded right after the DPRK-US summit depicted Kim Jong Un as a great negotiator who saved the Korean Peninsula from crises (*Kyŏreŭi minsim* 2018b). In a similar vein, the video posted on June 23 stressed that the first summit with the United States was the result of Kim Jong Un's initiative, referring to the event as a "centurial meeting prepared by Kim Jong Un's firm decision and will"; this clip was posted with a Japanese caption as well (see figure 9.7).

Taken together, the captions imply that the protagonist of the Korean peace process is Kim Jong Un and attribute all the success to their great leader. The celebration of Kim is associated with the regime's deep anxiety toward the construction of a powerful socialist state

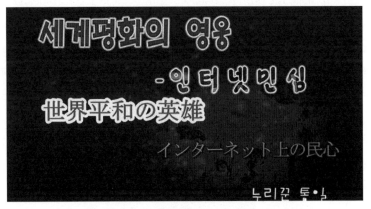

Figure 9.7. The Hero of World Peace (*Kyŏreŭi minsim* 2018c).

while diluting the image of a brutal regime. Through this process of representing the "glorious events," Koreans living outside the DPRK are able to link patriotism many feel toward their homeland directly to North Korea. The association of peace with the great achievements of the regime further glorifies Korea. To some extent, these representations of Kim Jong Un also imply North Korea's response to the perceived threat to its national sovereignty when encountering a foreign power. Although North Korea's important step onto the international stage means, in some respects, a weakening of the state, the official discourse continues to celebrate the series of summits, focusing on national unity and world peace through its power of independence rather than addressing cooperation with past enemies over decades.

The videos suggest a bright future for North Korea and for the Korean Peninsula. Borrowing the words of overseas Koreans, the clips mix together all the significant events worth celebrating. They make a connection between the powerful socialist state and ethnic Koreans abroad, as if what is significant for North Korea is significant for all Koreans. Further, as discussed, *Kyŏreŭi minsim* produces the clips with foreign subtitles, including Japanese, Chinese, and English, despite the emphasis on a common Korean common culture and, in particular, language. Embracing a population who has never been to North Korea is associated with global connectedness, which also partly reflects the regime's recognition of the heterogeneity of national culture through the new forms of diversity of the Korean nation.

– The United States: No longer an enemy?

The earlier regular criticism of the United States and South Korea by North Korean media has decreased recently, and its level of denouncement has weakened considerably with the advent of the country's peaceful outlook in 2018. However, members of the Liberty Korea Party are still seen as "internal traitors," and both Japan and the United States continue to be viewed as imperialist powers. A clip posted in March 2018 shows video footage of massacres of Korean "comfort women," women taken into sexual slavery by the Japanese military during World War II (*Kyŏreŭi minsim*, 2018d). And in both March and October of 2018, *Kyŏreŭi minsim* continued to criticize the United States, particularly Trump's October rejection of the idea of South Korea easing sanctions on North Korea (*Kyŏreŭi minsim* 2018i). Thus, the North Korean state's view does not necessitate the removal of all criticism of outside forces at work—meaning all those who fall in the category of the enemies—but rather continues its fight against what it perceives as imperialist forces. Moreover, North Korea's stance is seen as relatively heroic in its representation, because the North regards South Korea as a victim at the hands of foreign powers. Thus, the last two videos reinforce the importance of patriotism and heroics by openly identifying and criticizing the North's enemies.

Conclusion

North Korea has reconstructed the transborder nation as a national project, forming ties between the "homeland" state and its transborder "kin" through media. Analyses of Uriminzokkiri TV's *Kyŏreŭi minsim* section demonstrate the significant shift from antagonism in the presummit period to reconciliation in the postsummit period. The media representation illustrates not only the general inclination toward peace that started with the PyeongChang Winter Olympic Games but also the juxtapositions of the ethnic and political dimensions and of patriotism and nationalism. On the one hand, the representation of *Kyŏreŭi minsim* emphasizes ethnic oneness and national reconciliation. On the other hand, it protects the legitimation of the regime and national independence from the imperialist power, celebrating the leader's achievements and essentializing loyalty to the "great socialist state."

In the ethnic dimension, the kindred aspects of nation were emphasized, implying the responsibility of family obligations as members of a large family (Eriksen 2008). Interestingly, the Korean nation was imagined in primordial ways and portrayed as a community of suffering and coresponsibility in association with historical traumas and future destiny. In this process, the new space for potential unification of two Koreas invited not only those in the North and the South but also Koreans abroad. Identifying the transborder nation, ethnic nationalism is intended to reproduce a shared sense of ethnic unity, functioning as a unifying force aimed at "lasting peace."

In the political dimension, media representation reflects the regime's anxieties toward a powerful socialist state. The celebration of North Korea's diplomatic reach to the world and its leader's achievements reproduce the vision of the country. When it expresses hope for worldwide peace, the dream is for it to be accomplished through the work of the North Korean regime without losing its initiative. By borrowing the voices of Koreans living in Japan, the United States, and South Korea, "Koreanness" is achieved through the quality of *hwahae* (reconciliation), without having to include images of colonizing forces and without losing its *chaju* (independence). That is, when North Korean media conveys its ethnocultural messages to the Korean nationals existing outside North Korea, its stance is still rooted in the glorious socialist homeland.

This hybrid form of the coexistence of two loyalties—nationalism and patriotism—represents the ambivalent status as a state and as a nation as well as the complexity of the current dynamics surrounding the Korean Peninsula that North Korea is facing. To some extent, the advent of the peace process in 2018 blurred the incongruities found in the political and ethnic dimensions of Korean nationhood that were produced by ethnic and territorial division. Thus, most saliently, the making of transborder belonging interwoven with globalizing media reflects the media as a critical site in North Korea's nation-building.

Both Koreas have projected nationalist discourses and practices in the construction of transborder nationalism. South Korea has shaped the transborder ties by selective bureaucratic practices (J. Kim 2016). The recent South Korean efforts to reach Koreans abroad via government, business interests, and popular culture are visible (Lie 2017). Though renewed reckonings of "Koreanness" occurred in tandem with the Korean peace process, transborder Koreans are still embedded in the division system. The remaking of a transborder Korean nation involves dynamic and complex process between two Koreas and agents in various regions, which requires specific examination.

References

Altheide, David L. 1996. *Qualitative Media Analysis*. Thousand Oaks, CA: SAGE Publications.

Altheide, David L., Michael Coyle, Kate DeVriese, and Christoper Schneider. 2010. "Emergent Qualitative Document Analysis." In *Handbook of Emergent Methods*. Edited by Sharlene Naggy Hesse-Biber and Patricia Leavy. 127‒154. New York, NY: Guilford Press.

Anderson, Benedict. 1991. *Imagined Communities: Reflections on the Origin and Spread of Nationalism*, 2nd ed. London, UK: Verso.

Anderson, Benedict. 1992a. *Long-Distance Nationalism: World Capitalism and the Rise of Identity Politics*. Amsterdam, Netherlands: Centre for Asian Studies Amsterdam.

Anderson, Benedict. 1992b. "The New World Disorder." *New Left Review* 193:3‒13.

Anderson, Benedict. 1998. *The Spectre of Comparisons: Nationalism, Southeast Asia and the World*. London, UK: Verso.

Appadurai, Arjun. 1996. *Modernity at Large: Cultural Dimensions of Globalization*. Minneapolis: University of Minnesota Press.

Barker, Rodney. 2006. *Making Enemies*. London, UK: Palgrave Macmillan.

Brown, David. 2000. *Contemporary Nationalism: Civic, Ethnocultural and Multicultural Politics*. London, UK: Routledge.

Brubaker, Rogers. 1996. *Nationalism Reframed: Nationhood and the National Question in the New Europe*. Cambridge, UK: Cambridge University Press.

Calhoun, Craig. 1997. *Nationalism*. Minneapolis, MN: University of Minnesota Press.

Choi, Sunkyung, and Woo Yong Lee. 2017. "'Chosŏn minjok' kaenyŏmŭi hyŏngsŏngkwa pyŏnhwa" [The formation and change of the concept of "Choson minjok"]. *Pukanyŏnguhakoebo* [North Korean Studies Review] 21 (1): 1‒24.

Conversi, Daniele. 2012. "Irresponsible Radicalisation: Diasporas, Globalisation and Long-Distance Nationalism in the Digital Age." *Journal of Ethnic and*

Migration Studies 38 (9): 1357–1379.

Cumings, Bruce. 1993. "The Corporate State in North Korea." In *State and Society in Contemporary Korea*. Edited by Hagen Koo. 197–230. Ithaca, NY: Cornell University Press.

Ding, Sheng. 2007. "Digital Diaspora and National Image Building: A New Perspective on Chinese Diaspora Study in the Age of China's Rise." *Pacific Affairs* 80 (4): 627–648.

Duara, Prasenjit. 2006. "Nationalism in East Asia." *History Compass* 4 (3): 407–427.

Eriksen, Thomas. H. 2007. "Nationalism and the Internet." *Nations and Nationalism* 13 (1): 1–18.

Eriksen, Thomas H. 2008. *Ethnicity and Nationalism: Anthropological Perspectives*, 3rd ed. London, UK: Pluto Press.

Fuglerud, Øivind. 1999. *Life on the Outside: The Tamil Diaspora and Long-Distance Nationalism*. London, UK: Pluto Press.

Geertz, Clifford. 1963. "The Integrative Revolution: Primordial Sentiments and Civil Politics in the New States." In *Old Societies and New States: The Quest for Modernity in Asia and Africa*. Edited by C. Geertz. 105-157. New York, NY: Free Press of Glencoe.

Gellner, Ernest. 1983. *Nations and Nationalism*. Oxford, UK: Blackwell.

Giddens, Anthony. 1985. *The Nation-State and Violence*. Cambridge, UK: Polity Press.

Guarnizo, Luis Eduardo, Alejandro Portes, and William Haller. 2008. "Assimilation and Transnationalism: Determinants of Transnational Political Action among Contemporary Migrants." In *The Transnational Studies Reader: Intersections and Innovations*. Edited by Sanjeev Khagram and Peggy Levitt. 118–134. New York, NY: Routledge.

Hobsbawm, Eric. 1990. *Nations and Nationalism since 1780: Programme, Myth, Reality.* Cambridge, UK: Cambridge University Press.

Kapferer, Bruce. 1988. *Legends of People, Myths of State: Violence, Intolerance and Political Culture in Sri Lanka and Australia*. Washington, DC: Smithsonian Institution Press.

Kim, Il Sung. 1983. *Kim Il Sung sŏnjip 25* [Selected works, 25]. Pyongyang,

North Korea: Chosŏnrodongdangch'ul'pansa [Workers' Party of Korea Publishing House].

Kim, Jaeeun. 2009. "The Making and Unmaking of a 'Transborder Nation': South Korea during and after the Cold War." *Theory and Society* 38 (2): 133–164.

Kim, Jaeeun. 2016. *Contested Embrace: Transborder Membership Politics in Twentieth-Century Korea*. Stanford, CA: Stanford University Press.

Kim, Jong Il. 1998. *Kim Jong Il sŏnjip 13* [Selected works, 13]. Pyongyang, North Korea: Chosŏnrodongdangch'ul'pansa [Workers' Party of Korea Publishing House].

Kim, Jong Un. 2018. "Shinnyŏnsa" [New year address of supreme leader Kim Jong Un for 2018]. January 1, 2018.

Koo, Hagen, ed. 1993. *State and Society in Contemporary Korea*. Ithaca, NY: Cornell University Press.

Kyŏreŭi minsim. 2017a. "Chŏnjaeng bandae miguk bandae" [Anti-war, Anti-America]. November 8, 2017. Retrieved from http://www.uriminzokkiri. com/itv/index.php?ppt=minsimandno=36850.

Kyŏreŭi minsim. 2017b. "Chuhanmigun chŏlgŏ-ga" [The song for withdrawal of U.S. forces from South Korea]. June 13, 2017. Retrieved from http:// www.uriminzokkiri.com/itv/index.php?ppt=minsimandno=34628.

Kyŏreŭi minsim. 2017c. "Ssadŭnŭn ch'imnyagida" [THAAD is invasion]. September 14, 2017. Retrieved from http://www.uriminzokkiri.com/itv/ index.php?ppt=minsimandno=36089.

Kyŏreŭi minsim. 2017d. "Taetkŭllo ponŭn minjogŭi chaebu hwasŏng" [Value of nation, Hwasŏng]. September 6, 2017. Retrieved from http://www. uriminzokkiri.com/itv/index.php?ppt=minsimandno=35951.

Kyŏreŭi minsim. 2018a. "Korean peninsula free from war, the story just imagined in a dream." October 12, 2018. Retrieved from www.uriminzokkiri.com/ itv/index.php?ppt=minsimandno=41167.

Kyŏreŭi minsim. 2018b. "Ryŏksajŏgin 6.12 chŏngmal kkumman katta" [Historical 6.12! It's just like a dream]. June 17, 2018. Retrieved from http://www.uriminzokkiri.com/itv/index. php?ppt=minsimandno=39591.

Kyŏreŭi minsim. 2018c. "Segyepyŏnghwaŭi yŏngung: int'ŏnet minsim" [The hero of the world peace: Internet popular sentiment]. Retrieved from http://www.uriminzokkiri.com/itv/index.php?ppt=minsimandno=39680.

Kyŏreŭi minsim. 2018d. "Shipkuch'oŭi hwamyŏnŭl pon int'ŏnet minsim" [Public opinion from the scene of 19 seconds]. March 12, 2018. Retrieved from http://www.uriminzokkiri.com/itv/index.php?ppt=minsimandno=38399.

Kyŏreŭi minsim. 2018e. "Taetkŭlkwangjangŭl meun int'ŏnet p'yŏch'ang minsim" [Internet Pyeongchang popular sentiment]. February 21, 2018. Retrieved from http://www.uriminzokkiri.com/itv/index.php?ppt=minsimandno=38192.

Kyŏreŭi minsim. 2018f. "Taetkŭllo pon chŏlwŏlŭi int'ŏnet minsim (1)" [Popular feelings on Lunar New Year's Day seen from the comments (1)]. January 14, 2018. Retrieved from http://www.uriminzokkiri.com/itv/index.php?ppt=minsimandno=37719.

Kyŏreŭi minsim. 2018g. "Taetkŭllo pon p'anmunjŏm ch'unggyŏk (1)" [Panmunjeom shock seen from the comments (1)]. May 7, 2018. Retrieved from http://www.uriminzokkiri.com/itv/index.php?ppt=minsimandno=39084.

Kyŏreŭi minsim. 2018h. "Taetkŭllo pon p'anmunjŏm ch'unggyŏk (2)" [Panmunjeom shock seen from the comments (2)]. May 9, 2018. Retrieved from http://www.uriminzokkiri.com/itv/index.php?ppt=minsimandno=39106.

Kyŏreŭi minsim. 2018i. "Taetkŭllo ponŭn ch'iyogŭi hyŏnjuso" [Current state of humiliation from the comments]. October 19, 2018. Retrieved from http://www.uriminzokkiri.com/itv/index.php?ppt=minsimandno=41278.

Lie, John. 2004. *Modern Peoplehood*. Cambridge, MA: Harvard University Press.

Lie, John. 2017. "Korean Diaspora and Diasporic Nationalism." In *The Routledge Handbook of Korean Culture and Society*. Edited by Youna Kim. 245-254. London, UK: Routledge.

Ministry of Foreign Affairs, Government of Republic of Korea. 2018a. Panmunjom Declaration for Peace, Prosperity and Unification of the

Korean Peninsula. Retrieved from https://www.mofa.go.kr/eng/brd/m_5478/view.